Pain Pill Addiction:

A Prescription for Hope

By Jana Burson M.D.

First published by Dog Ear Publishing
4010 W. 86th Street, Ste H
Indianapolis, IN 46268
www.dogearpublishing.net

ISBN: 978-160844-698-8

This book is printed on acid-free paper.

Printed in the United States of America

This book is meant to provide information only. It is not intended to substitute for the advice of a doctor or other treatment professional. If you think you have an addictive disorder, please see a doctor. None of the information in this book should be used to diagnose anyone, or to recommend a specific treatment. Only a face-to-face evaluation and assessment with a physician or other treatment professional can give this information. This book has not been approved by any medical society or governmental agency.

Table of Contents:

Acknowledgements:

This book couldn't have been written without all of the thousands of addicts who taught me about the nature of opioid addiction, its treatment, and the possibility of recovery. This book is dedicated to the still sick and suffering addicts.

I am particularly grateful to the four anonymous people who granted me the interviews contained in this book. I appreciate their time and their candor.

Thank you, Dr. George Hall, M.D., FAAFP, FASAM, for being a friend and mentor. You taught me the joy of practicing Addiction Medicine.

My sister and first proofreader, Christie King, provided not just practical advice, but also the encouragement to complete the project. The love of my life, Greg Moon, also provided essential encouragement during bleak times, plus much needed input. Special thanks goes to Wanda Johnston and Gerri Sampson for their support and encouragement. Thanks also to DanaRae Pomeroy for her insightful editing. Katherine Boyle of Veritas Literary Agency deserves my special thanks, since she was the first publishing professional to show interest in my writing, and the subject matter.

Introduction

A tempest of pain pill abuse and addiction tore through many small and medium-sized towns in this country over the last decade. Thousands of lives were lost, numerous families destroyed, and countless people seriously and permanently affected. The consequences will be with us for years to come.

The economic costs of prescription drug addiction are overwhelming. The insurance industry estimates that diversion of prescription medication to addicts and abusers costs medical insurers an estimated *seventy-two and a half billion* dollars per year. (1)

But the costs to addicts and their families are incalculable. They pay with ruined marriages, careers, health, and reputations. Each addict directly affects an average of four close friends or family members, so many of us have felt the despair addiction brings, directly or indirectly.

How did this happen? How did we create, by conservative estimates, around 1.7 million prescription pain pill addicts? At least five factors contributed to this wave of addiction.

In the late 1990's, doctors were told we weren't doing a very good job of treating pain. We were called "opioiphobic," meaning we were overly concerned about causing addiction to pain medication and not concerned enough about treating the pain.

Legislature was passed, decreeing that all patients had the right to pain control. Pain medicine specialists said the risk of creating addiction in patients with true pain was about one percent. Primary care doctors, poorly trained in the management of chronic pain *or* in the identification and treatment of pain pill addiction, took these recommendations to heart, and began prescribing opioid pain pills in increasing numbers.

In 1996, a wonderful new drug for pain control was released. Oxy-Contin was heavily promoted not only for cancer pain, but also as a treatment for chronic non-cancer pain.

At this same point in time, internet technology expanded rapidly, providing people an opportunity to have prescription pain pills delivered overnight to their door. Most web sites didn't require a prescription, only a valid credit card number.

Our culture contributed to addiction. In many areas, it's culturally acceptable for people to share prescribed pain medication with friends and family. Most people who became addicted to opioid pain pills were given their first pill by a friend or family member. (2)

Rural areas with large numbers of blue collar workers holding physically demanding jobs became awash in pain pills. Since pain pills were prescribed by a doctor, many people thought they were safe, and didn't cause as much damage as "street" drugs, even if the person taking them wasn't the person for whom they were prescribed.

In 2001, I stumbled into the eye of the storm of opioid addiction, finding my niche in addiction medicine through luck and circumstance.

After completing my internship and residency in Internal Medicine, I entered private practice in a small Southern town. I liked it, but I didn't love it. I found it frustrating. Many of my patients had chronic diseases like diabetes, asthma, high blood pressure and high cholesterol, and didn't seem to improve. The diabetics remained obese and sedentary with poorly controlled blood sugars. Patients with high blood pressure forgot to take their medications, or completely stopped them because they didn't feel sick. The asthmatics kept smoking. Heart patients continued to eat cholesterol- laden foods and failed to exercise. Only a few of my patients made the behavioral changes necessary to improve their health.

My whole life and career changed when a friend of mine, who was the medical director of a nearby drug addiction treatment center, asked me to cover for him for a few days while he was out of town. I agreed, expecting I would do history and physical exams on addicts entering inpatient treatment. What I hadn't expected was seeing opioid addicts entering the methadone clinic.

I was appalled. I didn't believe in methadone treatment and had ethical concerns about this approach. I viewed patients on methadone as still using drugs, albeit legally prescribed. The only recovery from addiction with which I was familiar at that time was the twelve step recovery program, based on complete abstinence from all addicting drugs. Like many physicians, I didn't think methadone maintenance was a legitimate medical intervention, though I knew next to nothing about it. I considered it bit shady, something respectable physicians didn't get involved with.

I'd never been taught about the use of methadone to treat addiction, in medical school or residency. In fact, like many other physicians,

I hadn't really been taught about addiction as a disease, although the American Medical Association recognized it as such long before I graduated from medical school.

Working with methadone patients was an education, which led to a change in my career. I'd pictured a methadone clinic as some seedy place in a run-down section of New York City where heroin addicts came to clean up for a day or two, get some rest, then return to the streets to resume their drug addiction.

The patients I saw certainly didn't fit that picture. Most of them used prescription pain pills, mostly OxyContin. I was surprised that many snorted or injected these pills, and used them in fairly large amounts.

The average methadone patient was a blue collar worker who used pain pills for energy to get through the day, and to feel less pain from a physically demanding job. There were nearly as many women as men – hairdressers, waitresses, and housewives. These addicts were nice people. They could have been my neighbors. Some, in fact, were.

I was also surprised at my discussions with these patients on methadone. They were, after all, still using drugs in my view. Yet they were leading healthier and more productive lives than when they were under the burden of addiction. Their comments amazed me.

"Methadone saved my life."

"I have my wife and family back."

"I feel so much better and I don't wake up thinking about dope."

"I haven't spent a day in jail since starting methadone...I don't have to shoplift any more."

I was intrigued. These people were being helped. There was satisfaction in seeing lives being turned around, men and women going from helpless and hopeless addicts to happy and productive people.

I began researching the efficacy of methadone. I was amazed to find forty years' worth of research in the medical literature that clearly showed the effectiveness of methadone maintenance therapy. I read books and journals on opioid addiction, and attended conferences of ASAM (the American Society of Addiction Medicine). I saw that I could make a difference in the lives of my patients and their families working in the field of addiction medicine. After several years spent working in my friend's clinic, I had enough hours to qualify for the

ASAM certifying exam, passed it, and I began to work only with addicts. I found my niche in medicine.

Addiction is a chronic disease just like diabetes and hypertension. These diseases are treated with medication and lifestyle changes. Many addicts, especially those addicted to opioid medications, require the same combination.

While I will be exploring at some length the use of methadone and a newer drug, buprenorphine, I want to make it clear *no one treatment is best for everyone.* All too often, those providing treatment for opioid addiction are blinded by their own ideology.

Abstinence-based programs have actively discouraged opioid addicts from seeking help at centers which use medication-based treatments with methadone and buprenorphine. Some of their personnel, even doctors, completely discount the proven value of medication-based therapies.

Conversely, there are some opioid treatment centers who discount the possibilities of success with drug-free treatments, although this path works very well for some opioid addicts.

There are many roads to recovery.

The field of medicine is now emphasizing "evidence based" treatments. This stance emphasizes the importance of using treatments backed by good studies that prove they work. In opioid addiction treatment, medication-assisted treatments with methadone and buprenorphine have the most evidence to support their use. These treatments, combined with counseling, are the most effective manner of treating opioid addiction. Unfortunately, the stigma attached to these medications remains, and there's little reliable information available to opioid addicts and their families.

Prescription opioid addiction has increased dramatically since the late 1990's, reaching near epidemic proportions. In this book, we'll be discussing mistakes of the past, and treatments that have worked and those that have not. We'll look at why we must remove the stigma of treatment with methadone and buprenorphine, as well as the stigma associated with any type of addiction.

Endnotes

1. *Prescription for Peril*, Coalition Against Insurance Fraud 2007 http://www.insurancefraud.org/downloads/drugDiversion.pdf .
2. Substance Abuse and Mental Health Services Administration. (2009). *Results from the 2008 National Survey on Drug Use and Health: National Findings* (Office of Applied Studies, NSDUH Series H-36, HHS Publication No. SMA 09-4434). Rockville, MD.

CHAPTER 1

Kissing God

"I'll die young, but it's like kissing God"
> Lenny Bruce, who died at age forty-one of
> an intravenous morphine overdose.

"It did not feel like something that was going to take over my life and destroy it. It felt like a subtle flower instead of a manipulative demon. That's the mystery of heroin."
> Actor Corey Feldman

"The nice thing about being a heroin addict is that you either have no problems or one big one."
> Richard Schuldenfrei

Why do opioid drugs hold such power?

Throughout history, opioids ironically have given both great relief and great despair to humans who ingested their essence.

The opium poppy, *Papaver somniferum*, contains morphine and codeine, the raw materials that are made into opioid drugs. The ancient Sumerians, who lived in present day Iraq, called the opium poppy by a name that meant "plant of joy". (1) When shallow cuts are made into the poppy's unripe seed capsule, opium juice oozes out. After it dries, this material is scraped off the capsule, rendering the raw product of opium.

People are often confused by the words "opioid," "opiate," and "narcotic" and ask if they all mean the same thing. Technically, the word "opiate" includes only those substances made from the opium poppy.

The word "opioid" includes those compounds, plus the man-made or partially man-made drugs that have the same actions on the body as poppy opiates. All opioids act on receptors in the central nervous system to produce their desired effects. For ease of discussion, I will use the term "opioid" because it is more inclusive.

"Narcotic" is a legal term, and usually means any illicit drug, though the word's origin in Greek from "narco" means sleep and sedation. This technically could include not just opioids, but also prescription sedatives like benzodiazepines. Because different people use the word "narcotic" to mean different things, I will avoid its use in this book.

Some of the most common opioids are:

- heroin
- opium
- oxycodone (brand names include OxyContin, Percocet, Percodan, Roxicet)
- hydrocodone (brand names include Vicodin, Vicoprofen, Lortab, Lorcet),
- morphine (MS Contin, Avinza),
- methadone (brand names Methadose, Dolophine),
- fentanyl (Duragesic patches, Onsolis, Fentora)
- hydromorphone (Dilaudid)
- codeine
- meperidine (Demerol)
- pentazocine (Talwin)
- propoxyphene (Darvocet, Darvon)
- oxymorphone (Opana)
- butophanol (Stadol)
- tramadol (Ultram, Ultracet, also has an opioid-like action in some people, and has caused addiction with physical withdrawal symptoms identical to other powerful opioids)

In 1975, scientists began to learn how opioids produced their effects on the body. By the 1990's, three different opioid receptors had been identified, and were named *mu*, *kappa*, and *delta*. For our purposes, we'll focus on the *mu* receptor, since that's the receptor that produces euphoria, blockage of pain, and feelings of well-being when stimulated. These good feelings are caused when opioids attach to and activate these *mu* receptors in the brain and spinal column.

Opioids are also prescribed to treat diarrhea and cough. Opioid receptors located on the bowel walls slow peristaltic movements when activated. For this reason, opioids have been used for centuries as an effective treatment for diarrhea. Opioid receptors are also located in the cough center of the brain. When these receptors are stimulated, cough is suppressed, making opioids excellent medications to suppress a nasty cough.

The human body makes its own opioids, called endorphins. Endorphins activate the opioid receptors to cause feelings of wellbeing, and to a limited degree, relief of pain. The bodily effects of our endorphins are much weaker than the effect of opium and other opioids. Opioids administered from outside the body mimic the effect of endorphins, but are more powerful and cause intense euphoria and block severe pain. Opioids sometimes sedate, but some people get a feeling of energy from them. Endorphins made by the body have complex functions: they regulate stress response, regulate mood and feelings, and even influence learning and memory. Pain pills affect all these same functions, but more powerfully than the body's own endorphins.

Many different types of opioids are available today. In ancient times, available opium preparations varied a great deal in their potencies, but with modern methods of manufacturing, opioid pain pills are standardized in their opioid content. Each pill delivers a reliable amount of opioid. Street drugs like heroin still vary in potency due to adulteration by dealers, but overall the purity of heroin has risen over the past years.

Activities essential to human survival like eating, drinking, and mating (sex) all cause dopamine release in the pleasure centers of the brain, which in turn creates feelings of enjoyment, pleasure, and elevation of mood. Because these life-sustaining activities make us feel good, humans will continue doing things that keep us alive.

Addicting drugs, including opioids, alcohol, marijuana and others, also act on the sensitive pleasure centers of the brain. They also cause increases in brain dopamine, resulting in feelings of pleasure. In fact, in some people, these drugs seem to stimulate the pleasure centers even more strongly than food, water, or sex. In this way, addicting chemicals hijack the brain and substitute themselves for the things in life that are really life sustaining. The drugs can begin to tell an addict's brain that the drug is as necessary for survival as eating and drinking. This message from the pleasure center can be powerful, and difficult to drown out with voices of reason.

As research continues, scientists discover more about changes that occur in the brain during addiction. These changes are even more complex than previously thought. Multiple types of brain transmitters and other areas of the brain play important roles in both the development and continuation of drug addiction.

The pleasure people feel from opioid drugs has been described in different ways. Many opioid addicts say they feel energy, or describe a feeling of expansive well-being. Some use words and phrases like "bliss" or "peaceful" or "I feel straight (meaning normal, not in withdrawal)" or even "I don't feel anything. That's what I like". One memorable heroin addict said, "Doc, if you knew there was a drug you could inject and you would get a four hour orgasm, wouldn't you do it too?" It was a good question.

Clearly, all people don't get this same intense euphoria from opioids. In the future, we may discover that our individual genetic structure controls much of our response to opioids, other drugs of abuse, and many types of drugs and medications. Soon scientists will be able to predict a specific patient's response to a given medication based on his genetics. This exciting new field of medicine is called pharmacogenetics.

We know that physical and chemical changes occur in the brain after opioids are taken regularly for any reason. The brain adapts to the increase of opioids in the body, and makes changes to accommodate the extra opioids. Then, if the opioids are stopped suddenly, the chemistry of the brain becomes unbalanced, causing signs and symptoms of opioid withdrawal.

This is not in the patient's head... though it is in his brain and other places.

With daily use of opioids, these changes can occur in as little as two weeks. If opioids are stopped suddenly, the patient will get sick. The physical signs and symptoms can include sweats, chills, nausea and vomiting, diarrhea, insomnia, anxiety, profound muscle and joint pains, abdominal and muscle cramps, watery eyes, sneezing, runny nose, elevated blood pressure and heart rate, and fever. This is not psychological. It is physical.

And it feels awful. People have compared withdrawal to having the flu but in reality, it's more like having the flu... and then being run over by a tank.

However, this critical point must be made: *addiction is not just physical withdrawal symptoms*. Anyone who takes opioids for a long enough time will have withdrawal symptoms if he stops opioids suddenly. This is called physiologic opioid dependency, to differentiate it from opioid addiction.

Opioid *addiction* means there is mental craving and obsession with opioids. Therefore, it's possible for a pain patient to take opioid pain pills for many years and, though physically dependent, still not have addiction. Alternatively, it's also possible for an intermittent user of opioids to have the psychological symptoms, but no physical withdrawal symptoms. He would still meet the criteria for opioid addiction.

Is it Pain? Is it Addiction? Is it Both?

Many patients have both diseases: opioid addiction and chronic pain. An estimated thirty-five percent of patients enrolled in methadone maintenance clinics for treatment of opioid addiction also have chronic pain. (2) Having both of these medical conditions complicates the patient's care. Both medical conditions need treatment for the best patient outcomes.

Treating only one of the two diseases can make the other worse; for example, if an addict with chronic pain gets into recovery, but has no way to manage pain, the pain will be a relapse trigger. Preferably a non-opioid method can be found to manage pain, but this can be difficult to accomplish.

Conversely, if an opioid addict, untreated for his opioid addiction, is prescribed opioids for his chronic pain, he will probably have a bad outcome for both pain and addiction. He won't be able to take the pills as prescribed. He'll probably devour too many pills too soon, and then be in withdrawal, unless he can find another source of opioids. His life will get progressively worse when both the addiction and chronic pain spiral out of control.

The first step when evaluating a new patient who is in withdrawal from regular opioid use is to determine if this patient has true opioid addiction, or physiologic dependency. A person who is merely physically dependent can usually slowly reduce her dose of opioids without excessive difficulty, assuming that the underlying pain condition has been resolved.

A person with the disease of opioid addiction is unable to taper off the opioids, because the psychological aspects interfere. With true drug addiction, the following mental symptoms can be recognized: excessive time and energy spent thinking about the drug and planning to stay supplied with the drug, obsessive fear of running out of the drug, and continuing to use the drug even after bad things happen due to drug use.

The addict's obsession with the drug leads him to neglect important aspects of life, such as family, work, and health. The addict's tolerance and intake steadily increases. As one recovering addict said, "It takes more and more to do less and less." The addict spends much time recovering from effects of drug use. The addict often uses more of the drug, and for longer periods of time than she intended. She may make unsuccessful attempts to quit or cut down on drug use. An addict is unable to wean off the opioids because of both the mental obsession with drugs and the physical symptoms of withdrawal.

Addicts often underestimate the psychological aspect of opioid addiction and believe if they can get through the period of withdrawal, all will be well, and their addiction cured. This is usually not the case. In fact, even with medically assisted withdrawal in a detoxification unit, most patients relapse back to opioid use within the first month. (3) This is due both to the prolonged physical withdrawal symptoms, and to the mental portion of addiction, which causes persistent craving for the drug.

So how do doctors decide if a patient has physical dependency from appropriate use of pain medications, or if he has true opioid addiction? In some cases, addiction is obvious, but there can also be overlap between appropriate use of opioids, misuse of opioids, and actual addiction. There's no bright red line between misuse and addiction.

Pain patients do have situations occur where they have to take extra pills and run out of medication early. This is a behavior that is worrisome for addiction, but not necessarily diagnostic of it. Sometimes patients use illegal drugs. This does not necessarily mean they have addiction, though illegal drug use is a serious warning sign. Sometimes addiction can only be diagnosed by following the patient over time and accumulating enough information to determine if there is a pattern of prescription drug misuse.

Physicians look for certain behaviors when trying to decide if a patient may be developing addiction. Taking more pills than directed per dose, or taking pills more frequently than directed by the prescribing doctor are both worrisome signs. Doctors should be troubled by family reports of sedation or intoxication in the patient, and by any drug overdoses, or near overdoses. Some patients get pills from more than one doctor and these doctors are unaware of each other. This is called "doctor shopping," and is a frequent behavior seen in patients with addiction.

Other warning signs are running out of pain pills early, being given extra pills by friends or family, or buying them from other people. Using pills in ways they are not intended, like grinding the pills to snort or inject, is a clear sign that the patient has developed addiction. Addicts use pills in these ways to get a faster onset, or "rush." It's worrisome if urine drug screens show unexpected results, like the presence of illicit drugs or the absence of the prescribed drugs. In this last situation, it can mean the patient is taking too many pills when he first fills the prescription, causing him to run out early, or it can mean the patient is selling his medication.

Patients who ask for a specific brand of opioid may cause concern for their doctors. Generics have a lower street value, so patients planning to sell their pills often insist on getting name brand opioids. Frequent reported "loss" of medication is a warning sign, though this can happen to anyone once, or maybe even twice, but not routinely.

When patients use pain pills for symptoms for which they were not intended, such as using a pain pill to induce sleep or get high, or for extra energy, addiction is likely to be present. Such patients are "chemical copers," meaning they use pills (or alcohol) to medicate feelings, rather than tolerating and accepting negative feelings. (using this definition, many people in the U.S. are chemical copers.) Addiction tells the brain that any bad feeling, no matter what the cause, must be medicated. In this way, addicts lose coping skills that allow them to endure painful emotional states. If physicians see this mindset developing in patients on opioids for chronic pain, it may indicate onset of addiction.

To compound the difficulty of correctly diagnosing addiction, the addiction itself has a way of fooling its sufferers into believing they don't have a problem. I remember a discussion with a heroin addict, who insisted that he injected black tar heroin only to treat his chronic back pain. That sounded ridiculous to me, and I thought at first he was purposely misleading me. As we talked, it became obvious that he was convinced that what he was saying was true. He was sure he had only a chronic pain issue, not an addiction. This is an example of denial, which is not the same thing as lying. Denial occurs when the disease of addiction convinces its sufferers to believe outrageous things. Denial is a defense mechanism that prevents the recognition of a painful truth, in this case, the diagnosis of addiction.

To help doctors make an accurate diagnosis, they turn to the DSM-IV (Diagnostical and Statistical Manual, published by American Psychiatric Association), which contains diagnostic criteria for major mental disorders, including substance abuse and dependency. Dependency is used by the DSM-IV to mean addiction. The DSM-IV is based on a consensus of many psychiatrists, though some physicians have suggested improvements for the criteria. The new version of this manual is due soon, and may contain major changes in diagnostic criteria.

DSM-IV TR Criteria for Substance Dependence:

"A maladaptive pattern of substance use, leading to clinically significant impairment or distress, as manifested by three (or more) of the following, occurring at any time in the same 12-month period:

1. Tolerance, as defined by either of the following:
    a. A need for markedly increased amounts of the substance to achieve the same intoxication or desired effect
    b. Markedly diminished effect with continued use of the same amount of the substance
2. Withdrawal, as manifested by either of the following:
    a. The characteristic withdrawal syndrome for the substance
    b. The same or closely related substance is taken to relieve or avoid withdrawal symptoms
3. The substance is often taken in larger amounts or over a longer period than was intended
4. There is a persistent desire or unsuccessful efforts to cut down or control substance use
5. A great deal of time is spent in activities necessary to obtain the substance (e.g., visiting multiple doctors or driving long distances), use the substance (e.g., chain smoking), or recover from its effects.
6. Important social, occupational, or recreational activities are given up or reduced because of substance use
7. The substance use is continued despite knowledge of having a persistent or recurring physical or psychological problem that is likely to have been caused or exacerbated by the substances

(e.g., current cocaine use despite recognition of cocaine-induced depression, or continued drinking despite recognition that an ulcer was made worse by alcohol consumption)" (4)

To further muddy the waters, some patients misuse their medications, but don't yet fully meet the criteria for a diagnosis of addiction. These patients can be diagnosed with opioid *abuse*. The DSM-IV also has criteria for this less serious disorder:

DSM-IV TR Criteria for Substance Abuse

"Substance abuse is defined as a maladaptive pattern of substance use leading to clinically significant impairment or distress as manifested by one (or more) of the following, occurring within a 12- month period:

1. Recurrent substance use resulting in a failure to fulfill major role obligations at work, school, or home (such as repeated absences or poor work performance related to substance use; substance-related absences, suspensions, or expulsions from school; or neglect of children or household).
2. Recurrent substance use in situations in which it is physically hazardous (such as driving an automobile or operating a machine when impaired by substance use).
3. Recurrent substance-related legal problems (such as arrests for substance-related disorderly conduct).
4. Continued substance use despite having persistent or recurrent social or interpersonal problems caused or exacerbated by the effects of the substance (for example, arguments with spouse about consequences of intoxication and physical fights).
   Note: The symptoms for abuse have never met the criteria for dependence for this class of substance." (4)

That last sentence means that once a patient meets criteria for addiction, later in life he can't be diagnosed with the milder diagnosis of abuse. As recovering people have phrased it, "Once you become a pickle, you can't go back to being a cucumber."

Unfortunately, different workers in the field of addiction have used different phrases to mean the same thing, and it can be confusing. What the DSM-IV calls "dependence," I will call "addiction." I do this because it makes my meaning clearer; many people think dependence means only the physical part of the addiction, rather than what the people who wrote the DSM-IV had in mind when they use the term, which is true *addiction*.

The main difference between abuse and addiction is that a person with abuse can still voluntarily stop using drugs and stay stopped, if he has a good enough reason to do so. He retains the power of choice over his consumption of the drug. With addiction, control over the drug is partially or completely impaired.

Some pain patients made bad choices to misuse their medications, either from curiosity or peer influence, pushing them farther over the line into addiction. Patients should recognize their own contribution to their addiction, but this doesn't mean they're bad people nor have weak characters. They made a mistake. With opioid addiction, as the disease progresses, the addict loses the power of choice she once had. If an addict is fortunate enough to have a moment of clarity before the disease progresses too far, she may be able to stop on her own, without treatment.

Opioid addiction is somewhat different than other addictions. Once patients get through the acute withdrawal phase, it is often followed by a period of post acute withdrawal, lasting weeks to months. In post acute withdrawal from opioids, patients feel persistently unwell. Though they don't feel the misery of acute withdrawal, they don't feel well. People describe feeling low grade, persistent fatigue, depression, and irritability. Not every addict who has stopped using opioids feels this post acute withdrawal, but many do. We don't know why it occurs in some recovering opioid addicts but not in others. The likelihood of post acute withdrawal probably increases with longer duration of opioid use and larger quantities of opioid drug use. This post acute withdrawal can be draining. Many newly recovering addicts relapse during the first weeks or months of complete abstinence from opioids.

Many scientists, including the methadone maintenance pioneer, Dr. Vincent Dole, postulated the body stops making its own endorphins when there's been an outside source of opioids. It's hypothesized that some people never start making their own endorphins again, giving the addict a perpetual post acute withdrawal state that is difficult to tolerate. (5) Presently, there is no way to know in advance which patients may have prolonged or even permanent post acute withdrawal from opioids. Nearly constant support and encouragement can help to sustain an addict's willingness to remain abstinent from opioids during this difficult time. For patients who chronically feel unwell off of all opioids, medication-assisted treatments with buprenorphine or methadone are a welcome and effective option.

To fully understand and appreciate what addiction means and how difficult recovery can be for someone addicted to opioid medications, we need to see this disease from the patients' point of view.

Endnotes

1. Michael J. Brownstein, *A brief history of opiates, opioid peptides, and opioid receptors*, in Proc. Natl. Acad. Sci., USA, Vol. 90, pp 5391-93 June 1993.
2. Haddox JD, Smith M, Colucci S, et al., Pain as a Reason for Seeking Admission to Methadone Treatment. Program and abstracts of the American Academy of Pain Medicine 23rd Annual Meeting; February 7-10, 2007; New Orleans, Louisiana. Abstract 104.
3. Eric Strain M.D. and Maxine Stitzer, PhD., *The Treatment of Opioid Dependence*, (Baltimore, MD, The Johns Hopkins University Press, 2003) p 336.
4. *Diagnostic and Statistical Manual of Mental Disorders, DSM-IV-TR*, 4th ed., (American Psychiatric Publishing, 2000).
5. David Courtwright, Herman Joseph, and Don DesJarlais, *Addicts Who Survived: An Oral History of Narcotic Use in America, 1923-1965*, (Knoxville, TN, The University of Tennessee Press, 1989). p 339.

CHAPTER 2

Craving a Cure – The Patients

No stars were visible in the long night of the opium habit,
Dr. Judas by William Cobbe

"I've never had a problem with drugs. I've had problems with the police."
-Musician Keith Richards

When I started working at a methadone clinic in a large Southern city in 2001, I expected the patients would be intravenous heroin addicts, and many patients fit that description. But I was surprised by the number of young adults from rural areas, so desperate to find treatment for their pain pill addiction, they would drive up to an hour and a half, one way, to our clinic.

I knew addiction is an equal opportunity destroyer, capable of affecting anyone, but I had no idea pain pill addiction was becoming so prevalent in Western North Carolina and surrounding Appalachian areas. Beginning around 2001, workers in treatment centers in these areas saw a leap in the number of rural prescription opioid addicts.

Many patients were in their early twenties, and were using Oxy-Contin, a drug I hadn't heard of until the patients described it to me. These young people were crushing the pills, to snort or to inject. I wasn't completely naïve about addiction, but I didn't know these pills could be snorted, much less injected. Patient after patient would describe how they filed off the pill's time release coating, then crushed the pill to snort. Some addicts mixed the crushed pill with water and drew this solution into a syringe to inject. They also described their use of pills containing hydrocodone, called "hydros" (as opposed to "oxy's" or "OC's" for OxyContin). Most patients took the hydrocodone pills by mouth, because they were so large, but some patients snorted these pills also.

Some patients used fentanyl patches. Some patients didn't wear them on their skin as intended, but either ate the gel contained in the patches, or dissolved the gel in water to inject into their veins. I had no idea this could be done and I am fairly sure most doctors would be surprised to learn this. Fentanyl is an extremely potent opioid, so the patients who injected this drug were taking an incredible risk.

I had a hard time imagining how pain pill addiction had seized the areas of rural Appalachia. I've always loved the beauty of the Appalachians Mountains and their foothills. I love their ancient peaks, rounded by the eons of time slipping over them.

I identified with the people of these mountains, whose hardscrabble lives mirror my own early years. I felt I understood these people, despite my years of schooling spent living in cities of at least moderate size. A chord of resonance was struck within me when I talked to these addicts. I was raised in Southeastern Ohio, on the northern side of the foothills of the Appalachians, and I heard the unusual words and phrases of my grandparents from the mouths of the addicts I treated.

To help you understand the power of opioids and addiction, I want to describe the people that I met. I want to speak for them and let people know they are nice, normal people. They're your grocery clerk, your hairdresser, the guy who works on your furnace. They sit beside you at the movies and behind you at church. They have built a tolerance to the opioids, so they don't look high. They look like normal people, unless they run out of opioids. Then, they experience the misery of withdrawal, and are usually unable to go to work or function at all.

Some people compare opioid withdrawal to having the flu, but it's much worse. Most addicts in opioid withdrawal are unable to work, because of the severe muscle aches, nausea, vomiting, and diarrhea. Many of these patients are blue collar workers with physically demanding jobs, who initially used pain pills to mask their physical pain. They thought it allowed them to work harder, better, and faster, never guessing that what seemed to be helping was actually causing more harm than they could imagine.

When I worked for a non-profit methadone clinic, I didn't see many white collar patients. Most were blue collar workers, like construction workers or waitresses. This wasn't surprising, since addicted professionals and middle to upper class patients with insurance usually went to inpatient residential rehabilitation programs. After buprenorphine (Suboxone), became available in 2003, middle and upper class patients could go to doctors' offices for treatment, instead of methadone clinics. However, since Suboxone treatment is still much more expensive than treatment at a methadone clinic, most blue collar opioid addicts can't afford that option, unless they have health insurance.

Few patients at the methadone clinic had any insurance, other than Medicaid. Medicaid covers the cost of treatment at some methadone clinics, but many clinics don't want to take Medicaid, due to the large administrative burden it brings to the clinic. Medicaid does pay for Suboxone prescriptions, but pays little for doctors' visits, so most doctors who prescribe Suboxone take few, if any, Medicaid patients.

Some of the patients who came for treatment had already tried inpatient treatment and had relapsed, or had tried to get into an inpatient program, but were unable to afford it. There was a state funded inpatient program for indigent patients, but the waiting list was long. Recently, their program cut their length of stay to seven to ten days, instead of twenty-one to twenty-eight days, as in the past. A week or so is enough time for detox, now termed "withdrawal management," but that's not long enough to teach patients the skills they'll need to remain drug free. Relapse rates with detox treatment alone are as high as ninety-six percent in the first year. Most relapses occur within the first month.

Many patients were active in their church and communities. Most were not social misfits; they were trying to participate in their families and communities, but addiction interfered. Many addicted patients hadn't embraced a subculture identity of a drug user; in fact, most would recoil in horror when I asked them if they had ever used heroin, because they saw that drug as more destructive, and somehow worse than their own pill addiction. Quite often, the patient cited inability to participate in work or family activities, or the threatened loss of work or family, as factors that prompted them to seek help. Most didn't glamorize their addiction as did some of the young heroin addicts, particularly the college students, who seemed more likely to embrace a subculture value system.

The majority of opioid addicts that I met were average Americans.

My descriptions of patients are generalizations, but I want to give you an example of a patient seeking admission to the methadone clinic. What follows is a composite of a typical history given by a patient

"I started using pain pills in high school. I had friends who used them and I thought it would be OK. I didn't realize how addicting they were. Gradually, I started using them every day and once I didn't have any and I felt really sick. You know, with bad pains all over my body and throwing up and diarrhea. I didn't know what was happening. Then my friend said, 'You're dope sick,' and I took a pain pill and it all went away. That's when I knew I was addicted.

"At first, you know, I just wanted to get that high feeling. And I took more and more to get it and then started snorting the oxys. I didn't ever use a needle. I had more sense than that, thank God, like some end up doing. But now it's getting expensive and that's money I could be spendin' on my kids. They deserve better than that. But every time I try to quit, I can't. I make it a few days, but then feel so bad I have to use drugs again.

"I have to work every day. I can't be out of work sick for a week, waiting for the withdrawal to go away. I have to support my family. My cousin was just as bad addicted as I am and he got on this methadone program and he's doing a lot better now. He's saving money and doing things with his kids and his old lady isn't mad at him the whole time. He looks a lot better. He told me I should come here and get help too.

"I just want to feel normal again. I can't even remember what normal feels like."

Not many of the patients I saw at the methadone clinic became addicted only to the prescription opioids which were prescribed for them. Many of the addicts I saw started taking pain pills prescribed by their doctor, but they continued to get pain pills from a variety of sources. Sometimes this meant they returned to a different doctor, but often they obtained pills from friends or relatives. Opioid pain medications were more available, because they were being prescribed more frequently, due to the national movement to treat pain more aggressively. Prescription pain pills were easy to find on the black market.

After talking to thousands of opioid addicts over the course of seven years, a common theme emerged: these patients were surprised that prescription medication could be so harmful. Many addicts said that because they were prescription, they thought it meant they were safe. Most of the addicts had no idea how easy it was to develop a physical and psychological dependence on the pills. How could they? Even pain management specialists were wrong about the risk of addiction.

Many of the addicts were in tears as they told me that if they'd known what could happen, they never would have taken the first pill.

I was surprised how casually people shared controlled substances with one another. As a physician, it seems like a big deal to me if somebody takes a schedule II or schedule III controlled substance that wasn't prescribed for them, but the addicts I interviewed swapped these pills with little apprehension or trepidation. Taking pain pills to get through the day's work seemed to have become part of the culture in some areas. Sharing these pills with friends and family members who had pain was acceptable to people in these communities.

In the past, most of the public service announcements and other efforts to prevent and reduce drug use focused on street drugs. Many people seemed to think this meant marijuana, cocaine, methamphetamine, and heroin. The patients I saw didn't consider prescription pills bought on the street as street drugs. They saw this as a completely different thing, and occasionally spoke derisively about addicts using "hard drugs." Most addicts didn't understand the power of the drugs they were taking.

Some opioid addicts came for help as couples. One of them, through the closeness of romance, transmitted the addiction like an infectious disease to their partner. Most were boyfriend/girlfriend, but some were married. The non-addicted partner's motives to begin using drugs seemed to be mixed. Some started using out of curiosity, but others started using drugs to please their partner. I was disturbed to see that some of the women accepted the inevitability of addiction for themselves as the cost of being in a relationship with an addicted boyfriend. Often, addicted couples socialized with other addicted couples, as if opioid addiction bound them like a common fondness for bowling or dancing. Addiction became a bizarre thread, woven through the fabric of social networks.

We saw extended family networks in treatment for pain pill addiction at the methadone clinics. One addicted member of a family came for help, and after their life improved, the rest of the addicted family came for treatment too. It was common to have a husband and wife both in treatment, and perhaps two generations of family members, including aunts, uncles, and cousins. Many addicts who entered treatment saw people they knew from the addicted culture of their area, and sometimes old disputes would be reignite, requiring action from clinic staff. Sometimes ex-spouses and ex-lovers would have to be assigned different hours to dose at the clinic, to prevent conflict.

When the non-profit methadone clinic where I worked began accepting Medicaid as payment for treatment, we immediately saw much sicker people. Over all, Medicaid patients have more mental and physical health issues. Co-existing mental health issues make addiction more difficult to treat, and these patients were at higher risk for adverse effects of methadone. However, data does show that these sicker patients can benefit the most from treatment.

When I started to work for a for-profit clinic, I saw a slightly different patient population. I saw more middle class patients, with pink and white-collar jobs. Occasionally, we treated business professionals. The daily cost of methadone was actually a little cheaper at the for-profit clinic, at three hundred dollars per month, as compared to the non-profit clinic, at three hundred and thirty dollars per month. However, the for-profit clinic charged a seventy dollar one-time admission fee, to cover the costs of blood tests for hepatitis, liver and kidney function, blood electrolytes, and a screening test for syphilis. The non-profit clinic had no admission fee, but only did blood testing for syphilis. I believe the seventy dollars entry fee was enough to prevent admission of poorer patients, who had a difficult enough time paying eleven dollars for their first and all subsequent days.

The patients at the for-profit clinic seemed a little more stable. Maybe they hadn't progressed as far into their disease of addiction, or maybe they had better social support for their recovery. This clinic didn't accept Medicaid, which discouraged sicker patients with this type of health coverage. Both clinics were reaching opioid addicts; they just served slightly different populations of addicts. The non-profit clinic accepted sicker patients, which is noble, but it made for a more chaotic clinic setting. This was compounded by a management style that was, in a few of their eight clinics, more relaxed.

For the seven years I worked for a non-profit opioid treatment center, I watched it expand from one main city clinic, and one satellite in a nearby small town, to eight separate clinic sites. The treatment center did this because they began to have large numbers of patients who drove long distances for treatment. This indicated a need for a clinic to be located in the areas where these patients lived. Most of this expansion occurred over the years 2002 through 2006.

Three of these clinics were located in somewhat suburban areas, within a forty-five minute drive from the main clinic, located in a large

Southern city. The other four clinics were in small towns drawing patients from mostly rural areas. One clinic was located in a small mountain town that was home to a modest-sized college. Nearly all of the heroin addicts I saw in the *rural* clinics were students at that college. But by 2008, we began to see more rural heroin addicts, who had switched from prescription pain pills to heroin, due to the rising costs of pills.

Within a few years, clinics near the foothills of the Blue Ridge Mountains of Western North Carolina were swamped with opioid addicts requesting admission to the methadone clinics. These clinics soon had many more patients than the urban clinic.

I saw racial dissimilarities at the clinic sites. In the city, we admitted a fair number of African Americans and other minorities to our program. Most of them weren't using pain pills, but heroin. I don't know why this was the case. Perhaps minorities didn't have doctors as eager to prescribe opioids for their chronic pain conditions, or perhaps they didn't go to doctors for their pain as frequently as whites. If they were addicted to pain pills, maybe distrust kept them from entering the methadone clinic. In the rural clinics, I could count the number of African-American patients on one hand. They were definitely under-represented. The minorities we did treat responded to treatment just as well.

A recent study of physicians' prescribing habits suggested a disturbing possibility for the racial differences I saw in opioid addiction. (1) This article showed statistically significant differences in the rate of opioid prescriptions for whites, compared to non-whites, in the emergency department setting. Despite an overall rise in rates of the prescription of opioid pain medication in the emergency department setting between 1993 and 2005, whites still received opioid prescriptions more frequently than did Black, Asian, or Hispanic races, for pain from the same medical conditions. In thirty-one percent of emergency room visits for painful conditions, whites received opioids, compared to only twenty-three percent of visits by Blacks, twenty-eight percent for Asians, and twenty-four percent for Hispanic patients. These patients were seen for the *same* painful medical condition. The prescribing differences were even more pronounced as the intensity of the pain increased, and were most pronounced for the conditions of back pain, headache, and abdominal pain. Blacks had the lowest rates of receiving opioid prescriptions of all races.

This study could have been influenced by other factors. For example, perhaps non-whites request opioid medications at a lower rate than whites. Even so, given the known disparities in health care for whites, versus non-whites in other areas of medicine, it would appear patient ethnicity influences physicians' prescribing habits for opioids. The disparities and relative physician reluctance to prescribe opioids for minorities may reduce their risk of developing opioid addiction, though at the *unacceptably high cost of under treatment of pain*.

Interestingly, we had pockets of Asian patients in several clinics. We admitted one member of the Asian community into treatment, and after they improved, began to see other addicted members of their extended family arrive at the clinic for treatment. Usually the Asian patients either smoked opium or dissolved it in hot water to make a tea and drank it. When I tried to inquire how much they were using each day, in order to try to quantify their tolerance, the patient would put his or her thumb about a centimeter from the end of the little finger and essentially say, "this much." Having no idea of the purity of their opium, this gave me no meaningful idea of their tolerance, so we started with cautiously low doses.

One middle aged patient from the Hmong tribe presented to the clinic and when I asked when and why he started opioid use, in broken English and with difficulty, he told me he had lost eight children during the Vietnam War, and was injured himself. After the pain from his injury had resolved, he still felt pain from the loss of his family and he decided to continue the use of opium to treat the pain of his heart, as he worded it. I thought about how similar his history was to the patients of the U.S. and how they often started using opioids and other drugs to dull the pain of significant loss and sorrow. I thought about how people of differing ethnicities are similar, when dealing with addiction, pain, and grief.

I always asked the addicts entering treatment where they lived. I heard the names of the same small towns over and over again. No wonder many addicts at our clinics knew each other.

The methadone clinic near the Tennessee border had a great influx of patients from that state. This clinic was extremely busy. Before Suboxone was approved as an effective treatment for opioid addiction in 2002, our methadone clinic was the only option for medication-assisted treatment within a two hours' drive for many of these addicts.

Officials in Tennessee were not receptive when our organization (and others) tried to open methadone clinics in their state. They said it would create addicts were none existed, and bring the wrong element into their region.

That's not an unusual response to addiction. It's not only addicts who can be in denial about the extent of this disease. State and local governmental officials can be in as much denial as the addicts. Ironically, we had relatives of city or state officials dosing in our methadone program, but they suffered alone, scared to speak of their addiction, due to the stigma that was so obvious in this area. Fortunately, after 2002, doctors in that area began to prescribe buprenorphine, which likely saved the lives of many opioid addicts in that region. However, citizens in this area are trying to prevent the availability of even that life saving treatment.

The Johnson City Regional Planning Commission actually voted to stop the establishment of any further substance abuse treatment facilities. Given the numbers of opioid addicted citizens in this area, their decision is appalling. The following is taken from the minutes of the Johnson City Regional Planning Commission, 4/6/08:

"To recommend the City Commission enact a temporary moratorium on the establishment of any future substance abuse treatment facilities."

The motion carried by a 10 – 0 vote. (2)

Preventing the establishment of substance abuse treatment centers won't help this area recover. The National Survey of Drug Use and Health, in its 2008 report, found that Eastern Tennessee was one of a handful of sub-state areas with the very highest rates of nonmedical use of opioids, at 6.62%, compared to the national average of 4.9%. In comparison, Western North Carolina, by the time of this 2008 report, had a rate of nonmedical use of opioids that was a little less than the national average at 4.59%. (3) Below is the pictorial representation of this data:

As the map shows, Eastern Tennessee is one of a handful of areas with the highest rate of nonmedical use of prescription pain pills. It's difficult to attribute the actions of local Eastern Tennessee politicians to anything other than denial, fear, or ignorance. They'll reap the bitter

Figure 1. Nonmedical Use of Pain Relievers in the Past Year among Persons Aged 12 or Older, by Substate Region*: Percentages, Annual Averages Based on 2004, 2005, and 2006 National Survey of Drug Use in Households

harvest of their actions for years to come in the forms of increased crime and human misery.

Difficulties

Troubling issues arose when I worked at the non-profit clinic. I knew what the studies had shown, but I wasn't always sure our clinic was giving the best care possible. Some of our clinics were overwhelmed with the numbers of opioid addicts who wanted help. Our clinics admitted addicts to treatment on the day they asked for help. This is called "treatment on demand" and it's an ideal policy in addiction treatment. When an addict has a moment of clarity and willingness, it's best to get that addict into treatment quickly, before he changes his mind.

This is a good strategy, but quality of care should not be sacrificed to achieve it. On intake days at one of the clinics, we often had thirty or more addicts arrive, desiring admission. With the number of staff we had, there was no way we could safely admit all of these people in one day. The amount of time that should be spent with each new patient prohibits entry of that many patients in a single day. And yet, I hated to send away addicts who were seeking help, without receiving treatment, with only an exhortation to try to come back next week, a bit earlier, to be first in line. On these days, I saw as many as I could, and sometimes admitted as many as twenty people in one day.

Even though we had to turn some people away, we took a great many into treatment, and the clinics grew quickly. I worried that the quality of our care suffered. The counselor's case loads were frequently above federal limits of fifty patients per counselor. The counselors and nurses were wonderful, but one human can only do so much in an eight hour day. On some days, patients stood in line for an hour to get their dose at some clinic sites. I know they had to be frustrated and angry, as anyone would be. Maybe growing pains are the best kind of pains to have, but I was uneasy, and many of the staff echoed my concerns. I discussed the overcrowding with the administrators of the clinic, but I didn't feel like my concerns were heard. In fact, those administrators pressured me to admit even more new addicts to treatment.

Yet what were the options? If we were overwhelmed and couldn't admit addicts to our program, we recommended other treatment alternatives. However, many other resources, like detoxification units, were full with waiting lists. Most patients couldn't afford the subsequent inpatient treatment that should follow a detoxification, which needs to last a month to prevent a relapse, when treating opioid addiction. Some of the patients who *could* afford inpatient treatment refused to consider it as an option for a variety of reasons: fear of going through withdrawal, fear of an unfamiliar environment, or because they weren't yet willing to be completely opioid-free.

That methadone clinic was the only realistic treatment option for most of these addicts. People have faulted methadone clinics for starting patients on methadone before other treatment options have been tried. But in the real world, or at least in the part of the country where I worked, other workable treatment options didn't exist for patients without health insurance. And few of the patients we saw had health insurance.

Prior to their admission, I talked to patients about all treatment options, and explained how difficult it is to taper off methadone. The few times when a patient agreed to go to inpatient treatment – detox, to be followed by a twenty-eight day rehab – I could not find a place to accept him. If an inpatient program could be found, they didn't do detox, and demanded the patient be drug free and out of withdrawal before he could enter. Sometimes I could find a detox bed, but no inpatient program to take them immediately after the withdrawal was finished. If there's any gap between detox and inpatient rehabilitation, the patient will usually relapse. When treating an opioid addict who prefers to go a drug-free route of recovery, they need to go directly from the detoxification center to the inpatient rehabilitation, with no chance to go home to get clothes (and drugs), etc.

I've spent hours on the phone, trying to arrange an inpatient admission. More often I asked a counselor to do this frustrating job, and he or she spent hours on the task. The very agencies who talked bad about the methadone clinics were the ones who couldn't help us when we had an addict who agreed to go to an inpatient program. Many drug treatment facilities asked that the patient pay a significant sum of money prior to admission, and the patients didn't have that money.

Both the counselor and I would get frustrated with the difficulties and run-arounds we got from various agencies. And if we felt frustrated, how much more would an addict, in withdrawal and seeking help, when met with these obstacles?

The next closest methadone clinic was over seventy-five miles away. Suboxone was an option, but again, its expense put that out of reach for most addicts. I gave Narcotics Anonymous meeting schedules to patients, never knowing how many went to these free meetings for help.

People sometimes say if addicts could afford their dope, then they have enough money to pay for treatment. That's only partially true. Most addicts live day to day, and can find only enough money for that day's drugs – one way or another. Many times, this means resorting to criminal acts. Up to seventy percent of addicts sell drugs to help finance their own addiction. Some women resorted to prostitution. Many addicts can't pay a treatment center that asks for two-thousand dollars or even two-hundred dollars prior to admission. Some areas of the country may have inpatient addiction treatment readily available for the poor, but not in the area where I worked.

I have a doctor friend who works at a very posh, very good, rehabilitation center. I was talking to her about my problems with the opioid addicts, and she said their center would be willing to give scholarships for addicts. I deeply appreciated that....and I know she has helped some indigent addicts. It was a tremendous help for those few addicts, but it feels like removing several teaspoons from a swimming pool.

We were trying to balance patient safety and quality of care against a tidal wave of opioid addicts, rushing toward us, demanding help. More counselors were slowly added, but it never seemed enough. It felt like we were frequently teetering on the edge of chaos, but I always left work feeling that I'd helped a great many people. I felt I did more good in one day, prescribing methadone to help stabilize these opioid addicts, than I could do in a month working in primary care.

Now I work in a for-profit clinic that takes the counselor/patient ratio requirement seriously. New counselors are hired before long before the existing counselors have fifty patients. Overall there is a marked difference in management style from the first clinic where I worked. It's smaller, with less chaos, and I feel I know the patients much better. That means I'm able to make better treatment decisions, and the patients get better care.

Patients at the methadone clinics can be difficult. Addicts develop coping behaviors that work well on the streets, but cause problems in a treatment center, and can alienate the staff. Addiction can at times manifest as bad behavior. Not all patients who enter treatment actually *want* treatment. Some patients have divided hearts. Part of them wants treatment, and part of them wants to keep using drugs and getting high. This isn't uncommon; many addicts enter treatment with this ambivalence. Multiple studies show these patients can still have good outcomes if they can be retained in treatment. If they can engage in counseling, their focus can change from the drugs onto positive things they wish to accomplish.

Addiction is a disease that entices people to lie. In order for the addiction to continue, lies must be told. For example, if patient X asks her Aunt Sara for a forty dollar loan, her request is more likely to be granted if she says she needs it for gas money to get to work than if she says the forty dollars is going to buy OxyContin pills to snort.

Usually I'm able to accept lying as a part of a difficult disease. Addiction can cause honest people to lie. Usually, I don't take it personally. It's about the disease of addiction, not the character of the addicted person, or me.

There is an exception. I get very angry when addicts in treatment at a methadone clinic lie about the clinic to other doctors or to people in the community. When addicts tell untrue tales about the methadone clinic, public opinion of methadone treatment plunges further. This form of treatment already has enough bias against it.

I've had patients who told other doctors, "They won't let me bring my dose down. They want me to stay on a high dose." But clinics can't keep patients from reducing their dose, if this is what they want. If a patient tells their clinic that they're drowsy or fatigued on their dose of methadone, the clinic will immediately decrease the dose. If they want to come off methadone, we'll honor their wishes, though ideally we'd first like to give them our best recommendations about tapering methadone, in order to help them be successful. But we do *not* keep someone on a methadone program against their will. Patients may tell their family that the methadone clinic won't let them reduce their dose so the family won't blame the addict for being on methadone. ("It's not my fault. I want to get off methadone, but they won't let me").

Other stories that ex-patients tell include things like, "They just cut me off cold turkey." The only time I've cut patients off methadone suddenly was when we discovered the patient was getting methadone, or another strong opioid, from another source, or they were dosing at a second clinic. A methadone clinic may stop dosing a patient suddenly if he's been violent on clinic premises, but usually a transfer to a different clinic is offered.

Some clinics will taper a patient off of methadone rather quickly, if he or she can't afford to pay the daily fee. I've seen clinics do this over a four day period, which is very fast. But if the patient's urine drug screen is negative, most clinics will keep the patient for at least several weeks, to see if another solution can be found. If the patient's urine drug screen is positive for illicit drugs, most clinics will not waive dosing fees, since the clinic would then be subsidizing the patient's illicit drug use. In cases of financial hardship, most clinics cut the patient's dose of methadone over ten to twenty-one days, which is still fast.

It does seem harsh to discharge a patient from treatment because of an inability to pay – but that's what happens to people in this country with all types of illnesses.

I get angry when a patient tells people in the community, "There's just a bunch of people selling drugs in the parking lot of that clinic." Often, this means that *this patient* was selling drugs, and he had to be dismissed from the clinic. Drug dealing does occur at treatment centers, but most clinics try to make their clinics a safe place. We need the patients to help us, by alerting us to people trying to sell drugs on clinic property.

Unquestionably, the best part of my job working at a methadone clinic is watching people get better, and most patients do get better on methadone. When I see them on admission day, most look tired and disheartened. When I see them after a week or two, they look like younger, happier versions of themselves. I'm honored to be able to witness these changes. Not every patient has such a positive change, but most do.

Am I painting too positive a picture? I don't think so, given the alternatives. Some patients appear to have little chance of success. Some patients tell me on admission that they don't want to get off all drugs completely, and they only want to stop their opioid use. At least that's a starting point.

I remember an addict whom I'll call Carl. When I admitted Carl to the methadone clinic, I didn't like him very much. He was a thug, with thuggish ways, and he seemed to go out of his way to be unpleasant to all staff. He took particular pains to irritate me. He dressed like a drug dealer, because he was a drug dealer. Other patients said he used to be their "dope man," because he had several "hook ups for Oxys," in their lingo. I watched Carl closely, concerned that he might try to sell drugs to other patients while on our premises. Carl probably sensed my scrutiny, and responded with barely concealed hostility.

I was surprised when Carl made an appointment to see me at the clinic. He came into my office and stammered about anxiety, and how difficult life was. He had difficulty coming to the point, but eventually revealed he had unbearable anxiety. With his swagger, he didn't seem to have had an anxious feeling in his entire life, but the swagger was his façade, hiding an immense store of anxiety. I tried to view this as a medical problem, because some anxiety disorders are caused my chemical imbalances, and there were medications I could prescribe, though not benzodiazepines, that could help him. At the end of our visit, I started to explain this to Carl, but he interrupted me. I don't recall his exact words, but he said something like this:

"No, doc. You don't understand. I've been selling dope for years, and I think...maybe I just don't....I'm...really sorry for all of that. I've been thinking and thinking and I don't know how to make up for all of that. Selling drugs, I mean. Then I get real anxious, you know?"

I didn't know, but I let him talk. He had real guilt about bad things he had done in his life, and wanted to know how to get rid of this guilt. It seemed like he needed a way to atone for his past actions. I directed him to one of our counselors who had extensive experience with 12-step programs, since I knew the 12-step programs have steps that deal with past wrongdoings. I also asked if he had any particular religious affiliations that could provide answers. I felt lame. The best I could do was medicalize his problem, and I sensed that wouldn't work in this case.

I saw him several months later and he looked completely different. His walk, his clothes, his expression, even his voice was different. He looked happy. He had followed through with some suggestions from his counselor. He'd started going to Narcotics Anonymous meetings, and also went back to church. He said he'd found meaning and purpose for his life and a way to let his past help him be a better person in the future. He told me the anxiety was gone, and he felt good about the direction his life was going.

Watching one patient totally change makes up for the daily challenges of the methadone clinic. The complete change that happens in some people when they find recovery is astounding. I wish all addicts seeking recovery could find this.

Following is an interview with a successfully recovering opioid addict. He received treatment at methadone clinics off and on for years, and finally achieved medication-free recovery after going to an inpatient treatment program for 42 days. Later, he began to work in the field of addiction treatment as a methadone counselor. He was promoted multiple times over the years to his present position as director of the narcotic treatment program at his clinic. This is his perspective about his own experience and what he's seen with methadone treatment.

JB: Can you tell me your title at the opioid treatment clinic where you work?

KS: Director of Narcotic Treatment, which is our opioid treatment program. [He supervises counselors working at eight clinic sites, with a total census of around thirty-four hundred methadone patients]

JB: Can you please tell me about your own opioid addiction, and how you got into recovery, including what kind of substances you may have used, what kind of treatments, and your experiences with them?

KS: I started out using pain killers, mostly Percodan tablets, back in the late 70's, which lead me to using heroin. Heroin wasn't easy to get [where I lived], so I started using Dilaudids [a name brand of the drug oxymorphone]. I started using Dilaudid on a regular basis in the county I lived in, Gaston County. That was the primary drug I used for quite a few years.

[My] first experience with methadone treatment started in 1978, with a brief episode of treatment, a matter of a month or so, with no success. Pretty much during the 1980's, I was on and off methadone programs with little or no success, because I refused to participate in group or individual sessions. At the time, there was very limited counseling going on [at methadone clinics]. If there was a problem, you saw your counselor, and that didn't happen a whole lot. Patients were simply trying to get more methadone. At that point, the methadone dosages were very low. I think the average dose back then was somewhere between forty and fifty milligrams. And we [patients on methadone] didn't know that. We didn't know that. We just found out through....

JB: You didn't know what dose you were taking?

KS: Oh, no. We didn't know what dose we were taking, for a number of years. As a matter of fact, that didn't change until right before 2001.

JB: Wow

KS: Yeah.

JB: Could the patient find out if they wanted to? [the dose they were taking]

KS: We were blind dosed then. That didn't change until just before 2001.

JB: Was that unusual for methadone clinics to do?

KS: To my knowledge, I think we [the clinic where he now works, and previously was a patient] were one of the last ones to keep doing that. It was just something we had done over the years and never changed it. [The patients] didn't know what their dose was.

Through the 1980's, I was on and off methadone programs, sometimes for a few years at a time, and sometimes had some success. The biggest benefit I had from taking methadone and being on the program was that I was able to work. I held a job the entire time, and I wasn't doing anything criminal. It served the purpose it was supposed to serve there, because I had to work, and I was able to function fairly normally. But I never moved into actual recovery, and still used some opiates from time to time. So that was pretty much the 80's. Two good things happened in the 80's. In 1981 my son was born, and in 1989, I got clean.

JB: Big things.

KS: Two monumental things in my life. So, I went through that period of time I had talked about, when I started using opiates, in about 1974. Then I started getting on the methadone programs, on and off, [starting] from '78, but I continued to use. I was using Dilaudids on a daily basis for a number of years. When I got on the methadone program, I would curtail that, but always wanted to go back to Dilaudid. That [Dilaudid] became my drug of choice.

I was on the methadone program in 1989, and having some problems with alcohol. Prior to getting on the program, I was told, "We're not going to allow you on the program, unless you go on Antabuse." So I did that and I was successful at stopping drinking, and had some success with methadone. I decided I wanted off the methadone, started detoxing off, and had a series of positive drug screens for a variety of opiates: morphine, Dilaudid, and several different things I had access to. The methadone center said, "We're going to make a recommendation that you enter residential treatment." And I said, "Sounds great to me, I'll do that in a couple months." And they said, "No. We're going to make a recommendation you do that... pretty quickly."

And that's what happened. I said, "I don't think I can do this. I've got some things to do." And I remember it like it was yesterday. The counselor got up and walked out of the room and he left me sitting there by myself. Then he walked back in, said, "We've got you a bed." And that's what lead me to [inpatient treatment].

So I went to forty-two days of residential treatment, and actually entered that program ready to quit using and get into recovery. And from that point on, recovery has been the most important thing in my life….family, of course…but I've pursued recovery since May 3, 1989. I followed all the suggestions. [I'm] still really involved with 12- step meetings, and still really involved with some of the same things I did when I first came in [to recovery]. Obviously, I don't go to as many meetings, but still go to meetings on a regular basis

JB: Do you have any regrets about either type of treatment? The forty-two day inpatient or the methadone?

KS: I do believe that in my case, I needed to be taken away from my environment, simply because of the people I was associated with. That's not the case for everyone. In my case, I needed to be away from my environment. So the detoxing from the methadone and going into a residential program, that's what worked for me. Obviously, people can do that other ways. But I still had people in my life that were negative influences.

JB: If you had an opioid addict who presented for treatment for the first time, what would you recommend? If money were no object?

KS: I'd recommend that individual seek inpatient treatment. Now, if they had an extended history of opiate dependency, then that person's success rate in residential treatment is obviously going to be limited….and…it would just depend on the individual. Methadone treatment might be the way for them to go. I know that's kind of teetering on the fence. I'm going to be somewhat….I'm going to hold on to how powerful residential treatment was for me. But I had failed at methadone treatment. And, there again, it was a different time, the methadone doses weren't enough at the time.

JB: Did you feel normal on your dose of methadone or did you [still] feel withdrawal?

KS: I was feeling normal, however, I could still feel drug use [other opioids].

JB: So it wasn't a blocking dose?

KS: It was not a blocking dose. You knew if you got medicated at 7:00 am, at 5:00 pm you could fairly well feel somewhat of a rush and feel the effects of [other opioids].

JB: How did you get started working in the field of addiction treatment?

KS: I came out of treatment, worked for a family business for a couple of years, and always, from day one, I thought, "What a fascinating thing….if I could somehow do this…to get into that line of work [meaning addiction counseling].

I started, after two years, as an evening counselor at a residential treatment program, and saw that I really wanted to do that. There was an avenue for non-degreed people to come in to a counselor position. You didn't have to have a degree in substance abuse or anything like that, so I pursued that, and followed the certification process. I didn't work in residential treatment but nine months, and then moved to methadone counseling. From that point on, I had found what I wanted to do. And I've been offered a promotion at the treatment center to another department when I was over the methadone program, and turned it down to stay with that population [meaning opioid addicts in treatment on methadone].

JB: So you obviously enjoy it.

KS: Oh yeah.

JB: What did you like about it?

KS: I think my ability to relate to that population, without having any thought or putting any real effort…I don't have to think about it. I *know* I can talk to that population, and I know I can make them feel normal, by just holding a conversation with them….it might not be about drug use. It might not be about anything pertaining to the treatment episode, but I feel like…that I know exactly where they're coming from, and I can give them some hope that they don't have to keep living that way. Just an identification with that population.

JB: That's a precious gift.

KS: I agree.

JB: Do you believe that your background in addiction helps you when you talk to patients?

KS: I do. I believe wholeheartedly that you can't teach that. I've had some people work for me who had a graduate degree, have never personally had an incidence of opioid addiction or any addiction in their family, and they're absolutely fantastic clinicians. And you know they're in that line of work for a reason. So [personal experience with addiction] does not need to be a criterion; in my case, it helps. I find it fascinating to watch someone work who has no self-history of addiction. They can be very effective.

JB: What are the biggest challenges you face now at your work?

KS: That would be...documentation. [The demand for] documentation in this field has really overcome the interpersonal relationship. I can't help but think as time goes on, that's going to continue. We don't have twenty or thirty minutes to sit down with a client, and get into one issue after another, or whatever [the client] may have on their plate. And in opioid treatment, a lot of times it's brief therapy. They [patients] don't want to talk to you for twenty or thirty minutes. But you don't have time to do that, because of the documentation. [The counselor has] three people waiting in the lobby, and you're kind of selling that person short.

The documentation standards continue to rise, and in methadone treatment, I don't know how that can go hand in hand with a fifty to one case load. Whereas, someone else might have the same documentation required in the mental health field, but they might have sixteen people they're seeing.

JB: So you're saying that the state and federal regulations about documentation actually interfere with the amount of counseling the patients get?

KS: Right. Right.

JB: That's sad.

The clinic where you work has eight different sites. Can you tell me about what sort of interactions you've had with the community leaders, local police, and medical community?

KS: Overall, with any opioid treatment program [methadone clinic], there's going to be a negative stereotype associated with it in the community, as you well know. Local law enforcement has a bias [against] the [methadone] program. What we've found is, any interaction we have with them, and the better understanding that they have [of what we do], the better. And I believe we can make a difference in what law enforcement, and other areas of the community [think about methadone programs]. It has to happen one person at a time.

An example of that would be when I got a call, a couple of weeks ago, to the Gastonia program at ten o'clock at night. An alarm is going off. So I meet the police out there, and we go in, make sure nobody's in the building. I'm trying to give him some information about it [the methadone program].

He says, "Is it true they come in every day and ya'll shoot 'em up?" (laughter) So he thinks that's what happens.

So, I educated him on what we do and followed that up with, "Why don't you stop by and get coffee any time you want to and we'll give you information." They were very receptive to that. That's how you've got to approach it. Be willing to talk to people and give them information. [Do the] same thing with community leaders. They're just not educated in outpatient opioid treatment. Once they get some information, they seem to have a different take on it.

JB: Can you tell me what you've seen, particularly over the last seven years, about the types of populations that are coming to the clinics, and if that's changed any?

KS: I started working in methadone treatment seventeen years ago. We used to have statistics on the methadone program. The average age of a person coming on the program was thirty-four years old, at that time. We had eighty or ninety people on the program and that was it. And they were long term users, primarily heroin as drug of choice. We've seen what's happening over the years.

Heroin has decreased somewhat. Prescription medications went wild. I just read information that forty-four percent of patients entering methadone programs in the nation were on prescription opioids. The age of the person coming on the program has dropped from thirty-four into their late twenties. I don't have that exact number. But we've seen them get younger, and we've seen prescription drugs take the place of heroin, in driving people into treatment.

JB: What seems to be the main type of prescription drug, or is there one?

KS: OxyContin changed the landscape in our setting. It's still a driving force, as far as putting people into treatment. We have an increase in heroin in Gaston county and Mecklenburg county [North Carolina], but the western part of the state...OxyContin and morphine are on the scene....and any painkiller.

JB: Do you have any opinion about why that happened? Why the incidence of pain pill addiction seemed to rise over the last seven to ten years?

KS: If there's a reason for it....I think it's generational. It's passed down. It's easy. You've got doctors giving the mother and the father painkillers for whatever reason, legitimate or not. It gets passed on...obviously there's a genetic link for some kinds of addiction or alcoholism. I think you know what you're getting there [meaning a prescription pill]. People addicted to opioid drugs have very few avenues to get quality heroin in those regions of the country. [Pain pills] are a sure bet. Patients say, "I know what I'm getting when I get that pill."

JB: If you had the ear of policy makers in Washington D.C., what would you tell them? What would you like to see happen in the treatment field for opioid addiction?

KS: I'm going to refer back to what I said earlier. In methadone treatment, there should be some kind of review, as far as what needs to be documented. Obviously, there needs to be accurate documentation, but not to put methadone or opioid treatment into the same mental health arena for documentation requirements. Because you're dealing with a different environment, a different population, and a different caseload.

JB: Would you like to see buprenorphine play a role [at the methadone clinic]?

KS: Yes, there's a need for it. You've got such a stereotype against methadone facilities, that's another avenue for people to be in treatment [meaning buprenorphine]....whether it's administered in the methadone facility or [community] doctor-based, there's a need for that.

This interview was with one of the many wonderful people I've had the honor of working with at methadone clinics. In my years of work in the medical field, I've never been surrounded by as many quality people, who had passion for their work, as I have in addiction medicine. I don't know if I've been extremely lucky, or if all addiction treatment centers draw dedicated individuals to work within their systems. Many of these workers try hard to dispel the stigma and social isolation that addicts feel. Sadly, even patients in treatment are sometimes treated badly, as we will see in later chapters describing the stigma that methadone and buprenorphine patients face.

End Notes

1. Pletcher M MD, MPH, Kertesz, MD, MSc et. al., "Trends in Opioid Prescribing by Race/Ethnicity for Patients Seeking Care in US Emergency Departments," *Journal of the American Medical Association*, 2008 vol. 299 (1) pp 70-78.
2. Johnson City Regional Planning Commission Minutes, 4/08. http://www.johnsoncitytn.org/uploads/Documents/Planning/Planning%20Commission/2008%20Documents/2008-04-08%20Minutes.pdf .
3. National Survey of Drug Use in Households, 2008, *Non-Medical Use of Pain Relievers in Sub-state Regions, 2004 – 2006.*

CHAPTER 3

Why Addiction Is a Chronic Disease

The American Society of Addiction Medicine, the most prestigious organization of addiction professionals, defines addiction as follows:

"Addiction is a primary, chronic, neurobiologic disease, with genetic, psychosocial, and environmental factors influencing its development and manifestations. It is characterized by behaviors that include one or more of the following: impaired control over drug use, compulsive use, continued use despite harm, and craving" (American Society of Addiction Medicine, 2001)

In other words, addiction is its own disease and not caused by anything else, though many other factors may influence its development and progression. Risk factors are both genetic and environmental. A person can be influenced by environment or personality characteristics to take drugs the first time, the second, and maybe even the tenth, but eventually an addict loses the power to control whether he takes the drug or not. The disease can be recognized by the behaviors of the addict, as discussed in Chapter 1, and by the mental obsession to use drugs.

Many families expect addiction treatment centers to "fix" their addicted loved ones forever. If the addict relapses, the family feels the treatment didn't work. Many other people, including politicians, policy makers, and even physicians, are disillusioned with the medical treatment of addiction, because relapse is so common. Sources cite relapse rates of forty to sixty percent in the first year of treatment (for all types of drugs, not just opioids). These families and community leaders make the mistake of assuming that addiction behaves like an *acute* disease. Like a broken bone or pneumonia, once it's treated, the problem is expected to be resolved.

We now know that addiction is a *chronic* disease, and it behaves like other chronic diseases, such as diabetes, asthma, and high blood pressure. While not everyone relapses, and all care should be taken to prevent a relapse, most addicts *do* experience periods of remission and relapse. As with other chronic diseases, there are two types of factors that influence the occurrence and course of disease: genetic makeup of the patient and environmental influences.

Genetic Factors

Diabetes and asthma are both recognized to run in families and have a genetic component influencing the development of disease. They both also have definite environmental factors that affect the development and course of disease. Some of the environmental factors are under the patient's control and some are not. The asthmatic may have no choice but to be exposed to smog and air pollution that makes the asthma worse. But the asthmatic does have the choice to avoid things that can make the disease flair, like cigarette smoke, or exposure to animals to which they are allergic. A diabetic may be genetically pre-disposed to high blood sugar, but if he maintains a healthy weight and exercises, he may never develop overt diabetes. If he doesn't exercise, and eats unwholesome foods and gains weight, the diabetes can emerge and worsen.

In this same manner, both genetics and environmental factors influence the risk of addictive disease. Dr. Thomas McLellan elegantly outlined this premise in his article *Drug Dependence as a Chronic Illness.* (1)

As he points out, we know genetic makeup influences addiction. One of the best ways to look for genetic influence on a disease is to compare disease rates in identical twins, compared to fraternal twins. Identical twins have 100% of the same genes, so if a disease is 100% genetically determined, both twins should have the disease – or not have the disease. This agreement between the disease or non-disease states is called "concordance." So in our 100% genetically determined disease, there should be 100% concordance between *identical* twins.

Fraternal twins share approximately 50% of the same genetic material. If we look at our disease that is 100% determined by genetics, we would expect a concordance rate in *fraternal* twins of around 50%, because fraternal twins share only 50% of the same genes. In other words, if one twin has the disease, there should be a 50% chance that the other twin will have the disease. Looking at the difference in concordance rates in *identical* versus *fraternal* twins helps us to estimate the degree of genetic influences of a disease.

However, very few diseases are completely determined by genetics. Most diseases, particularly chronic illnesses like diabetes and hypertension, have multiple genes that can influence risk to different degrees. There are very few "one gene" diseases.

We can take a disease, such as diabetes, and look at the differences in the concordance rates between identical and fraternal twins. The larger the difference, then the bigger role genetics plays in disease development. From this information, we can calculate heritability estimates. Heritability estimates are estimates of the risk attributable to genetic variations, which is not the same thing as twin concordance rates, but based on that information.

It's important to discuss what heritability estimates mean and what they don't mean. Genetics does not equal destiny. It's possible to have the genetic makeup that puts a person at high risk for addiction, but if that person never puts a drug, including alcohol, into her body, there's no way she can become addicted. Conversely, another person may have a genetic makeup that happens to put him at low risk for addiction, but if he grows up in an environment where drugs are plentiful and cheap, he may still develop an addiction.

Let's compare some heritability rates. For hypertension, or high blood pressure, the heritability rates have been estimated from .2 to .6. (2) This means that one forth to one half of the risk of developing high blood pressure is attributable to the genes inherited from parents. In type II diabetes, there is a high heritability estimate of around .5 in identical twins, compared to .37 in fraternal twins. (3) Asthma has a wide heritability risk of anywhere from .36 to .7. Different studies show somewhat different heritability estimates, but this gives an idea of the rates in some more common chronic diseases.

Alcohol dependency, or alcoholism, has a heritability risk of .55 to .65, at least among males. (1) This means that around half, or possibly a little more, of the risk of becoming alcoholic is attributed to genetics.

Not as many studies of heritability have been done with addiction to drugs other than alcohol, but in a twin study of heroin dependence, the heritability risk was .34, which means that about a third of the risk for heroin addiction was determined by genetic makeup. (4)

Some genes can actually protect against developing addiction. For example, many Asians have a variant of the gene that controls the metabolism of alcohol. This gene variant causes a buildup of acetalde-hyde, a by-product of alcohol metabolism. This product gives unpleas-ant symptoms of flushing, headache, and nausea. It's uncommon to see an alcohol addict with that genetic variant, because that person's experience with alcohol is so unpleasant. It is not impossible to develop alcoholism with this genetic variant, but it's certainly more difficult.

In summary, addiction's heritability rates are quite comparable to rates of other chronic illnesses, meaning that addiction is influenced by genetics as much as these other chronic diseases.

Many people say addicts have the ability to choose actions that will help their recovery, such as attending 12- step meetings, staying away from people who use drugs, and informing doctors that they have a history of addiction. If an addict makes a choice not to follow such good advice, people say it's not a disease effect, but bad personal choices. To some extent, this is true. However, the same complaint could be made about diabetics who have difficulty following their diet and getting the right amount of exercise.

Again, chronic illnesses are similar to addiction. For example, less than 60% of patients with type II diabetes, on insulin, comply fully with the medication they are prescribed. Less than 30% of people with dia-betes, high blood pressure, or asthma comply with their doctor's advice on diet, exercise, and other behavioral changes. Less than 40% of patients with asthma and hypertension take their medications exactly as prescribed. (1)

The point is, in most chronic diseases, there are behavioral changes that should be made, and many humans have difficulty making behavioral changes. Humans struggle when changing their behavior with something relatively easy, like taking a blood pressure pill daily. It's even more difficult to give up something enjoyable, such as food, drugs, remaining at leisure, or starting to do something relatively unpleasant, like exercise, taking insulin, eating vegetables, or going to counseling.

Factors such as poverty, poor family support, and psychiatric problems complicate behavioral change with the disease of addiction, just as these same factors make it harder to make behavioral changes for other chronic diseases like diabetes, asthma, and high blood pressure. Personal and environmental factors influence the risk of many diseases, including addiction.

Personal factors:

Personality traits influence the risk of addiction. People who are impulsive and playful are at higher risk, while more cautious people, who like to avoid danger, have a lower risk of addiction. These personality traits are at least partially genetically determined.

Life experiences influence risk. People who experience traumatic events are more likely to develop an addiction than those who have not experienced such events. Events like serious illness, natural disaster, and domestic violence all increase addiction risk. For example, seventy percent of the women entering treatment for an addiction have a history of physical or sexual abuse in their background. Post-traumatic stress disorder resulting from such events greatly increases risk of addiction. We can see this with the higher rates of addiction in soldiers returning from war, and its severe stresses.

Any psychiatric illness increases the risk for drug addiction. For example, patients with schizophrenia have ten times the risk of developing alcohol addiction than an average person without schizophrenia. (5) Unfortunately, consumption of alcohol often makes schizophrenia worse. Up to forty percent of patients seeking alcohol addiction treatment have mood disorders, including bipolar disorder and major depressive disorder. Among methadone maintained patients, one study showed that forty-eight percent had a psychiatric disorder in addition to their addiction disorder.

In times past, addiction treatment professionals thought that mental illness caused addiction; that is, because of a mental illness, the person would use drugs or alcohol to self-treat their mental state. This isn't always the case. If it were, once the mental illness is treated, the addiction should stop, but that's usually not what happens.

Other professionals thought the addiction caused mental illness, and if the drug or alcohol use stopped, the mental disorder would resolve. While it's true that addiction can mimic mental disorders of all types, in many patients, after the drug use stops, the mental illness remains.

Now, we know best results are obtained when both the addiction *and* the mental illness are treated. It may be wise to wait at least two to four weeks after the drug use stops, to see if the mental illness clears. If still present after that time period, the mental disorder also needs treatment, in order for the patient to have the best chance of a successful outcome for both disorders.

Age of first drug use influences risk for addiction. The younger a person begins to experiment with drugs, including alcohol, the more likely he is to develop an addiction. This is why it is so important to prevent adolescent experimentation with drugs. For each year that experimental substance use can be postponed, the risk of addiction is decreased by around five percent. (6) Ironically, the decision-making areas of the brain, the frontal lobes, don't fully develop until around age twenty-four, making it more difficult for youngsters to make good decisions about drug use and experimentation. Substance use may affect, and even damage, the developing brain in different ways than it affects the already formed adult brain. However, younger brains may be more resilient than adult brains.

Environmental factors:

Availability, affordability, and acceptability all influence the risk of drug and alcohol use, and thus influence addiction risk.

Drugs have to be available before people can become addicted to them. In other words, someone living in a neighborhood rife with illegal drug use and sales, will be at higher risk of using drugs and becoming addicted than someone living in a conservative town, where there aren't many drugs, if such a town still exists. It's easier to buy drugs in some locations than others. Density of drug outlets affects addiction rates. This means the more sources for obtaining the drug in a given community, the more addiction there will be in that community.

Affordability affects drug consumption, even for heavy users. If a drug is expensive, fewer people will try that drug. For example, when cocaine was a relatively expensive drug, sold in the powder form, fewer people used it. When it became available in the form of crack, small amounts could be purchased for as low as ten dollars, making it more affordable. Then it became more widely used. Presently, the cost of OxyContin on the street has gone up to as much as a dollar per milligram, so some opioid addicts have switched to the less expensive heroin.

People buy less legal drugs when the price increases. Sales decline when taxes are levied on alcohol and nicotine. During periods of U.S. history when the taxes on alcohol were relatively high, there were fewer deaths from cirrhosis due to alcohol dependency. Even heavy users consume less when prices increase.

Family characteristics influence a child's risk for addiction. Parents who give their children clear and consistent anti-drug messages reduce the children's risk for addiction, but risk increases if the parents are overly strict and authoritarian. Permissive and inconsistent parenting styles both increase their children's risk for addiction. (6)

Parents who abuse drugs or alcohol increase their child's risk of addiction. Risk increases if the child is involved in the parent's drug, alcohol or cigarette use. For example, asking the child or adolescent to "Go get me a beer" or allowing them to light the parent's cigarettes increases the child's likelihood of alcohol and tobacco addiction.

Children of parents who divorce have a higher risk of alcohol and drug use. However, high levels of conflict in the family home also increase risk for drug experimentation and addiction. Older siblings can have a strong influence on their younger brothers and sisters, both in positive and negative ways. Older siblings can reduce their younger sibling's risk, by endorsing and enacting anti-drug attitudes, or can increase their younger siblings' risk, by using drugs and being permissive toward drug use by their younger siblings. In some cases, sibling influence may be stronger than parental influence.

Outside of the home, other factors influence risk. Peer group use of drugs and alcohol is one of the strongest predictors of drug use by an adolescent. With younger children, parents have more influence over drug experimentation and addiction, but in older adolescents, peers are usually the stronger influence.

School experiences can either increase or decrease risk. Academic failure increases risk of drug use, as can an attitude that school is unimportant. Conversely, performing well in school decreases the risk of developing addiction, and having friends who support anti-drug attitudes can be a protective factor. (6)

Social acceptability of drug use affects addiction rates. When marijuana was regarded as being relatively harmless, use of that drug increased in the U.S. When public attitudes changed, and more people believed marijuana was harmful, its use went down, even in adolescents. In cultures where binging on alcohol and getting drunk are not considered social taboos, people have higher rates of alcohol abuse and addiction. People living in cultures that endorse moderate use of alcohol, and frown on intoxication, have lower rates of alcohol addiction.

Accepting Addiction as a Disease

Many people have a hard time accepting the fact that addiction is a disease. They fear it will let addicts off the hook for bad behavior. That implies an attitude of blame, which is not helpful when dealing with diseases. Besides, with many, if not most, chronic diseases there is a component of choice involved with the initiation or continuation of the disease.

With addiction, people may have a choice over whether they take a drug the first time or even the first few times. The much maligned "Just say no" campaign of Nancy Reagan in the 1980's does have value. It can help stop people from experimenting with drugs, and it can help if a person is dabbling with drugs, but hasn't yet become addicted. With opioids, many people didn't choose to take opioids. They had to start them for a painful medical situation, and developed drug addiction as a complication of the medication. This doesn't mean they are of low character or are weak willed; it means they've developed a chronic illness.

Some people refuse to consider addiction as a disease. Because statistics show that some heavy users of drugs and alcohol, who met the criteria for drug or alcohol dependency, were able to quit on their own, these people make a leap to the conclusion that all people should be able to stop, if they want to do so. This is like saying that since not all people with diabetes need insulin, no diabetic should need insulin. Or, to use the example of Dr. C. Everett Koop M.D., former Surgeon General, it's like saying that since some people get better from strep throat without antibiotics, no one with strep throat needs antibiotics. (7)

People who can quit using drugs on their own, remain abstinent from drugs, and live comfortably don't need addiction treatment. These people may not have been addicted in the first place. Perhaps they had a milder form of the disease, and it had not progressed to the point of taking away their ability to stop using drugs. Maybe they had better internal or external resources they could access for help. That's wonderful. They're fortunate. These people don't need treatment. But that doesn't erase the devastation of addiction in the lives of those who are unable to stop using drugs, even when they desperately want to do so.

Opioids carry the danger of producing addiction, and the danger is higher than experts have alleged in the past, but opioids are a blessing to the human race. No longer do we have to endure the severe pain of broken bones, cancerous destruction of the body, kidney stones, gallstones, and other painful diseases. Opioids can make intolerable pain tolerable. These drugs can cause great good or great harm, depending on how they're used. For lessons as to how best to use these medications, we need to learn from history.

Endnotes

1. A. Thomas McClellan, David C. Lewis, Charles P. O'Brien, Herbert D. Kleber, "Drug Dependence as a Chronic Illness", *Journal of the American Medical Association* 2000; 284: (13) pp. 1689-1695.
2. Joseph L. Izzo, Henry Richard Black, and Theodore L. Goodfriend, *The Hypertension Primer*, 3rd Edition (Chicago, IL, Lippincott, Williams, and Wilkins, 2003) p 227.
3. "Heritability of type II diabetes mellitus in abnormal glucose tolerance", *Diabetologia*, Vol. 42, #2 (January, 1999) pp. 139-145.
4. Pickens, Elmer, Labuda, *Genetic Vulnerability to Substance Abuse*, (Springer Verlag 1996)
5. Jean Kinney, *Loosening the Grip: A Handbook of Alcohol Information*, (Boston, McGraw-Hill, 2009) p. 478.
6. Richard K. Ries, David A. Fiellin, Shannon C. Miller, and Richard Saitz, *Principles of Addiction Medicine*, 4th ed. (Philadelphia, Lippincott, Williams, and Wilkins, 2009) ch.99, pp. 1383-1389.
7. Jack E. Henningfield, Patricia B. Santora, Warren K. Bickel, editors *Addiction Treatment: Science and Policy for the Twenty-first Century*, (Baltimore, MD, Johns Hopkins University Press, 2007).

CHAPTER 4

It's Déjà vu all Over Again...and Again

A man who cannot work without his hypodermic needle is a poor doctor. The amount of narcotic you use is inversely proportional to your skill.

Martin H. Fischer, circa 1900

History of Opioid Addiction and Treatment in the U.S.

Addiction trends, as with most human concerns, tend to repeat themselves. Contrary to popular belief, addiction to opioids, as medications, has been with us for over a hundred years. This provides us with a great deal of history to examine, in our search for ways to prevent opioid addiction, without interrupting access to pain medication for patients who need them.

Opioids have been used in the United States for centuries, beginning in colonial America. They were used as treatment for a variety of ailments. However, the amounts available were small and addiction was probably rare until the mid-1800's.

Prior to this time, opium came in several forms. Granulated opium was made from raw opium, and could be taken by mouth. Powdered opium could be placed directly on wounds. It was also mixed in liquids containing alcohol and called laudanum.   (1)

Until the early twentieth century, physicians had few effective medications to treat diseases, so they tended to overuse opioids. Even if no cures were produced, the patient felt better. Those physicians who freely prescribed opioids were more popular than their more cautious colleagues with parsimonious prescribing habits. However, opium products, as well as marijuana and cocaine, could be obtained without a prescription at the local druggist's. (1)

In addition to their legitimate use, for the treatment of pain, cough, and diarrhea, opioids were also used to treat nervous conditions of all sorts, asthma, gynecological disorders, skin rashes, hiccups, and masturbation. (2) The drugs were of questionable or of no value for such disorders, and exposed those patients to the risk of addiction.

Morphine, named for Morpheus, the Greek god of dreams, was first produced commercially in 1827, and soon was used for many painful conditions. Like the original opioids, morphine products could be purchased without a prescription, in the patent medicines of that era. Commercial morphine was a breakthrough because it had a higher potency than previously available opioids, and came in pill form, in predictable doses. When the hypodermic was invented, around the time of the Civil War, it was an ideal drug, as injections of morphine provided quick pain relief for injured soldiers. Civil War veterans were given morphine for relatively long periods of time. The public thought so many Civil War veterans were addicted to opioids that it was called, "the soldiers' disease."

In reality, the middle and upper classes, especially women, had the highest addiction rate of any demographic group in the late 1800's and early 1900's. Women went to doctors more frequently than men, especially if they could afford to do so. Many of these women were diagnosed with "nervous ailments," requiring opioids. Opioids did relieve anxiety, temporarily, but carried the risk of opioid addiction. Here we see the beginnings of iatrogenic (caused by a doctor or medical treatment prescribed by a doctor) addiction.

By the turn of the century, the average addict was a middle aged, middle class white female, found in greatest relative numbers in the South. This group of addicts was nearly inconspicuous, as they quietly continued their opioid addictions in the home, with over the counter, prescription, or patent medications containing opioids.

Chinese immigrants brought the habit of smoking opium with them, as they immigrated to the United States. Since these young immigrant males were of the lower social status, their addiction was viewed with alarm and disgust, while the war veterans and middle class female addicts were viewed with more compassion for their plight. The latter groups were perceived as more sympathetic, because they developed the disease of opioid addiction from medication prescribed by a doctor, and not through their own fault. (1)

In the late nineteenth and early twentieth centuries, patent medicines affected opioid addiction rates. Prior to the passage of the Pure Food and Drug Act, in 1906, manufacturers of non-prescription tonics or elixirs could legally include addictive substances into their potions, without disclosing the contents. Many Americans unknowingly took patent medications containing opioids, usually either morphine or opium. Some patent medications also contained alcohol and cocaine, which made them understandably popular. As a result, people using patent medicines developed addictions. The poor, less able to afford a visit to the doctor, were more likely to use, and become addicted to, these patent medicines. (1)

Laudanum, the liquid morphine combined with alcohol, was a popular ingredient in many of the patent medications. Ads for popular products claimed to do all things for all people.

"Has been used for over Sixty Years by Millions of Mothers for their Children While Teething with Perfect Success. It soothes the Child, Softens the Gums, Allays all Pain; Cures Wind Colic, and is the best remedy for Diarrhea."

What this ad for Mrs. Winslow's Soothing Syrup didn't disclose on the label was that each ounce of the syrup contained one grain, or sixty-five milligrams, of morphine. (3)

Lallermand Rheumatism, Gout and Neuralgia Treatment, another patent medication, contained seven and a quarter percent alcohol and nearly a grain of opium per ounce. (4)

There were many such concoctions on the market. Ironically, some were marketed not only for medical complaints, but for the treatment of addiction to alcohol or opioids. These patent medicines may have been the first cure touted for treatment of opioid addiction in this country.

"Opacura takes the place of opium, morphine, laudanum and liquor, while under treatment and finally effects a complete cure; no pain, no nervousness, no opiates after beginning treatment....Opacura treatment can then be easily discontinued as the cure is perfect and permanent."

The medication appeared to be the perfect cure. But the advertisement didn't mention that Opacura contained opium. As soon as the patient stopped the medicine, the usual opioid withdrawal began. (5)

Physicians assumed the patent remedies cut into their own business, and resented these products. They lobbied for their removal from the market.

It wasn't until 1906 that people had any way of knowing the contents of the remedies they were taking. When the Pure Food and Drug Act forced manufacturers of patent medicines to disclose the contents of their potions on the labels, many people became alarmed at the names of the powerful medications included. The popularity of the patent medicines waned at that point, partly because addiction was perceived to be a pressing problem in society around that time.

Heroin, first invented by the Bayer Company, was released in 1898 as a cough suppressant. Bayer released aspirin a few years later. Initially aspirin was a prescription medication, as opposed to heroin, which was legally sold over the counter at that time. Heroin is a partially man-made substance, with molecules added to morphine that allow the drug to cross from the blood into the brain more quickly. This produces a faster "rush". Heroin was also found in patent medicines of the day. (1)

Heroin was marketed by Bayer in both pill and elixir forms. It certainly did suppress coughs, as any opioid will do. It was also believed, wrongly, to improve lung function. The drug was initially touted by the manufacturer as having a low risk of causing addiction, a false assurance that would be echoed throughout the twentieth century, for drugs such as Quaaludes, Valium, and OxyContin. Fortunately, prescription heroin came on the market at a time when physicians were a bit more cautious about prescribing practices for opioids, but there were still some patients who developed iatrogenic addiction as a result of their doctor's prescriptions. (6)

Sometimes heroin was prescribed as a cure for morphine addiction, with predictable results. The patients were then addicted to heroin. The medical community debated the risks of heroin and it was taken off the market in 1911.

Despite the problems patent medicines caused, physicians inadvertently created the most opioid addicts in the era between the end of the Civil War and 1906. (6) A number of doctors indiscriminately and inappropriately prescribed large amounts of opioids. As a result, many of their patients became addicted. Gradually, better trained, younger physicians were able to influence prescribing practices.

Increasing numbers of citizens were becoming addicted and the liberal access to addicting drugs alarmed many people, who thought the fabric of society was being damaged.

It's estimated that around 1900, around 4.59 people out of a thousand, living in the United States, were addicted to opioids. (7) For comparison, over one hundred years later, best estimates of the number of pain pill addicts are around 1.7 million people. In our population of just over three hundred and seven million people, this gives a rate of approximately 5.5 people out of a thousand.

By 1910, the practice of medicine was more advanced. Physicians were able to treat the causes of diseases, rather than relying on opioids to mask symptoms. Living conditions improved as overall hygiene and sewage disposal improved, reducing the rates of dysentery. This further reduced the need for opioids.

By the early nineteen hundreds, the numbers of opioid addicts began to drop, as both the Civil War veterans and the middle class female addicts aged and died.

This relatively free access to addicting drugs during the era of patent medicines was the United States' first experiment with legalization of addictive drugs. The majority opinion was that it didn't go well. The public eventually came to believe opioids, cocaine, alcohol, and marijuana presented hazards to the community, and clamored for laws to regulate these drugs. Politicians of the day listened, and passed laws against their free distribution and consumption. Among such legislation was the 1914 Harrison Narcotic Act.

Eventually, the number of opioid addicts dropped, but there was still the question of treating those who remained.

End Notes:

1. David Musto, *The American Disease: Origins of Narcotic Control*, 3rd ed., (New York: Oxford University Press, 1999)
2. Hodgson, B, *In the Arms of Morpheus*, (Buffalo, NY, Firefly Books, 2001) p 20.
3. National Museum of American History, Smithsonian Institute, accessed June 7, 2009, http://americanhistory.si.edu/collections/group_detail.cfm?key=1253&gkey=51
4. National Museum of American History, Smithsonian Institute, accessed June 7, 2009, http://americanhistory.si.edu/collections
5. Self Culture magazine 1900, digitalized by Google, accessed 1/4/09.
6. David T. Courtwright, *Dark Paradise: A History of Opiate Addiction in American*, (Cambridge, Massachusetts, Harvard University Press, 2001), pp. 45 – 60.
7. Ibid., p. 33.

CHAPTER 5

History of Addiction Treatment

Again, we can learn much from the past about the best ways to treat addiction. We particularly need workable ideas to help deal with our current rise in opioid addiction. There have been some approaches that worked, and many that didn't.

The Harrison Narcotic Act of 1914 was eventually interpreted by the U.S. courts as a prohibition against the prescription of opioids by doctors, as a means to treat withdrawal in treating opioid addicts. A few hardy doctors bravely held firm to the opinion that opioid addiction was a disease best treated by physicians, without interference from law enforcement. These doctors usually prescribed morphine, in quantities sufficient for the prevention of withdrawal, with the hope that the dose could gradually be reduced to zero.

However, a small percentage of unscrupulous doctors did run "pill mills" where there was little, if any, true clinical interaction between doctor and patient. At these sites, the patient would tell the doctor which drug they preferred and the doctor complied with a prescription, usually for a hefty fee. These script doctors, called "croakers" by some addicts, gave a bad name to doctors who sincerely tried to prescribe opioids to treat suffering opioid addicts. (1)

Sadly, there were then, as now, other unscrupulous people who took advantage of addicts' desperation by offering easy, expensive, and bogus cures for addiction. A plethora of false cures were sold, including personalized diets, colonic enemas to detoxify the system, vitamins, sun baths, cures with metals, magnets, and hydrotherapies. The types of potions and regimens were legion. These old, unproven cures occasionally re-appear.

Prior to the 1920's there were maintenance clinics in various larger cities, created to treat opioid addicts. These clinics varied in their effectiveness.

By all accounts, one of the most successful was run by Dr. Willis Butler, in Shreveport, Louisiana. He was a careful and diligent physician, and able to impress the local authorities with the way he ran his clinic. Although he enjoyed the support of his community, the politics of the nation during this Prohibition era were shifting away from medical treatment of addiction, towards supply reduction and criminalization of opioid addiction. Eventually all the maintenance clinics folded, from pressure applied by law enforcement.

The interpretation of the Harrison Act by the courts was a major turn of policy for the United States. For the first time, laws were enacted that dictated what medications physicians could prescribe for the treatment of a disease: the disease of opioid addiction. From that point, until the passage of the Drug Addiction Treatment Act of 2000, it was illegal for physicians to treat opioid addicts from their offices with replacement medications.

The Harrison Act marked a sharp turn in attitudes towards addiction, and had a huge impact on opioid addicts for the rest of the twentieth century, making it more likely they would be jailed because of their addiction.

The strict enforcement of the drug laws during this period filled the jails and prisons to overflowing with youthful addicts, and overwhelmed incarceration systems. By the end of the 1920's, approximately one-third of all federal prisoners were incarcerated on drug charges. (2) Wardens, with little experience in treating the problems of these unruly addicts, were distressed to discover addicts were able to smuggle drugs into the prisons. They felt the addicts were a bad influence on the other prisoners.

To deal with this problem, the Public Health Service and the Bureau of Prisons joined forces, to create a unique facility, part jail and part treatment hospital. Founded in 1935, it was initially named the United States Narcotic Farm, but later changed to the U.S. Public Health Service Narcotics Hospital. Even after this name change, most people called it the Narcotic Farm.

This facility was located on twelve acres of Kentucky farmland, and served a dual purpose. It was a treatment hospital, where drug addicts could voluntarily be admitted for treatment of their addiction, and it was also a federal prison, where drug offenders were sent to serve their sentences. About two thirds of the inpatients were prisoners and the other third were addicts, voluntarily seeking help for opioid addiction. Both types of patients were treated side by side. For over forty years, it was the main drug addiction treatment center in the United

States, along with a similar facility in Ft. Worth, Texas, which opened in 1937. (3)

The Narcotic Farm was a massive institution for its time. It had fifteen-hundred beds, and housed tens of thousands of patients over its forty years of operation. It was located in a rural area of Kentucky, which gave it space for numerous operations to engage the prisoners – now called patients - in all types of job training. (3)

The Narcotic Farm really *was* a farm. Besides growing many types of vegetables, there was a working dairy, and livestock including pigs and chickens. These operations provided food for the patients and staff of the facility and provided work for the patients. The patients provided the labor to keep the farm going and it was hoped they would simultaneously learn useful trades. In addition to farming, they learned skills in sewing, auto repair, carpentry, and other trades. Besides teaching new job skills, it was hoped that fresh air, sunshine, and wholesome work would be beneficial to the addicts. (3)

For its time, the Narcotic Farm was surprisingly progressive in its willingness to try multiple new treatments. For the forty years it operated, many different treatments were tried for opioid addicts. It offered individual and group talk therapies, job training, psychiatric analysis, treatment for physical medical issues, Alcoholics Anonymous meetings, art therapy, shock therapy, music therapy, and even hydrotherapy, with flow baths to soothe the nerves. Despite these options, the Farm apparently retained many of the characteristics of a prison, with barred windows and strict security procedures. (3)

The Narcotic Farm had its own research division, the Addiction Research Center (ARC), which became the forerunner of today's National Institute on Drug Abuse (NIDA). The Narcotic Farm did pioneering work, using methadone to assist patients through withdrawal, and helped establish the doses used to treat opioid addiction. Methadone was used only short term, for the management of withdrawal symptoms, and not for maintenance dosing at the Narcotic Farm. The Farm also trained a dedicated group of doctors and nurses, who were pioneers in the field of addiction treatment. It provided new information on the nature of addiction. (3)

Admission to the Narcotic Farm allowed an opioid addict some time to go through opioid withdrawal, eat regular meals, work in one of the farm's many industries, and have some form of counseling. However, after leaving the hospital, the addicts were entirely released from care and supervision, with no assistance to help re-enter their communities. Most times, they returned to their same living situation and old circumstances encouraged relapse back to drug use and addiction. As a result, two follow up studies of the addicts treated at the Narcotic Farm showed a ninety-three percent and ninety-seven percent relapse rate within six months, with most of the relapses occurring almost immediately upon returning home. Many addicts cycled through the Public Health Hospital multiple times. (3)

The Narcotic Farm was eventually turned over to the Bureau of Prisons in 1974, as the treatment for addiction was de-centralized. Since the studies found high relapse rates for addicts returning to their previous communities, it was hoped by moving treatment centers into communities, these addicts could have ongoing support after they left inpatient treatment.

The two Narcotics Farms were built to handle the expanding prison census from the fervent enforcement of the nation's new drug laws. From 1930 until 1962, Mr. Harry J. Anslinger was the commissioner of the Federal Bureau of Narcotics, the forerunner of the Drug Enforcement Administration of today. He heartily endorsed the movement toward criminalization of addiction, because he thought it would reduce the demand for illicit drugs. He was fierce and tireless in his quest to arrest drug users and drug dealers alike. As a practical point, it's difficult to clearly delineate the two. Around seventy percent of addicts sell small amounts to friends and acquaintances, to finance their own use.

During Anslinger's reign, the number of opioid addicts actually did drop, at least during and immediately after World War II. This was probably not due to his fanatical law enforcement approach to treating addiction, but to the interrupted supply of the raw materials for heroin. Supplies of opium were requested by the U.S. and other governments, to make more pain medications needed to treat injured soldiers. That left less opium to be made into heroin, and the addicts' supply became scarce, as well as expensive. Also, the usual supply lines were disrupted. When an addictive drug becomes harder to acquire, or more costly, fewer people use the drug, and become addicted. The numbers of opioid addicts were relatively lower just after WWII, but not for long. (4)

After the war, Italian and French crime rings began selling illicit opioids, mostly heroin, and mostly moved through the French city of Marseilles. The movie, "The French Connection," immortalized this criminal organization. By 1960, the Federal Bureau of Narcotics estimated that as much as five thousand pounds of heroin were imported yearly into the U.S., and by 1969, most of the heroin that reached the U.S. came through this drug ring. The U.S. citizenry became alarmed at the escalating numbers of opioid addicts.

These new addicts tended to be younger, minority races, and from urban areas. Again, whereas war veterans and middle aged, middle class females were viewed with compassion, these new addicts were viewed with apprehension and distain. The public panicked at the image of these addicts, and supported politicians who advocated for harsher drug laws. During this time, as in all times, the public's opinion of drug addicts depended on who was addicted.

Anslinger advocated for the passage of the Boggs Act, which dictated heavy financial penalties and long sentences, even for first time possession of a controlled substance. The Narcotic Control Act, passed in 1956, five years after the Boggs Act, went even further. Under that law, sale of heroin to a minor could be punishable by death. Some states followed with legislation authorizing longer sentences. In a few states, drug addiction itself was defined as a crime, punishable by arrest. (4) By the late 1950's and early 1960's, U.S. jails were filling with people addicted to an assortment of drugs. As ever, minorities were disproportionally represented in the jail populations.

In the earliest days of contemporary heroin addiction, it was most often snorted by addicts who were accustomed to snorting cocaine. Over time, heroin became more available in larger cities, and eventually most addicts used it intravenously. By the 1950's, most opioid addicts were inner city teenagers, and a larger percentage of them were either black or Hispanic. A mere decade later, in the mid-1960's, the number one cause of death in New York City in people aged fifteen to thirty-five, was heroin-related.(5) Heroin use became part of a subculture and its use symbolized that the user was hip or cool. Then as now, a great many musicians and other artists became addicted to heroin.

By the 1960's, the public attitude towards drugs, addicts, and addiction treatment began to change. The psychological sciences were gaining acceptability and people were hoping that science would have better success treating addiction than imprisonment. As the psychiatric medical science gained credibility, the U.S. public was more willing to considering addiction as a disease, not a sign of social deviance. By 1962, the U.S. Supreme Court ruled that addiction was a disease, not a crime. The medical establishment, judges, and the prisons system all became opposed to mandatory sentencing. It was against this background that doctors began trying to find an opioid substitute to treat addicts.

Dr. Vincent Dole was an intelligent, accomplished, and politically well-connected physician, who studied metabolic disorders. In the early 1960's, he was elected chairman of the Health Research Council's Committee on Narcotics. As a conscientious and open minded man, he took pains to talk to leaders in the field of addiction. An earnest young physician named Dr. Marie Nyswander came to his attention. He'd read extensively about addiction and its treatment, and read a book she had published, quite advanced for its time, *The Drug Addict as Patient*. She worked at the Public Health Hospital in Kentucky, and had prescribed methadone short term to manage opioid withdrawal symptoms.

Dr. Dole invited Dr. Nyswander to leave the Public Health Hospital in Kentucky, to join him in his research project in New York City. She agreed, and they began experimenting with new ways to treat opioid addiction. They admitted heroin addicts to an inpatient unit and began to dose them with different opioids, at various doses. They'd gone about two months into their research when they noted patients dosed with methadone were looking and acting much better.

As their research progressed, they found that methadone controlled patients' cravings for drugs, and allowed patients to live normally. They found that methadone, unlike the short-acting opioids codeine and morphine, kept a steady level of opioid in the body, due to its long duration of action. Methadone prevented withdrawal, and after stabilization, it didn't sedate or impair their patients. As an additional benefit, the methadone blocked the euphoric effect of heroin or similar drugs, if an opioid addict relapsed.

They had remarkably good success and began to publish their results. Fortunately, Dr. Dole already had an excellent reputation as a research scientist, and he had enough prestige in the medical community that his findings were not discounted. In spite of this, he and Dr. Nyswander faced considerable hindrances from both the government and the scientific community.

In this era, the Federal Bureau of Narcotics still operated under the assumption that addiction was a crime which must be stamped out. Drs. Dole and Nyswander were intimidated and bullied by the Federal Bureau of Narcotics, and were even threatened with arrest. Dr. Dole, in *The Addicts Who Survived*, described an episode of being threatened with arrest by an agent. (6) Dr. Dole instructed the agent to arrest him, so there could be a hearing in court of this issue and an end to the harassment. The astounded agent abruptly left. Dr. Dole further alleges that the agents stole records and started false rumors to discredit them. Thankfully, Drs. Dole and Nyswander had the full support of the Rockefeller University, and the University's lawyers.

Initially, the medical community responded to Dole and Nyswander's work with little interest. Physicians had been chased out of the field of addiction medicine by the heavy handed approach of law enforcement. Since 1914, maintenance therapies - maintaining an opioid addict on prescription opioids to prevent withdrawal and illicit opioid use - were illegal outside of research settings and the Narcotics Farms. Eventually, data accumulated that showed the benefits of methadone treatment. Slowly, the medical community began to have an interest in the treatment of opioid addiction. (6)

The years of the 1970's were unique. Nixon was president, and was faced with the specter of heroin-addicted American soldiers returning from Vietnam. Heroin in Vietnam was cheap and pure, and many young men used heroin for the first time there, during the stress of wartime. Some of Nixon's advisors estimated that fifteen to twenty-five percent of the soldiers used heroin at least once while they were in Vietnam, and the president worried these soldiers would return home with heroin addiction. To address this, Nixon hired Jerome Jaffe, one of the most knowledgeable doctors in the field of addiction medicine. Dr. Jaffe had trained at the Narcotic Farm in Lexington, and had also learned about methadone from Dr. Dole. He had set up pilot opioid treatment clinics in Illinois, which included methadone clinics and therapeutic communities. His programs were enormously successful.

Jaffe recommended that instead of prosecution, the military should offer treatment to young soldiers addicted to heroin. Jaffe thought that only a minority of the soldiers using heroin were actually addicted. He believed that given a proper incentive, most soldiers, who weren't daily users, would be able to quit without formal treatment.

Dr. Jaffe arranged for a massive urine drug testing program, Operation Golden Flow, to be done on soldiers prior to their departure from Vietnam. This was the first attempt at large scale screening of urine samples for drugs. Any soldier testing positive couldn't board the plane for home. This was an enormous incentive to stop using heroin, if they were able to do so. Only four percent of the soldiers tested positive, rather than the feared twenty-five percent. It became obvious that the situation in Vietnam was unique. The soldiers used heroin during that very stressful time, but most were able to quit, without difficulty, when they returned home. (7) Soldiers with addiction, who couldn't stop using heroin, underwent detoxification in Vietnam, and then were referred for treatment once they arrived in the U.S., instead of being court-martialed. (8)

Just prior to this, congress passed the Controlled Substance Act in 1970. This act defines the federal drug policy of the U.S. It governs production, possession, use, manufacture, and importation of potentially addictive drugs. The Act classified drugs into five categories, or schedules, according to their addictive potential and usefulness as medications.

Classification	Description	Examples
Schedule I	Drugs with no legitimate medical use, and a high potential for abuse	GHB, cannabis (marijuana), PCP, heroin, MDMA, mescaline
Schedule II	Drugs with a high potential for abuse, but currently has an acceptable medical use	Cocaine (when used as an anesthetic), methylphenidate (Ritalin), methadone, morphine, oxycodone, fentanyl, amphetamines (Adderall), hydromorphone (Dilaudid)
Schedule III	Potentially addicting, but not as much as Schedule II Currently accepted medical use	Anabolic steroids, buprenorphine (Suboxone), Marinol (pill containing THC), paregoric, Ketamine, hydrocodone, dihydrocodeine
Schedule IV	Lower potential for addiction, has an accepted medical use	Alprazolam (Xanax), clonazepam (Klonipin), diazepam (Valium), zolpidem (Ambien), eszopiclone (Lunesta), modafinil (Provigil), phenobarbital, butalbital (Fioricet)
Schedule V	Minimal risk for addiction, has an accepted medical use	Promethazine (Phenergan) with codeine, small doses of codeine

Prescription medicines that have no potential for addiction, such as high blood pressure medications and antibiotics, aren't placed on any schedule, and are not controlled substances.

The laws surrounding the manufacture and prescribing of scheduled drugs vary, and Schedule II drugs have many more restrictions than Schedule V drugs. For example, a Schedule II drug can't be called in to a pharmacy. The patient must have a written prescription. Drug companies are concerned about the schedule their drug is placed in, because this will affect the number of prescriptions written.

At the same time the new treatment options of using methadone and other opioids to maintain opioid addicts were being studied and explored, new drug-free methods of treating opioid addiction were created.

Therapeutic communities (TC's) were started in the 1960's and have continued to this day, though in a much altered form. Therapeutic communities are drug-free residences, where recovering addicts live for months, or years, to learn how to live a life free from drugs.

Since the inception of TC's over forty years ago, there have been major differences between various therapeutic communities, but the basic concept is the same. The influence of the community helps the addict learn new life skills in important areas of function, including communication, education, social skills, acceptance of responsibility, and job skills. The community consists of both patients and staff, with some overlap. Some TCs have staff members who were previously patients. Many TCs reward the resident addicts with different levels, corresponding to their progress acquiring basic life skills. Duration of treatment at a TC has varied. Since people progress in their recovery at different rates, the amount of time needed to learn and apply skills differs. In the past, most opioid addicts stayed in TCs eighteen to twenty four months, but now, with reduced funding, many have been reduced to six to twelve months. This is still a long time for the addict to be away from home and for this reason is not acceptable to many addicts.

The first therapeutic community, Synanon, was started by a recovering addict, named Charles Dederich, in 1958. He had originally been helped by Alcoholics Anonymous, but was still searching for meaning in his life and started a discussion group to aid that search. (9) A group of people trying to recover from drug addiction were drawn to Dederich, who has been described as exceptionally charismatic. The group moved into his apartment. Later, as the group expanded, a clubhouse was rented and became a place where addicts could both go through drug withdrawal (without the help of medications), and live together as a community of recovering people. This group held meetings that used brutal honesty as a means of breaking through psychological resistance. Physical violence wasn't allowed, but all nature of verbal abuse was dispensed, in the name of helping the addict. Other recovering addicts were leaders of the Synanon meetings.

Over time, Synanon expanded in numbers and in locations. They were touted as having high success rates, but the data they released was misleading. Because of the harsh confrontational tactics, many addicts dropped out, early in their treatment. Eventually, the focus of Synanon shifted towards retaining addicts in the Synanon community indefinitely, and its leader Dederich became despotic, leading the organization towards what he saw as a utopian society. (10)

As time passed, Synanon became more cultish and redefined itself as a religion by 1974. Dederich, becoming ever more paranoid, began to demand proof of loyalty from group members. He became lavishly and conspicuously rich, at the expense of the other members, and generally behaved in an increasingly unstable manner. Finally, he was arrested in 1978 for the attempted murder of a lawyer for one of Dederich's opponents in a lawsuit. Dederich pled *nolo contendere* to the conspiracy to commit murder, by placing a rattlesnake in the lawyer's mailbox.

Though Synanon ended in ignominy, some of the people involved took the positive aspects of what they had found in Synanon and established different types of therapeutic communities. Some of the more successful were Daytop Village, Phoenix House, and Delancey Street Foundation. These newer versions of therapeutic communities intended to treat the addict, then return him back to his or her community. These organizations also hired professionals, as well as ex-addicts, as counselors. Because most accepted federal money, they also had to abide by monitoring guidelines, which kept them accountable and adherent to more mainstream methods.

Therapeutic communities have claimed high success rates, with around ninety percent of graduates achieving drug abstinence at one year, but only a small percentage actually stay through all stages of treatment and graduate. Many TC's screen out many candidates during the admission process, and of the addicts they do accept, around half leave their TC during the first year. The patients who do stay through all phases of treatment at their TC have shown marked reductions in drug use and criminal activities, and have an increased likelihood of gainful employment. Successful outcomes are correlated with length of time in treatment. (11)

One criticism of therapeutic communities has been the potential for abuse of power. With their strict hierarchal structure, those in a position of respect could do much damage if their power is misused, as occurred with Synanon. Also, with the long amount of time required for treatment, the cost may be prohibitively high. In the 1960's, the amount spent on one patient in a therapeutic community could finance three addicts on methadone maintenance treatment or drug-free out-patient counseling. (10)

Therapeutic communities continue to operate around the world in sixty-five countries and have been shown to be effective at treating some of the sickest addicts. (12) TCs have been shown to reduce drug use, unemployment, criminal activity, and help with mental health issues. TCs have in common the basic concepts of using community to help people change behaviors. They tend to have structured activities and help the patients address problems in all areas of their lives. The approaches used may differ in different cultures, but the concepts remain the same. In the United States, around three to four thousand people residing in therapeutic communities say that opioids were their primary drug. (12)

The original therapeutic community, Synanon, was started by an ex-member of Alcoholics Anonymous, and AA had some influence on its beginnings. Alcoholics Anonymous also influenced the development of the residential treatment program, another medication-free treatment for addiction.

In 1907, Minnesota passed laws increasing taxes on liquor licenses in order to fund treatment centers for alcoholism. For the next fifty years, several treatment centers blossomed, and became models for the delivery of effective inpatient drug addiction treatment. Willmar State Hospital and Hazelden were the first two such programs. Hazelden in still recognized as one of the premier residential addiction treatment programs in the U.S. First created for treatment of alcohol dependency, they now treat addictions to drugs other than alcohol as well.

Inpatient residential treatment programs are often referred to as the "Minnesota Model," because of their origins in that state. Treat-ment programs using the Minnesota model usually consist of individual and group counseling sessions, educational lectures about the nature of the disease of addiction, informal contact between patients, contact between patients and counselors, and the use of films and books as resources. Inpatient programs have the advantage of completely removing the addict from a drug setting and immersing them in a recovery milieu. Such exceptionally supportive treatment, concentrated in space and time, can advance an addict's recovery much faster than is possible with outpatient programs. Most treatment centers using the Minnesota model keep patients for twenty-eight days.

Eventually, many programs recognized the importance of involving the family of the addict in recovery, and started programs for family members affected by addiction to alcohol or drugs.

Many addictionologists still consider the Minnesota model of inpatient residential treatment to be the gold standard of opioid addiction treatment. Professionals, such as doctors, dentists, and celebrities, most often get this form of treatment. Because it can be costly, it's difficult for addicts of limited financial means to afford. Because of the nature of addiction, by the time the opioid addict is ready to seek treatment, he or she often has no health insurance.

Some treatment centers helped create the dilemma of unaffordability. When reimbursement for drug and alcohol addiction treatment was at its height, in the early 1980's, before managed care, the number of treatment centers exploded. Many were for-profit organizations. Few guidelines existed for ethical business practices. Some of these treatment facilities would gouge the insurance companies, by admitting every patient to inpatient treatment, whether it was needed or not, and deemed them ready for discharge the day their insurance benefits ran out. Many specialty programs were created with a focus on a certain subpopulation of addicts, such as women, younger addicts, or those with co-existing mental health disorders, though many times these programs had no particular expertise, except good marketing.

Not all treatment centers were well-run facilities, like Hazelden, and not all were staffed by qualified personnel. Some treatment centers employed marginally educated people, whose only qualification for their job as an addictions counselor was that they were in recovery from addiction.

The bad programs tainted the reputation of the good programs.

As insurance companies paid greater amounts for questionable treatments, they hired people to investigate the appropriateness of admissions. In many cases, studies showed no difference in treatment outcomes for outpatient treatment, as opposed to the much more expensive inpatient treatments, when treating alcohol and other addictions. Insurance companies began insisting that cheaper treatment methods be tried first, reserving inpatient treatment for patients with repeated relapses.

The poorly regulated treatment industry killed the insurance goose that laid the golden egg.

By the 1980's, twelve step recovery programs had exploded with ever-increasing numbers of new members. Alcoholics Anonymous, formed in 1935 by a businessman and a doctor, Bill W. and Dr. Bob, was the first 12- step program. Because of the success of alcoholics who became members of AA, recovery groups for other substances and behaviors sprang up, using the same twelve steps as guiding principles. Narcotics Anonymous began in the mid-1950's, and has grown impressively. Narcotics Anonymous doesn't separate one drug from another. They consider any use of addicting drugs, including alcohol, to be a relapse in one's recovery program. Later 12-step groups include Cocaine Anonymous, Overeaters Anonymous, Sex Addicts Anonymous, and Gamblers Anonymous.

As the 1980's continued, President Reagan helped guide the thinking of the nation, and emphasized law enforcement as the solution to the war on drugs. Spending increased for police and other enforcement agencies, but decreased for addiction research and addiction treatment. When crack cocaine captured the attention of America in the mid-1980's, it re-ignited old fears.

As in times past, what people thought of drug addicts depended in part on who was addicted. There was much rhetoric about the nature of crime committed by minorities, addicted to drugs, and of crack babies, based more on media exaggeration than on science. As a result, the drug laws were again re-written.

During the Reagan years, laws were passed that were quite similar to the Boggs Act of the 1950's. The death penalty was even re-introduced for drug dealers, under certain circumstances. Laws mandating sentences for simple possession were resurrected, and in general, drug laws were set back to the way they were thirty years prior.

Parents of the 1980s observed with alarm the rise in cocaine abuse, with its hazards and easy availability. They leapt into action, by forming the Parent's Movement. They were a powerful political voice that helped coerce lawmakers into passing tougher drug laws. The American public had once again demanded more punitive drug laws.

Laws passed against the possession of crack were different from those for powder cocaine. The penalty for five grams of crack was the same as the penalty for five hundred grams of powder cocaine. African Americans, of lower socioeconomic status, tended to use crack because it was cheaper than powder cocaine. Therefore, African Americans were more likely than whites to receive a mandatory sentence for drug possession, because it took so little crack, a hundred-fold less, to carry the same sentence. (12)

State and federal laws differed considerably, because federal convictions could not, by new law, be shortened by more than fifteen percent. This meant that being convicted in federal court lead to longer sentences than being convicted in state courts. District attorneys had the power to decide in which jurisdiction to try an offender, and this gave them considerable influence over the fates of arrestees.

Predictably, prisons filled around the country, and prison censuses doubled, at both state and federal levels. (13)

Shortly before the first of the George Bushes took office in 1989, the 1988 Anti-Drug Abuse Act was passed, which re-organized the bureaucracies assigned to overseeing the drug addiction problems of the nation. Under this Act, the Office of National Drug Control Policy (ONDCP) was formed, and William Bennett was designated drug czar. This agency was given the task of monitoring all of the anti-drug programs in government agencies. The forerunner to the Center for Substance Abuse Prevention (CSAP) was formed in the Substance Abuse and Mental Health Services Administration (SAMHSA). There was much fanfare about new policies, which would both emphasize a zero tolerance toward drug use and also give more attention to treating addiction. However, Bennett resigned abruptly and the fanfare fizzled.

When Clinton took office in 1993, he cut funding for the ONDCP by eighty-three percent, and exhibited a general lack of interest in addiction and its treatment. His Surgeon General, Jocelyn Elders, angered many when she appeared to advocate legalization of drugs. (14) Probably in response to public pressures, and concerns about the rising rate of marijuana use among adolescents, Clinton publically announced a new attack on drugs, just before the next election year, and nominated Barry McCaffery to head the revived ONDCP.

Throughout the 1990's, heroin purity on the U.S. streets was gradually increasing. In 1991, heroin was about twenty-seven percent pure, while by 1994, it had risen to forty percent. That was a dramatic increase in purity, compared to 1970's and 1980s, when an average purity of three to ten percent was found in U.S. cities. Many potential addicts, scared off cocaine by high profile deaths of people like Len Bias and John Belushi, turned to experimentation with heroin. (13). Columbian drug cartels, diversifying from dealing only with cocaine, began selling heroin to meet an increasing demand by the U.S. Because heroin was so pure, it could be snorted, rather than injected, and many people who balked at injecting a drug would snort it, and did. By 1997, heroin accounted for more treatment center admissions than did cocaine. (14). "Heroin chic", a trend of thin and ill-looking models as the ideal of beauty, came into vogue in the mid-1990s.

At that same time, in the mid-1990s, several more ingredients besides higher potency heroin were thrown into the simmering caldron of opioid addiction: the pain management movement and access to controlled substances over the internet. Then, with the release and deceptive marketing of OxyContin, the cauldron began to boil.

End Notes

1. William S Burroughs, *Junky*, 50th anniversary ed., (New York, Penguin Books, 2003).
2. David T. Courtwright, *Dark Paradise: A History of Opiate Addiction in American*, (Cambridge, Massachusetts, Harvard University Press, 2001), pp. 168-175.
3. Nancy P. Campbell, *The Narcotic Farm: The rise and fall of America's first prison for drug addicts*, (New York, Abrams, 2008).
4. David T. Courtwright, *Dark Paradise: A History of Opiate Addiction in American*, (Cambridge, Massachusetts, Harvard University Press, 2001) pp 45 – 60.
5. U.S. Department of Health and Human Services, Substance Abuse and Mental Health Services Administration, *Medication-Assisted Treatment For Opioid Addiction in Opioid Treatment Programs: TIP 43* (Rockville, MD, 2005) p 7.
6. David Courtwright, Herman Joseph, and Don Des Jarlais, *Addicts Who Survived: An Oral History of Narcotic Use in*

America, 1923 – 1965 (Knoxville, TN, University of Tennessee Press, 1989) p 337.

7. David T. Courtwright, *Dark Paradise: A History of Opiate Addiction in American*, (Cambridge, Massachusetts, Harvard University Press, 2001).

8. Michael Massing, *The Fix*, (New York, Simon and Shuster, 1998) pp 108 – 118.

9. Lewis Yablonsky, *The Tunnel Back: Synanon*, (New York, The Macmillan Company, 1965).

10. William L.White, *Slaying the Dragon: The History of Addiction Treatment and Recovery in America*, (Bloomington, IL, Chestnut Health Systems, 1998) pp 241-244.

11. National Institute on Drug Abuse, *Research Report Series: Therapeutic Community*, http://www.drugabuse.gov/ResearchReports/Therapeutic/default.html .

12. Gregory C. Bunt, Britta Muehlbach, and Claire Moed, "The Therapeutic Community: An International Perspective," *Substance Abuse* 39 (2008): pp. 81–87.

13. David Musto, *The American Disease: Origins of Narcotic Control*, 3rd ed., (New York: Oxford University Press, 1999) p 274.

14. David T. Courtwright, *Dark Paradise: A History of Opiate Addiction in American*, (Cambridge, Massachusetts, Harvard University Press, 2001) pp. 180-181.

CHAPTER 6

Lighting the Fire

It is easy to get a thousand prescriptions but hard to get one single remedy.

~Chinese Proverb

Medical men do not know the drugs they use, nor their prices.

Francis Bacon

One doctor makes work for another.

~English Proverb

In the 2006 National Survey of Drug Use in Households (NSDUH) study, *5.2 million people* in the U.S. population over age twelve used prescription pain medications, for non-medical reasons, within the month prior to the survey. This means they took prescription opioid pills for reasons other than for the treatment of pain as prescribed by a doctor, inferring they took them to get high. In 2006, the number of *new* users of prescription pain pills for non-medical reasons, at 2.2 million people, was higher than the number of new users of marijuana, at 2.1 million people. This was the first year – ever – that any drug beat marijuana for number of new drug users, and indicates that the prescription pain pill addiction will be with us for some time to come. (1)

The percentage of young adults, age eighteen to twenty-five, currently using prescription pain pills rose *from 4.1% to 4.6%* in the years between 2002 and 2007. (2) While these numbers are overwhelming, not everyone who misuses prescription pain pills will develop addiction. Presently, best estimates given by governmental studies are that *1.7 million* people in the U.S. can be diagnosed with opioid addiction or abuse. (1)

Beginning in the late 1990's, several factors contributed to the biggest epidemic of pain pill addiction in more than a hundred years in the U.S. The most obvious reasons included an overzealous pain management movement, which coincided with OxyContin's release and inappropriate marketing. But less well-recognized factors kindled our present conflagration of opioid addiction.

Cultural norms and beliefs in the U.S. were fuel for the fire of opioid addiction that started to spread in the late 1990's. *We tend to share our medications.* People in this country are sharing powerful and potentially dangerous prescription medications, even controlled substances, like opioids. The 2008 National Survey of Drug Use in Households study surveyed the people over twelve who said they currently used prescription pain pills to get high, and fifty-six percent of these people said they got their prescription opioid drugs from friends or relatives, free of charge. Nine percent bought them from friends or relatives, and about five percent took them from a friend or relative without asking. Eighteen percent of people misusing prescription opioids got them by prescription from one doctor. Only about four percent said they bought drugs from a drug dealer, and only half of a percent said they got their prescription opioids from the internet. (2)

We don't just share with adults. Among 12th graders who were current nonmedical users of prescription opioids, *sixty-six percent* got them from a friend or relative. Nineteen percent were prescribed the opioids they misused by one doctor. Only eight percent bought them from a dealer. Of the kids who got their pills from a friend or relative, thirty-three percent of these youngsters were given their pills. Twenty-one percent bought them and twelve percent stole them. (3)

The image of a villainous drug dealer enticing our nation's youth to use drugs is a myth. Young people get opioids to abuse from their friends and relatives, not from drug dealers. Young adults trade medication ("I'll give you my Ritalin if you give me your Vicodin") and don't know – or care -that it's illegal and dangerous. Powerful prescription opioids were viewed as relatively less dangerous than street drugs. Many people mistakenly believed that prescription drugs were safe.

Young people often have mistaken ideas about the risk of prescription drugs. According to one study, forty percent of adolescents in grades seven through twelve believed that prescription drugs are safer than street drugs. (4) Thirty percent believed prescription drugs aren't addictive. As we learned from Chapter 1, when a drug is perceived as less dangerous, more people use it.

We have a pill-taking culture. Possibly due to bombardment with drug company advertisements, many people believe there is "a pill for every ill." Experts have a term for these people, who feel the need to medicate even routine negative feelings with drugs or medications: "chemical copers." When a person uses medications to cope with any negative feelings, he loses the ability to handle unpleasant feelings and learn from them. Sometimes, negative feelings are essential, to prod us into making beneficial life changes.

The over- prescription of opioids by physicians, and the release of OxyContin certainly contributed to the opioid addiction conflagration, but the ways our cultural regard controlled substances added to the rate of addiction. Other contributing factors were the lack of prescription monitoring programs in most states, and poor physician education, regarding addiction, pain, and their treatments. According to several studies, internet access to prescription pain pills didn't appear to contribute as much to the numbers of people who became addicted to pain pills as most people have suspected.

Thankfully, the most recent NSDUH shows a drop in the number of people over age twelve using pain pills in a nonmedical way. An analysis of the 2008 data showed the number had dropped to 4.7 million people, down from the peak of 5.2 million in 2006. (2)

The Pain Management Movement

In the late 1990's, organizations like the American Pain Society and the American Academy of Pain Management declared that doctors in the U.S. were doing a lousy job of treating pain, and were under-prescribing opioid pain medications, due to a misguided fear of causing addiction. As a result, there was a national push to treat pain more aggressively. Some states even passed pain initiatives, mandating treatment for pain. Lawsuits were brought against doctors who didn't adequately treat pain. The Joint Commission on the Accreditation of Healthcare Organizations (JACHO), the organization that inspects hospitals to assess their quality of care, made the patient's level of pain the "fifth vital sign," after body temperature, blood pressure, heart rate, and respiratory rate. Pain management specialists encouraged more liberal prescribing of pain medication. These experts told their primary care colleagues that the chance of developing addiction from opioids prescribed for pain was about one percent.

With these limited facts, the pain management movement was off and running. Many pain management specialists, some of whom were paid speakers for the drug companies that manufactured powerful opioid pain medications, spoke at seminars about the relative safety of opioids, used long term for chronic pain. Pain management specialists taught these views to small town family practice and general medicine doctors, who were relatively inexperienced in the treatment of either pain or addiction.

The problem was...the specialists were wrong.

These specialists, in their well-intentioned enthusiasm to relieve suffering, used flawed data when reciting the risk for addiction. The one percent figure came from a study looking at patients treated in the hospital for acute pain, which is quite different from treating outpatients with chronic non cancer pain. (5) In other words, they compared apples to oranges.

To many addiction specialists, an addiction risk of only one percent seemed improbable, since the general population has an addiction risk estimated from six to twelve percent. Surely, being prescribed pain pills would not *lessen* the risk for addiction. Yet the one percent figure was often cited by many pain management professionals, as well as by the representatives of the drug companies selling strong opioids.

Some pain management specialists even took a scolding tone when they spoke of some primary care physicians' reluctance to prescribe strong opioids. They often muddied the waters, and grouped patients with cancer pain, acute pain, and chronic non-cancer pain together, and spoke of them as one group. This can feel insulting to doctors who, though reluctant to prescribe opioids endlessly for a patient with chronic non cancer pain, are adamant about treating end-of-life cancer pain aggressively with opioids. No compassionate physician limits opioids for patients with cancer pain *or* with acute, short term pain, but chronic non-cancer pain is different, with different outcomes than acute pain or cancer pain.

We didn't learn from history, or we would have learned that when many people have access to opioids, many will develop addiction. We are scientifically more advanced than one hundred years ago, but we still have the same reward pathway in the brain. The human organism hasn't changed physiologically. The present epidemic of opioid addiction is reminiscent of the early part of the twentieth century, just after the Bayer drug company released heroin, which for a short period of time was sold without a prescription, before physicians recognized that over prescription of opioids caused iatrogenic addiction.

Following is a composite of a typical history given to me by a patient entering the methadone clinic:

"I had back pain and I went to my family doctor. I work construction and my back was always hurting. He gave me hydrocodone pills and they helped a little, but he had to keep increasing the dose. He took X-rays and couldn't find anything wrong, so he sent me to the pain clinic. They took me off the hydrocodone and started me on OxyContin.

I started on twenty milligrams twice a day, but we had to keep going up on the dose. The doctor increased me to two-hundred and forty milligrams a day, and it started to be that wasn't enough and I still had back pain. Then one of my friends said, 'Hey, you can get more out of them if you crush them and snort them.' So I tried it once, to see what it was like. Since it was a prescription medicine, I didn't think it was dangerous.

"I got a really good feeling after I snorted that pill, and knew I wanted to keep snorting Oxy's so I could feel that way. I felt like I had energy, was in a good mood, and didn't have a care in the world. I felt like I could work longer and get more done. And my back didn't hurt. But I ran out of pills early once I started snorting them, so I had to buy them from people I knew. Where I live, it seems like everyone is on pain pills. I started snorting more and more and then one day I couldn't get any and wow....I felt bad. I couldn't go to work, couldn't eat....my friend told me I was dope sick.

"After that, it just got worse and worse. I was using three to four hundred milligrams of Oxy's a day, easy. Then the price started goin' up. Used to be you could get a forty for twenty dollars, [meaning a forty milligram pill for twenty dollars], but now you're lucky to find them forty milligrams for forty dollars, if you can find them at all.

"I never would have started the pain pills if I'd known what they'd do to me. The doctor never told me I could get addicted to them. Of course, I didn't tell him I'd been snorting them. I know that was wrong, but I didn't think it could cause all this. [meaning addiction]"

This is a typical history from people who started taking pain pills under the direction of a physician. These patients didn't intend to become addicted. Some addicted people blame their doctors for causing their opioid addiction, but most doctors were conscientiously trying to treat the pain reported by their patient, and the pain management experts had told these doctors the risk of addiction was so low they didn't have to worry about it.

Certainly many patients made bad choices to misuse their medications, either from curiosity or peer influence, pushing them farther over the line into addiction. Patients need to recognize their own contribution to their addiction. But with opioid addiction, *as the disease progresses, the addict loses the power of choice that he once had. If the addict is fortunate enough to have a moment of clarity, before the disease progresses too far, he may be able to stop on his own, without treatment.*

By their very nature, opioids produce pleasure. Any time doctors prescribe something that causes pleasure, we should expect addiction to occur. Some people, for whatever reason, feel more pleasure than others when they take opioids, and seem to be at higher risk for addiction. As discussed in previous chapters, genetics, environment, and individual factors all influence this risk.

Opioids treat pain – both physical and emotional. Many of the neuronal pathways in the brain for sensing and experiencing pain are the same for both physical and psychological pain. For example, the brain pathways activated when you drop a hammer on your toe are much the same as when you have to tell your spouse you spent the rent money while gambling. Opioids make both types of pain better. Chronic pain patients with psychological illnesses are at increased risk for inappropriate use of their pain medications.

In a recent study, the rate of developing true opioid addiction in patients taking opioids for chronic pain was found to be increased fourfold over the risk of non-medicated people. (6) Instead of a one percent incidence, as estimated by pain medicine specialists in the past, it now appears eighteen to forty-five percent of patients maintained long-term on opioids develop true addiction, not mere physical dependency. (7) If this information had been available in the late 1990's, doctors may have taken more precautions when they prescribed strong opioids for chronic pain.

Researchers have identified the risk factors for addiction among patients who take opioids long-term (more than three months) for chronic pain. Studies now show that a personal past history of addiction is the strongest predictor of future problems with addiction, as would be expected. A patient with a family history of addiction is also at increased risk for addiction, as is a patient with psychiatric illness of any kind. (8)

However, at the height of the pain control movement, there were no good studies of the addiction risk when opioids were used for more than three months. The little information that did exist was misused, resulting in an incredible underestimation of the risk of addiction in patients with chronic pain, who were treated with opioid medications for more than three months.

Speakers at the American Society of Addiction Medicine (ASAM) meeting in 2009 explained that in new guidelines, published by the American College of Occupational and Environmental Medicine, the routine use of opioids for the treatment of non-cancer pain was **not** recommended, because of the lack of studies showing clear benefit. Speakers also discussed hyperalgesia, a condition where patients on opioids for long periods of time actually become more and more sensitive to painful stimuli. (9)

To their credit, some pain medicine specialists have acknowledged that, in their enthusiasm to promote the appropriate treatment of pain, they understated risks of addiction. In 2001, Dr. Steven Passik, a renowned pain management specialist, wrote a letter to the editor in the Journal of Pain and Symptom Management, saying, "In effect, we have told primary care doctors and other prescribers that the risk was so low they essentially could ignore the possibility of addiction." He conceded that, in some groups of patients, the rate of addiction can be as high as forty-five percent, such as patients with previous addictive disorders. (7)

With the momentum of the movement for better control of pain, both acute and chronic, the number of prescriptions for opioid pain pills increased dramatically. In the years from 1997 through 2006, prescription sales of hydrocodone increased 244%, while oxycodone increased 732% during that same time period. Prescription sales for methadone increased a staggering 1177%. (10)

It's not just patients who are at risk for abuse and addiction. The increased amount of opioids being prescribed meant there was more opioid available to be diverted to the black market. When an addicting drug is made more available, it will be misused more often. As we've seen, giving or selling pills to friends or family occurs regularly in this country.

OxyContin

The increase in opioid addiction coincided not only with the movement toward aggressive treatment of chronic pain with opioids, but also with the release of OxyContin by its manufacturer, Purdue Pharma, in 1996. Their other drug for pain, MS Contin, had become well-established in the treatment of severe cancer pain, but this drug was due to come off patent. This meant the other drug companies could then manufacture and sell a generic version of the same drug at a cheaper price. Purdue obviously wanted physicians to switch to their new drug, still under their patent, to maintain their share of this market.

OxyContin was marketed aggressively to small town family doctors who didn't have much experience treating chronic pain with powerful opioids, or with identifying and treating pain pill addiction. In rural areas, family doctors had few places they could refer patients who developed problems with their opioid pain medications. (11)

The drug company marketed OxyContin as an appropriate treatment for chronic, moderate to severe, non-cancer pain. In the past, such strong opioids were used only for intractable, severe pain. OxyContin was marketed as the pain medicine to "start with and stay with." OxyContin was even prescribed for such ailments as menstrual cramps, oddly mirroring the misuse of opioids like laudanum and morphine a century earlier.

Purdue Pharma believed OxyContin was tamper-resistant and less likely to be abused, due to its time release coating. The drug company was still touting this as a selling point in 2001, when addiction medicine doctors all over the country were seeing hundreds of OxyContin addicts. These addicts described how easy it was to moisten the pill, crush it, snort it, inject it, or just file off the coating and chew it.

Purdue Pharma didn't do pre-release testing of their new drug, to assess its desirability to addicts seeking to get high. At first, they didn't have a post-market release system to monitor for signs of abuse and diversion, as other companies have done. In fact, Purdue Pharma seemed to go out of their way to ignore early warnings and complaints about the drug. Doctors, who tried to warn the drug company about the patients they were seeing who were addicted to OxyContin, were ignored and discounted. (11)

Sales representatives for Purdue Pharma made deceptive statements. Besides telling doctors that the drug was less likely to be abused, the sales representatives also gave false information about the risks of opioid withdrawal after stopping the pill. (12)

OxyContin became such a commonly known drug to both abusers and the media that the U.S. General Accounting Office (GAO) asked for a report about the promotion of OxyContin by Purdue Pharma, information on factors affecting its abuse and diversion, and recommendations of how to curtail its misuse. This report, released in 2003, stated that by 2001, the sales of OxyContin were over 1 billion dollars per year, making it the most commonly prescribed brand of opioid medication for moderate to severe pain. (12)

By 2002, prescriptions written for OxyContin for non-cancer pain constituted eighty-five percent of its total sales. The type of non-cancer pain for which it was prescribed included both acute pain, like kidney stones, broken bones, and post-operative pain, and chronic pain like arthritis and fibromyalgia. By 2003, primary care doctors, with little or no experience or training in the treatment of long-term pain, were prescribing about half of all the OxyContin prescriptions written in the country. By 2003, the FDA had cited Purdue Pharma twice, for using misleading information in its promotional advertisements to these doctors. (12)

The GAO's report recognized the unique timing of the release of OxyContin. "Fortuitous timing may have contributed to this growth, as the launching of the drug occurred during the national focus on the inadequacy of patient pain treatment and management." (12, Page 9)

Purdue Pharma could have re-formulated their pill, to reduce the risk of abuse and addiction. Sterling Drug, manufacturer of the pain medication Talwin, re-formulated their medication, to make it less likely to be abused. The active drug in Talwin is pentazocine, an opioid that had a brief rise in abuse when it was first released in the 1980s. To prevent intravenous injection of their drug, Sterling re-formulated Talwin within a year, adding naloxone, a drug that reverses the effects of opioids. This is the same medication used by doctors to treat opioid overdoses. Naloxone is not absorbed when taken by mouth, because it is inactivated by stomach acid. But when the pentazocine/naloxone pill is ground and injected, it puts addicts into immediate withdrawal, thus making it a much less desirable drug for intravenous addicts. This action by Sterling curtailed the abuse of Talwin/NX, their new product.

Other manufacturers have taken different precautions, when concerned about the abuse of a prescription drug. For example, the drug

Rohypnol, commonly called the date rape drug, is illegal in the U.S., but is legally prescribed in Europe and Latin America. Because they were concerned that the drug was being used illicitly, to facilitate rapes, the manufacturer, Hoffman-LaRoche, re-formulated Rohypnol so that instead of being clear, colorless and tasteless, it becomes milky white when added to any other liquid. This can warn unsuspecting people that something has been added to their drink.

A Purdue Pharma representative testified before congress in 2002, saying that the company was working on a re-formulation of OxyContin, to make it harder to use intravenously, and that they expected to have the re-formulated pill on the market within a few years. (13) Eight years later, there still is no such re-formulation of OxyContin. Purdue Pharma said it would take three or four years to reformulate the drug, though Sterling, with Talwin, managed to accomplish this within a year, more than a decade earlier.

In May of 2007, three officers of Purdue Pharma, a privately held company, pled guilty to misleading the public about the drug's safety. Their chief executive officer, general counsel, and chief scientific officer pled guilty, as individuals, to misbranding a pharmaceutical. The executives did not serve jail time. Though they plead guilty, they claimed they personally had done nothing wrong, but accepted blame under the premise that an executive is responsible for the acts of the employees working under him. (14) The three executives' fines totaled 34.5 million dollars, to be paid to Virginia, the state that brought the lawsuit.

The Purdue Pharma company agreed to pay a fine of $600 million. Though this is one of the largest amounts paid by a drug company for illegal marketing, Purdue made 2.8 billion dollars in sales revenue, from the time of its release in 1996 until 2001 alone.

To be fair, the drug company and addiction specialists had data that showed the most common opioid to be abused is actually hydrocodone, a short acting opioid, often marketed under the brand names of Vicodin or Lortab. While this is technically correct, the strength of a single hydrocodone pill is usually 5, 7.5, or 10 milligrams, while OxyContin came in 10, 20, 40, 80, and, for a brief time, 160 milligrams. In addition, hydrocodone is slightly weaker, milligram per milligram, than oxycodone. In other words, the opioid firepower in one OxyContin is much higher than in one hydrocodone, so they are hardly comparable. An addict would need more than eight hydrocodone 5 milligram pills to equal one OxyContin 40 milligrams.

This much opioid, packed into one pill, produces a powerful high when it's released all at once, as it is when the time release coating is removed. Many patients I've talked to have said they knew OxyContin would cause problems from the first use. "After that first high, I knew I would keep using. I wanted that feeling," is an example of a typical quote.

Since the debacle of OxyContin, Purdue Pharma has donated money towards helping communities treat opioid addicts, and has paid money as ordered by the court. Much of the $600 million award will go to states heavily afflicted by OxyContin addiction. This money will help to establish programs to help prevent and treat opioid addiction.

Not all states in the U.S. have been beset with dramatic increases in opioid addiction. Some regions of the U.S. have been hit harder than others over the last ten years. In late 2004, the Department of Justice released a bulletin, with information about OxyContin diversion to the black market and its illicit use. The information presented suggested that the Southeast had more OxyContin diversion and illicit use. (15)

The backbone of the Appalachian Mountains and its foothills, from the southern part in Alabama and Georgia, to the northernmost part in Maine, has been the most dramatically affected. Rural Appalachia has become a hotbed of opioid addiction. This increase started at the very end of the twentieth century.

At an American Society of Addiction Medicine conference in 2003, participants speculated about possible reasons why this increase occurred. The Appalachian region has much heavy industry, like mining and logging, which can lead to musculoskeletal injuries. These types of injuries often require prescriptions for opioids. These patients may then become addicted, or they may divert them to a black market, taking advantage of the potential supplement to their income. Other doctors speculated that these patients may have the genetic makeup that makes them more susceptible to addiction. Some doctors theorized that these are the grandchildren of bootleggers, inferring either that they are genetically more prone to addiction, or may find drug using and trafficking more acceptable given the cultural milieu.

The General Accounting Office report stated that some states — Tennessee, Kentucky, Virginia and West Virginia — historically have been areas of high intensity for drug trafficking of prescription opioids.

This report opines the poverty of the area, and the potential for large profits from illicit sales of opioid drugs, has driven the demand for prescriptions in this area. (12)

People who sold their prescriptions for OxyContin did get hefty profits from the black market. Patients entering treatment for opioid addiction in 2001 told me the local black market rate was usually twenty dollars for a forty milligram pill, or fifty cents milligram. For a modest prescription of forty milligrams, taken every twelve hours, one month's total of sixty pills would bring twelve hundred dollars per prescription, though after deducting the amount paid to the pharmacy to fill the prescription of approximately two dollars per pill, the clear profit would be around just over a thousand dollars. By 2006, OxyContin became harder to find in black markets in rural Western North Carolina, and my patients told me the cost of OxyContin rose to about one dollar per milligram, doubling the profit for even a relatively small prescription to several thousand dollars. This would be quite a temptation to an otherwise law-abiding person, who badly needed money. Many addicts deal drugs to support their own addiction. Opioid- addicted patients with prescriptions for stimulants like Ritalin and Adderall, or benzodiazepines like Xanax or Klonipin, often trade or sell these for money to buy opioids, their drug of choice.

Other factors contributed to the rapid increase in prescription opioid addiction. Use and abuse of the internet, the refusal in some states to create prescription monitoring databases, combined with the sad lack of addiction education for doctors in training and in private practice, also fuel the fire.

End Notes:

1. Substance Abuse and Mental Health Services Administration. (2007). *Results from the 2006 National Survey on Drug Use and Health: National Findings* (Office of Applied Studies, NSDUH Series H-36, HHS Publication No. SMA 09-4434). Rockville, MD.
2. Substance Abuse and Mental Health Services Administration. (2009). *Results from the 2008 National Survey on Drug Use and Health: National Findings* (Office of Applied Studies, NSDUH Series H-36, HHS Publication No. SMA 09-4434). Rockville, MD.

3. Johnston, L. D., O'Malley, P. M., Bachman, J. G., & Schulenberg, J. E. (December 11, 2008). "Various stimulant drugs show continuing gradual declines among teens in 2008, most illicit drugs hold steady." University of Michigan News Service: Ann Arbor, MI. http://www.monitoringthefuture.org .
4. Partnership for a Drug-Free America – The Partnership Attitude Tracking Study Teens 2008, Report http://www.drugfree.org/Files/full_report_teens_2008 .
5. Porter and Jick, *New England Journal of Medicine*, 302 (2) (Jan. 10, 1980) p. 123.
6. Michael F. Fleming, Stacey L. Balousek, Cynthia L. Klessig, et al. "Substance Use Disorders in a Primary Care Sample Receiving Daily Opioid Therapy," *Journal of Pain*, 207; Vol. 8, issue 7: pp. 573-582.
7. Steven Passik M.D., *Journal of Pain and Symptom Management*, Vol. 21 No. 5, (May 2001), pp. 359 – 360.
8. Chou, R, Fanciullo, G, Fine, P, et. al., "Opioid Treatment Guidelines: Clinical guidelines for the use of Chronic Opioid Therapy in chronic, non-cancer pain." *The Journal of Pain*, 2009, Vol. 10, No. 2. pp. 113-130.
9. Melvin Pohl M.D., "Recovery from Chronic Pain, Opioid Free"; lecture, annual meeting of Pain and Addiction: Common Threads, New Orleans, LA, April 30, 2009.
10. Andrea Trescott, MD, Stanford Helm, MD, el. al., "Opioids in the Management of Chronic Non-cancer Pain: An Update of American Society of the Interventional Pain Physicians' Guidelines," *Pain Physician* 2008: Opioids Special Issue: 11:S5 – S 62.
11. Barry Meier, *Pain Killer: A "Wonder" Drug's Trail of Addiction and Death* (Rodale Books, 2003).
12. General Accounting Office *OxyContin Abuse and Diversion* report GAO-04-110, 2003.
13. United States Senate. Congressional hearing of the Committee on Health, Education, Labor, and Pensions, on *Examining the Effects of the Painkiller OxyContin*, 107th Congress, Second Session, February, 2002.
14. Washington Times, "Company Admits Painkiller Deceit," May 11, 2007, accessed online at http://washingtontimes.com/news/2007/may/10/20070510-103237-4952r/prinnt/ on 12/18/2008.

15. 13. U.S. Department of Justice, *Intelligence Bulletin: OxyContin Diversion, Availability, and Abuse,* (Johnstown, PA, National Drug Intelligence Center, 2004) http://www.usdoj.gov/ndic .

CHAPTER 7

Feeding the Flames

Internet Pharmacies

Internet pharmacies offered addicts new channels for obtaining opioids. Since 2004, The National Center on Addiction and Substance Abuse at Columbia University (CASA) has done surveillance of internet pharmacies offering controlled substance prescriptions. Their latest report, released in July 2008, found that out of one hundred and fifty-nine sites, only two were legitimate pharmacies, certified by the National Association of Pharmacy Boards. Eighty-five percent of rogue sites offered to sell addicting prescription drugs *without* requiring a pre-scription. (1) Of the few sites that did ask for a prescription, half allowed a faxed prescription, which can be falsified with ease. CASA found no controls to prevent the access of these drugs by children. In some cases, CASA posed as an underage person, and the internet sites still offered to sell them the drugs.

About ninety-five percent of the prescriptions filled by rogue internet pharmacies are for controlled substances. Of these, the most commonly offered drugs for sale were the benzodiazepines (Valium, Xanax, and others), offered by ninety percent of the internet sites. Next were the opioids, offered by fifty-seven percent of the sites. The most common opioids for sale were hydrocodone, oxycodone, and propoxyphene. These came in many different brand names. Stimulants, like methylphenidate (Ritalin, Concerta) and dextroamphetamine (Adderall, Dexedrine), were offered by twenty-seven percent of the internet pharmacy sites. Because these websites have a very high turnover, it's difficult to detect and prosecute the people operating them. (1)

The Ryan Haight Act was signed by President George W. Bush in October of 2008. This law requires a face-to-face meeting and exami-nation of each patient with a licensed physician, before a controlled substance can be prescribed and dispensed. The medication must be prescribed for a legitimate medical reason, with clear documentation in the patient's chart. There must be at least one face–to-face meeting of physician and patient per year. The dispensing online pharmacy must post their physical location, the license numbers of their pharmacists, and must have an endorsement by the DEA to conduct business over the internet.

This act was named after Ryan Haight, who died of a hydrocodone overdose at age eighteen, from pills he had ordered off the internet. They were prescribed by a doctor who never saw him, and an internet pharmacy delivered them to his house. More information about Ryan can be found at http://getsmartaboutdrugs.com. Ryan was a highly intelligent, athletic, and loving young man, according to a description of his story by his mother. His mom was so outraged at the ease with which Ryan was able to order hydrocodone from the internet, she testified before the U.S. Senate and organized other families to advocate for stronger laws to prevent deaths like his.

Many of the young people who have died of overdoses have been great kids, like Ryan, who weren't even addicted to drugs, but were curious. They may have made one bad choice, and it cost them their lives. Many young people have no idea how harmful prescription drugs can be. In the past, most of the anti-drug messages for youth have focused on illicit street drugs, not prescription drugs.

Internet companies are adjusting to the changing laws. One company is recruiting doctors from all over the country, for the mandated face–to-face meetings, and the yearly follow up examinations. In January of 2009, I saw an advertisement on Craig's List for a physician job. The ad offered a disproportionately large sum of money to doctors willing to meet with patients for one initial visit, and then once per year, and prescribe medication for them for the rest of the year. Suspicious, I contacted the company. At first, they were quite vague and said their patients needed prescription medications, but were prevented from seeing a doctor because they were too poor or lived too far away. This made their company sound like a humanitarian organization.

Finally, I was referred to a doctor in Illinois who talked openly. He admitted that around ninety percent of the patients he saw needed medications for chronic pain, and they couldn't afford to go to expensive pain clinics. He said it was a way for the poor to be able to get needed pain management, like the wealthy who can go to pain clinics. When I asked him if he was concerned about the potential for addiction, he said that if he suspected addiction, he would refuse to prescribe. He felt his actions met a physician's standard of care.

But how would this doctor know if his patients were having problems with addiction, since he saw them only once a year? He had no office visits for random urine drug screens, and no way to do pill counts periodically. Patients could progress far into addiction, before he knew they needed help. He stated that he believed misuse of medication by a patient would be a rare event, and he would know when it happened, though he didn't say *how* he would know. It's a convenient belief for him to hold, considering he's apparently reimbursed handsomely for his limited contact with these patients. For a year at a time, he is authorizing the affiliated pharmacy to dispense opioid medications, with essentially no oversight.

Intrigued, I began trolling Craigslist, to see if this company has continued to advertise for doctors. They ran an advertisement recently, and now appear to be much more forthright about their intent. They now advertise for "pain physicians" and the ads say that doctors in thirty-five U.S. cities are participating in this "exciting new program." They also tell doctors reading the ad "there is little or nothing for you to do." They're right. Easy money for doing next to nothing, except authorizing prescriptions for opioid pain pills, with very little oversight. I've seen such advertisements as recently as early 2010.

Because the internet is a relatively new way to obtain addicting opioids and other drugs, regulation has taken some time, because new laws have to be passed to address new concerns. Though it is illegal in this country to sell controlled substances with no physician prescription, it is not illegal in other countries. Many of the web sites are based in countries with markedly less restrictive laws. Because many of these organizations are foreign, it's harder for the DEA to close down these rogue websites. Many times, after they're closed, they quickly re-open under a new name.

Because these online pharmacies are rather expensive, addicts can spend large sums feeding their addictions, adding to their financial chaos and worsening family tension. I had a patient, whom I will call Greg, who ordered nearly all his opioids from online pharmacies, and built a large pain pill tolerance, over a period of five years. Greg nearly lost his family, due to the great sums of money he spent on internet pharmacies. He said that once he ordered from one pharmacy site, he got repeated emails from other sites, and just started ordering from one after another. When a new prescription was due, he got reminder emails. Obviously the internet companies had shared his email address, because he was contacted by companies he didn't know, asking if he would like to order pain pills.

Initially, money was not an obstacle for Greg, since he had a good job and some savings. He kept his addiction secret from his wife, until he spent tens of thousands of dollars. He then came to my office, seeking help, hoping to get into treatment before his wife found out. He hoped that if he were already in treatment when she found out, she would be less likely to leave him. He had to stay off his computer completely, because it was a trigger to order and use pain pills. Ultimately, he told his wife everything, and she stayed with him, though she insisted on installing controls on their computer, to prevent nefarious online drug companies from sending ads and reminders.

Opioids are not cheap on these sites. While writing this book, I priced oxycodone on several sites. On one site, oxycodone eighty milligrams costs four hundred and seventy-nine dollars for ninety pills. The website says no prescription is needed. Since oxycodone is sold for up to a dollar a milligram on the street, a person willing to commit a felony for easy money can order online and still resell for quite a profit.

Even though the internet provided prescription opioids to some addicts, studies like the 2008 National Survey on Drug Use and Health (NSDUH) indicated that little of the abused opioids in this country originated from these pharmacies. (2)

Prescription monitoring plans

Many states with high rates of prescription pain pill addiction didn't have operational prescription monitoring programs until very recently. Prescription monitoring programs keep electronic records of all controlled substances prescribed for each patient. The data under each patient's name includes the type of drug, milligram dose, number of pills dispensed, prescribing physician's name, and the location of the pharmacy where it was filled.

This data base is accessible to any physician in that state, who prescribes controlled substances. It allows doctors to discover patients who are "doctor shopping," a term for patients who see multiple doctors for opioid prescriptions at the same time, and these doctors are unaware of each other. Patients who are addicted to prescription opioids resort to doctor shopping because their tolerance increases, but the amount the physician is willing to prescribe stays the same, so the addict needs an ever increasing amount of opioids.

In the states with monitoring programs in place early in the rise of prescription pain pill abuse, it was harder for patients to receive opioids from more than one physician. As a result, many addicts travel to doctors in neighboring states, which didn't have prescription monitoring programs in place. Most states now either have operational systems, or are working on getting them.

States that want to set up a prescription monitoring plan can get federal money from the Harold Rogers Prescription Monitoring grant. These programs can be costly to both start and continue. Estimates for the cost of starting a program are about three hundred and fifty-thousand dollars, and it costs and it costs up to one million dollars per year to operate. In 2005 money became available from NASPER, National All Schedules Prescription Electronic Reporting Act, funded through Substance Abuse and Mental Health Services Administration, which created grant programs for states to start or enhance their existing programs. Grants provided from this fund require the sharing of data across states lines. It's hoped that ultimately, there will be a nationwide program, so prescription pill addicts cannot just cross state lines to get additional drugs from unsuspecting doctors in a different state.

North Carolina's program started in mid-2007, after much resistance from the state legislature. Apparently, the measure to create a monitoring system was passed by lawmakers by a slim margin, due to concerns about the confidentiality of the information. By January of 2009, only about ten percent of North Carolina physicians were registered to use the database.

The state prescription monitoring program is a valuable tool to keep patients safe. I've used the program to screen patients I admit to methadone clinics since I first got access in December, 2007. I need to know if a patient receives other controlled substances which could be fatal when combined with methadone. I also screen patients several times per year, and also if a counselor requests it due to unusual behavior on the part of a patient.

The first time I screened methadone patients using the prescription monitoring database, it was on a group of thirty-one hundred established patients. I was amazed to see all the controlled substances being prescribed to them. We had no knowledge of these medications. In some cases, our patients were getting methadone both from us and from a doctor in the community. Of course, they neglected to tell either doctor about the other. Many patients prescribed benzodiazepines didn't tell us about these drugs. Often, the prescribed drugs weren't present on the patient's drug screens. If they weren't, it's likely the patient was giving or selling their medications to other people. Many times, these were the patients we had already suspected of drug dealing on our clinic premises.

My experience convinced me that screening all patients at a methadone clinic with the prescription monitoring database is essential. Screening also reduced drug dealing on clinic premises. Checking such data bases should be a standard of care at all methadone clinics and pain clinics, because it's such a vital safety measure.

Lack of Physician Training

Most medical schools and residency programs place little emphasis on educating future physicians about addiction. A survey conducted by the Center on Addiction and Substance Abuse at Columbia University (CASA) revealed that physicians are poorly trained to recognize and treat addictive disorders. (3)

CASA surveyed nine-hundred and seventy-nine U.S. physicians, from all age groups, practice settings, and specialties. Only nineteen percent of these physicians said they had been trained in medical school to identify diversion of prescribed drugs. Diversion means that the drug was not taken by the patient for whom it was prescribed. Almost forty percent had been trained to identify prescription drug abuse or addiction, but of those, most received only a few hours of training during four years of medical school. More shocking, only fifty-five percent of the surveyed doctors said they were taught how to prescribe controlled drugs. Of those, most had less than a few hours of training.

This survey indicates that medical schools need to critically evaluate their teaching priorities. Surely, medical schools should train their students about how to prescribe controlled substances. Distressingly, my own experience mirrors this study's findings. My medical school, Ohio State University, did a better job than most when they taught us in our first year about alcohol addiction, but I don't remember any instruction about how to prescribe controlled substances. Is it possible that I've forgotten I had such a course? Well, yes. But if I can still remember the tediously boring Krebs cycle, then surely I would have remembered something juicier and more practical, like how to prescribe potentially addicting drugs. Similarly, less than half of the surveyed doctors recalled any training in medical school in the management of pain, and of those that did, most had less than a few hours of training.

Residency training programs did a little better. Of the surveyed doctors, thirty-nine percent received training on how to identify drug diversion, and sixty-one percent received training on identifying prescription drug addiction. Seventy percent of the doctors surveyed said they received instruction on how to prescribe controlled substances. (3)

This last finding is appalling, because it means that thirty percent of doctors received *no training on how to prescribe controlled substances in their residency programs.* Could it be true that nearly a third of the doctors leaving residency – last stop for most doctors before being loosed upon the populace to practice medicine with little to no oversight – had **no** training on how to prescribe these potentially dangerous drugs? Sixty-two percent leaving residency had training on pain management. This means the remaining thirty-eight percent had no training on the treatment of pain.

Could it be that many of these physicians were in residencies or specialties that had no need to prescribe such drugs? No. The participating doctors were in family practice, internal medicine, OB/GYN, psychiatry, and orthopedic surgery. The study included physicians of all ages (fifty-three percent were under age fifty), all races (though a majority at seventy-five percent were white, three other races were represented), and all types of locations (thirty-seven percent urban, thirty percent suburban, with the remainder small towns or rural areas). This study reveals a hard truth: medical training in the U.S. does not do a good job of teaching future doctors about two diseases that causes much disability and suffering: pain and addiction. (3)

When I recall my residency days, I shudder, as I remember how we treated patients addicted to prescription medications. By the time we could identify a person as addicted to opioids or benzodiazepines, their disease was fairly well established, and it didn't take much clinical acumen to detect. They were the patients with thick charts, who were in the emergency room loudly proclaiming their pain and demanding to be medicated. Overall, the residents were angry and disgusted with such people, and treated them with thinly veiled contempt. I think we regarded them more as criminals than patients. We mimicked the attitudes of our attending physicians. Sadly, I did no better than the rest of my group, and often made jokes at the expense of patients who were suffering in a way and to a degree I was unable to perceive. I had a tightly closed mind and made assumptions that these were bad people, wasting my time.

Heroin addicts were not well treated. I recall a discussion with our attending physician concerning an intravenous heroin user, re-admitted to the hospital. Six months earlier, he was hospitalized for treatment of endocarditis (infected heart valve). Ultimately his aortic heart valve was removed and replaced with a mechanical valve. He recovered and left the hospital, but returned several months later, with an infected mechanical valve, because he had continued to inject heroin. We discussed the ethics of refusing to replace the valve a second time, because we felt it was futile.

I didn't know any better at the time. I didn't know we could have referred him to a nearby methadone clinic after his first admission. Maybe he wouldn't have gone, but maybe he would. He may have done well on methadone and stopped using heroin, thus avoiding the second surgery. We could have started him on methadone in the hospital, stabilized his cravings, and then referred him to the methadone clinic, when he left the hospital. Instead, I think we had a social worker ask him if he wanted to go away somewhere for treatment, he said no, and that was the end of that. Small wonder he continued to use heroin.

At a minimum, the attending physician should have known that addiction is a disease, not a moral failing, and it can be treated. The attending physician should have known how to treat heroin addiction, and conveyed this information to the residents he taught. Instead, we were debating whether to treat a man whose care we had mismanaged. Fortunately, he did get a second heart valve and was able to leave the hospital. I have no further knowledge of his outcome.

Despite having relatively little training in indentifying and treating prescription pill addiction, physicians tend to be overly confident in their abilities to detect such addictions. CASA found that eighty percent of the surveyed physicians felt they were qualified to identify both drug abuse and addiction. However, in a 1998 CASA study, *Under the Rug: Substance Abuse and the Mature Woman*, physicians were given a case history of a 68 year old woman, with symptoms of prescription drug addiction. Only **one percent** of the surveyed physicians presented substance abuse as a possible diagnosis. In a similar study, when presented with a case history suggestive of an addictive disorder, only six percent of primary care physicians listed substance abuse as a possible diagnosis. (4)

Besides being poorly educated about treatments for patients with addiction, most doctors aren't comfortable having frank discussions about a patient's drug misuse or addiction. Most physicians fear they will provoke anger or shame in their patients. Physicians may feel disgust with addicted patients and find them unpleasant, demanding, or even frightening. Conversely, doctors can feel too embarrassed to ask seemingly "nice" people about addiction. In a CASA study titled, *Missed Opportunity*, forty-seven percent of physicians in primary care said it was difficult to discuss prescription drug addiction and abuse with their patients, for whom they had prescribed such drugs. (4).

From this data, it's clear physicians are poorly educated about addiction at the level of medical school and residency. Even when they do diagnose addiction, are they aware of the treatment facilities in their area? Patients should be referred to treatment centers who can manage their addictions. If patients are addicted to opioids, medications like methadone and buprenorphine can be a tremendous help.

Thankfully, the yearly NSDUH study and other studies are beginning to show a slight reduction in the prevalence of opioid addiction in this country. Many of the factors discussed in this chapter are beginning to be recognized, and changes made.

Pain specialists have revised what they teach to general practitioners, and are much more cautious about monitoring for addiction in their chronic pain patients on opioids. The company that manufactures OxyContin has been called to account for its marketing mistakes and is paying money in fines, to fund addiction prevention and treatment programs. Laws have been passed and are being enforced, to shut down rogue internet pharmacies dispensing controlled substances. Most states already have, or are getting, prescription monitoring plans. Many addiction experts have been encouraging medical schools and residencies to include more hours of training in identifying and treating addiction.

These measures will reduce new cases of opioid addiction, but how do we help the people who became addicted before changes began to occur? Preventing addiction is always better than trying to treat it after it occurs, but the people who are already suffering from opioid addiction need to access compassionate and effective treatment. This leads us to a more extensive discussion of medication-assisted therapies with methadone and buprenorphine.

End Notes:

1. Center on Addiction and Substance Abuse at Columbia University, *"You've Got Drugs" V, Prescription Drug Pushers on the Internet*, White Paper 7/08. Available online at http://www.casacolumbia.org

2   Substance Abuse and Mental Health Services Administration. (2007). *Results from the 2006 National Survey on Drug Use and Health: National Findings* (Office of Applied Studies, NSDUH Series H-36, HHS Publication No. SMA 09-4434). Rockville, MD.

3   *Missed Opportunity: A National Survey of Primary Care Physicians and Patients on Substance Abuse*, Center on Addiction and Substance Abuse at Columbia University, April 2000. Also available online at http://www.casacolumbia.org

4. *Under the Rug: Substance Abuse and the Mature Woman*, Center on Addiction and Substance Abuse at Columbia University, 1998. Available online at http://www.casacolumbia.org

CHAPTER 8

Methadone: Just the Facts

Poisons and medicine are oftentimes the same substance given with different intents.

~Peter Mere Latham

Discussions of methadone maintenance to treat opioid addiction cause disagreements even among addiction treatment professionals. This country, unlike European countries, has believed the only worthwhile recovery from addiction is drug-free recovery. Other countries long ago decided that reduction of harm done by addiction was a worthy goal in its own right, but the U.S. has been slow to embrace this view. We tend to have an "all or nothing" attitude.

This may be a holdover from days past, when people still believed that addiction was a choice, not a disease, despite all of the accumulated scientific evidence to the contrary. This view may be a result of our unique "up by your bootstraps" approach to overcoming adversity in the U.S., or it may be due to the success of 12-step recovery groups like Narcotics Anonymous, which believe that complete abstinence from all drugs is the goal of recovery.

Methadone has advocacy groups, dedicated to promoting or restricting the use of methadone. NAMA, or National Association for Methadone Advocates, is a group that advocates for the use of methadone in the treatment of opioid addiction. HARM'D, for Help America Reduce Methadone Deaths, is critical of methadone use, and though it falls just short of advocating its abolition, favors even more severe governmental regulation of methadone and methadone clinics than we have now. Our country already has more rigorous regulations on methadone treatment than many other countries.

Why does this medication possess such power to inflame passions?

Most addiction treatment centers in the U.S. are abstinence-based, meaning they define recovery as freedom from all addictive drugs. Present-day centers were influenced by the Minnesota model of the earliest treatment centers, as previously discussed. In fact, only recently have many treatment centers allowed the use of even non-addicting medications for the treatment of alcoholism, such as naltrex-one or acamprosate. Ten or twenty years ago, some centers eschewed even antidepressants, though most reputable treatment facilities now realize these can be of great benefit, when used appropriately.

Methods of opioid addiction treatment that don't use opioid sub-stitution medications, such as inpatient residential treatment, or thera-peutic communities, can be effective for patients who are able – and willing – to accept those forms of treatment, but it is difficult to retain patients in those treatments.

Few studies have been done to show the success rates for opioid addicts who underwent inpatient detoxification, followed by an inten-sive outpatient treatment. This is because opioid addicts don't often complete abstinence-based outpatient programs. Several studies were attempted, hoping to compare success rates of outpatient treatment versus medication-assisted treatment, but the studies couldn't be com-pleted. The patients refused to be randomized! They voted with their feet, and flocked to treatment using methadone. It appeared that out-patient treatment alone was an unacceptable option to many opioid addicts.

Many addicts have been through terrible opioid withdrawals in the past, and are unwilling to endure this agony again. Without using effective medications which ease the withdrawal, it's difficult to keep opioid addicts in treatment of any kind. In the past, clonidine was the only drug used by detoxification units.

Clonidine is a blood pressure medication that blocks some of the withdrawal symptoms, but at best, it's mildly to moderately effective. Most addicts say it helps a little, but not much (See Appendix B). Most reputable detoxification units now use buprenorphine (sometimes bet-ter known under the brand name Suboxone) to ease opioid withdrawal symptoms, but since it too is an opioid, addicts still feel withdrawal after the buprenorphine leaves their opioid receptors.

As described previously, many opioid addicts have a post-acute withdrawal syndrome from opioids, which can last for weeks to months after the acute withdrawal is over. They feel achy, sluggish, fatigued and perhaps a bit depressed. This is an emotionally and physically draining state, and most addicts can't tolerate it for long. This prolonged low-grade withdrawal is a trigger for relapse back to opioid use. Not all addicts experience this post-acute withdrawal, and we have no way of predicting who will be affected. The likelihood of post acute withdrawal probably increases with duration and intensity of opioid use.

Heroin Addiction: A Typical Addict

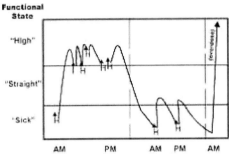

*Wide swings in opioid levels with heroin use

For a patient who feels chronically unwell off all opioids, methadone or buprenorphine may be the best course of treatment. Even in the 1960's, Dr. Vincent Dole postulated that after taking opioids from outside sources, the body stops making its own opioids, called endorphins. These endorphins are required to feel normal. He conceptualized addiction as a metabolic disorder, with chronically reduced endorphin levels after prolonged use of opioids. Presently we have no way to measure endorphins, so this remains a theory.

Methadone replaces this lack of endorphins. Because it is an opioid, it stimulates the opioid receptors. Because it is long-acting, it can prevent withdrawal for twenty-four hours or more, in most patients. At the proper dose of methadone, patients should feel normal, not feel intoxicated, or high, and should not feel withdrawal symptoms. Methadone gives the opioid addicts a fairly steady level of opioid, compared to short-acting opioids usually used for intoxication.

Former Addict Treated With Methadone Maintenance

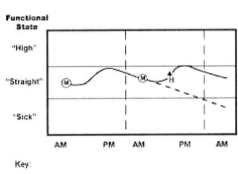

Key:
Ⓜ   Methadone Dose
↑   Heroin Injection
----- Course Of Mood And Function
- - - Course Of Mood And Function
      If Methadone Dose is Skipped

*Fairly stable opioid level on stable once daily methadone dosing

*Taken from NIDA's Methadone Research Web Guide (1)

Freed from the endless cycle of intoxication and withdrawal, addicts on methadone can participate in their own lives again. They can focus on the tasks of recovery. They can participate in individual and group counseling, and purge their social networks of drug users. They can focus on securing employment and getting treatment for co-existing mental and physical health issues. Addicts are able to function normally on methadone.

Using methadone and buprenorphine, which works by the same principle, to treat opioid addiction is *not* "like giving whiskey to an alcoholic," as has incorrectly been asserted by opponents of medication assisted therapies. *The valid difference lies in the unique pharmacology of methadone and buprenorphine.* Opioid addicts can lead normal lives on either of these two medications, when they are properly dosed.

They take an oral dose of methadone once daily, instead of injecting or snorting an opioid every few hours, or searching for the next pill or balloon of heroin. Other than coming to the clinic each day for their dose, life can be normal for them. Most addicts enrolled in an opioid treatment program are able to save money, work, and participate in family life. They are also much more likely to get counseling, which is an essential element in the treatment of opioid addiction.

Active addiction leads to chaotic and dangerous life styles (or death styles, as one patient said), and most people need time, support, and guidance to make positive changes. Admittedly, not all methadone clinics do a great job of providing counseling.

Methadone doesn't work for everyone. There are some patients who tried methadone, but found it left them feeling tired, sedated, or nauseous, despite multiple dose changes. Sedative drugs like benzodiazepines and barbiturates can be deadly with methadone, as can alcohol. Patients with coexisting addictions to these drugs are at higher risk for an overdose death, if they remain in methadone maintenance programs. Some patients have mental illness so severe it prohibits safe treatment with methadone. Methadone is not a panacea for all opioid addicts. Just as methadone opponents say methadone should never be used, some of methadone's advocates can swing too far in the other direction and believe methadone is the answer for every opioid addict.

History of methadone

Methadone was invented by German scientists in the 1940's, during the Second World War. Because of war embargoes, the Germans were running short of morphine for their soldiers and were looking for another drug to use as a pain killer. Though it was developed by German scientists, they never used it for pain management.

After the war, the FDA granted approval to the drug company, Eli Lilly, so they could sell methadone as a cough suppressant and pain killer. Because they named it Dolophine, rumors circulated then, as now, among addicts that it was named after Adolph Hitler, though it was actually named after the Latin word for pain: *dolor* (2). Methadone, though available to treat pain or cough, was rarely used except at the Federal Narcotic Farm to help manage withdrawal symptoms, short-term, in the opioid addicted patients.

Then in the 1960's, Drs. Dole, Nyswander, and Kreek began to use methadone experimentally on inpatients, in an attempt to find a drug that could treat both opioid withdrawal symptoms and the opioid craving that comes with abstinence from opioids. After their positive results were released in medical journals, methadone treatment slowly gained momentum, despite heavy pressures from politicians and law enforcement personnel.

Dole and Nyswander's results were markedly different from those of the earliest maintenance clinics in the 1920's, because they were using a drug with unique pharmacology. In the 1920's, the only drug available to use for maintenance was morphine, but it didn't work well, since addicts needed three to four doses per day to stay out of withdrawal. But methadone can prevent withdrawal for over twenty-four hours, meaning it can be dosed only once daily. The addicts of Dole and Nyswander's methadone experiments were able to function normally for the whole twenty- four hours.

The results seen with methadone were quite impressive. Besides publishing their work, Dr. Dole also gave lectures about their findings. One such lecture was attended by Dr. Jerome Jaffe, a psychiatrist with an interest in treating drug addiction. Dr. Jaffe had become familiar with methadone when he worked at the Lexington Narcotic Farm. Jaffe, intrigued by Dole's results, began prescribing methadone for a few outpatients. All of Dole and Nyswander's patients had been treated as inpatients, but Dr. Jaffe thought methadone could be given safely to outpatients. Eventually, Dr. Dole also switched to outpatient dosing.

Dr. Jaffe gave lectures at a nearby medical school, and Dr. Alfred Gilman, of the famous text Goodman and Gilman's *The Pharmacological Basis of Therapeutics*, heard Dr. Jaffe and was impressed by him. He asked Jaffe to author the chapter on drug addiction and narcotic analgesics for this text. (3)

Because of the stature his contribution to the textbook gave him, Jaffe was offered a job at the University of Chicago and was also asked to become the advisor to the Illinois Narcotic Advisory Council. After this, he was asked to run the Illinois Drug Abuse Program, funded by the Illinois Department of Mental Health.

Dr. Jaffe opened the drug abuse program in 1968, with seventy-five methadone patients. Within just a few weeks, he was overwhelmed with hundreds of addicts, applying for admission to this program. Jaffe didn't focus only on methadone maintenance treatment, but understood that addicts need a variety of available treatments, noting that no one type of treatment will work for everyone. He had been dismayed by the infighting he'd seen in the past between advocates of therapeutic communities and advocates of methadone. He felt all treatment providers should work together, rather than participate in petty bickering. Jaffe opened an inpatient detoxification ward with outpatient aftercare, and a therapeutic community. (3)

Dr. Jaffe wanted to do randomized controlled trials, to see which treatment worked the best for opioid addicts: methadone maintenance, or inpatient detoxification followed by outpatient aftercare, but the addicts refused to be randomized. Most of them demanded treatment with methadone, and he allowed them to enter the treatment program of their choice. The methadone treatment expanded to seven sites that treated five hundred people. He also had a therapeutic community, which combined abstinent addicts with those on methadone who needed more structure than was possible as an outpatient. By 1976, his successful program grew to fifteen methadone clinic sites serving over nine hundred patients. (3)

Nixon was in the White House when Dr. Jaffe started his methadone clinic experience. Nixon was focused on reversing the nation's rising crime rate, particularly in Washington, D.C. As White House staff investigated ways to reduce crime, it became obvious that much of the crime was drug related. To reduce crime, drug addiction had to be addressed.

The White House sought advice from Dr. Robert DuPont, a respected and experienced physician working in the drug addiction treatment field. Dr. DuPont had heard of Jaffe's successes, and went to Illinois to look at Jaffe's programs. Impressed with what he saw in Illinois, Dr. DuPont returned to D.C. and started a pilot methadone clinic program there. That program was so successful, it was soon besieged with applicants requesting addiction treatment. At a time when the rest of the nation's crime rate increased, D.C.'s crime rate fell, after the start of the addiction treatment programs. This is significant, because Washington D.C.'s crime rate had been the highest in the nation. (3)

On the heels of this success, the White House asked Dr. Jaffe to head a group of professionals and asked them to formulate recommendations for a national drug addiction treatment policy. Dr. Jaffe put together a group of experts. The report they produced advocated methadone as treatment for heroin addiction, among other recommendations. Jaffe's completed report languished until 1971, when the Nixon administration became concerned about heroin addiction in soldiers returning from Vietnam.

By the end of 1972, there were sixty thousand patients in federally funded methadone clinics in the United States. But then, the parents' anti-drug movement gained momentum. In the late 1970's and into the early 1980's, parents all across the country became alarmed at what they perceived as rampant drug use in the nation, and began organizing themselves on a large scale, from a grass roots beginning. They demanded dramatic action from their government and pushed for new legislation, to address various aspects of drugs and addiction. Politicians, seeking election or re-election, courted the parents' votes with anti-drug rhetoric and complied with their demands for stricter drug laws. In 1973, New York Governor Nelson Rockefeller proposed harsh laws, with mandatory sentencing, which were ultimately passed and known as the Rockefeller Laws. The sentence for selling heroin then became longer and harsher than the sentence for murder. (3)

Caving to the pressure of the parent's movement, politicians strived to appear tough on drugs. Throughout the 1980's, drug enforcement spending swelled by twenty percent while demand reduction, or addiction treatment spending, plunged twenty-five percent. Available treatment slots for all types of addiction treatment, including methadone maintenance, dropped and crime rates increased.

When crack cocaine broke into the U.S. like a festering boil, there were too few treatment centers available to treat the large numbers of addicts. By the mid-1980's, eighty percent of the nation's drug budget was spent on supply reduction and only twenty percent on demand reduction (treatment). Cutbacks in federal funding meant that methadone clinics were full to capacity, with waiting lists, and their quality had declined as well. Reagan, more concerned with marijuana, was opposed to methadone, even as HIV, a new blood borne disease, began prowling our nation. (3)

Acceptance of methadone as a valid treatment option grew in the 1990's, after reports from several government agencies highlighted its benefits. The General Accounting Office (GAO), after fully investigating methadone treatment, issued a report criticizing the low cap on methadone dosing. They saw the multiple studies that showed higher doses predicted better outcome in treatment. The GAO encouraged methadone clinics to avoid under- treatment with doses which were too low. (4)

In 1995, the Institute of Medicine (IOM) issued a report that recognized the benefits of methadone treatment, and criticized the over-regulation of methadone clinics. The IOM further recommended the federal regulations be modified, so more addicts could have access to effective treatment with methadone. (5)

In 1997, the National Institute of Health issued a consensus statement that emphasized that opioid addiction was a treatable medical disease, and that addiction is not caused by a failure of willpower. (6)

In 2001, a new national accreditation system was created, with the goal of transferring oversight of methadone clinics from the FDA to the Substance Abuse and Mental Health Services Administration (SAMHSA), since drug addiction was recognized as a treatable medical illness. This system, which operates today, started with the goal of standardizing and improving methadone treatment in the U.S. Under this new system, SAMHSA emphasizes best practice guidelines and accreditation standards, in an effort to encourage improved treatment, rather than relying on regulatory criteria.

As of 2006, there were a total of 1,108 separate methadone clinics in the United States and around 263,000 patients in treatment at these clinics. (7) To put this in perspective, our best guess is that there are around 600,000 to 1 million active heroin addicts, and around 1.7 million prescription pain pill addicts. From this, one can see that only a fraction of people with opioid addiction are getting treatment in methadone clinics. Most are not getting treatment anywhere.

What is the basis for these learned organizations to endorse the treatment of opioid addiction with methadone? Let's examine the science.

Benefits of methadone

More research has been done on methadone than most other prescription medications.

Many studies, ever since Dole and Nyswander's groundbreaking study of 1966, have conclusively shown the benefits of methadone for the treatment of opioid addiction. It works for any type of opioid addiction, both heroin and pain pills.

"Evidence-based" is a frequently used phrase in medicine today. It means that a certain treatment is backed by quality studies that prove its effectiveness. Treatment of opioid addiction with methadone is one of the most heavily evidence-based treatments we have in medicine today. Study after study has shown multiple benefits: reduced transmission of HIV, reduced rate of crime, reduced use of heroin and other opioids, reduced use of other drugs, reduced death rates, and increased employment.

Because of the negative stigma linked to methadone, we need to review the studies and their conclusions. These studies have been listed in Appendix A for further review. It would take a firmly closed mind to remain opposed to methadone in the face of all this evidence, but some people remain blinded by their own ideology.

Methadone reduces illicit opioid drug use

Methadone reduces illicit opioid drug use. By occupying opioid receptors, methadone alleviates the physical withdrawal symptoms, which can become the driving force of addiction. Many addicts continue to use opioids long after their ever-increasing tolerance makes it difficult to become intoxicated, or high. These addicts continue to use opioids to prevent the dreaded physical illness that follows cessation of opioids.

With methadone, opioid addicts don't have to face this awful withdrawal. As explained earlier in the chapter, methadone can be dosed only once per day and lasts long enough to keep the patient out of withdrawal for at least twenty-four hours. Once the opioid addict is on a sufficient dose of methadone to occupy opioid receptors, other opioids are blocked from having their effects. If the addict then uses heroin or oxycodone, he won't feel high from it, realize it's a waste of money, and stop using these illicit opioids.

Tolerance doesn't develop to the blocking dose, so patients can continue on the same dose for months or even years. Methadone works well in most patients. We have many studies that show the dramatic drop in illicit opioid use when addicts start methadone treatment, as you will see in Appendix A.

Patients do better with adequate doses

In the past, methadone clinics mistakenly tried to keep the methadone dose of their patients as low as possible, and rarely went above sixty or seventy milligrams per day. Since that time, multiple studies have shown that patients on low doses are more likely to drop out of treatment, or keep using other opioids. Now, good opioid treatment centers try to get their patients to a blocking dose, so that patients get the maximum benefit. Like chemotherapy, if a patient is going to use methadone as a treatment, they need to take enough for it to be effective.

Most patients do best on a dose in the range of eighty to one hundred and twenty milligrams of methadone per day. Occasionally, an opioid addict wants to keep her dose at around thirty to forty milligrams, just enough to keep her out of withdrawal, but not so much that it blocks the euphoria of illicit opioids. In a situation like this, treatment staff should encourage such a patient to increase the methadone dose.

Not understanding the optimum doses for methadone, many family members will pressure the addict to bring their dose down, mistakenly thinking that if they have to be on methadone, it would be better to stay on a small amount. However, studies show that patients use less illicit opioids if they're on adequate doses of methadone. Patients on sixty milligrams of methadone or more are more likely to be retained in treatment for their addiction.

Longer treatment works better

The Ball and Ross study of 1991 (8) showed that the longer patients were retained in methadone treatment, the less illicit opioids they used. At six months or more of treatment, heroin use in patients dropped from ninety-seven percent to twenty-three percent. When patients stayed on long term methadone maintenance for more than four and a half years, the number dropped to eight percent. Of the patients that left methadone maintenance treatment, eighty-two percent injected heroin within 1 year. Therefore, we know that longer treatment is better than shorter treatment.

Use of other illicit drugs

While we expect the rate of illicit opioid use to go down in a patient on methadone, it should have no effect on illicit use of non-opioid drugs. Methadone has no effect on cravings for cocaine, alcohol, marijuana, methamphetamine, or benzodiazepine nerve pills. However, as an added bonus to methadone treatment, some studies show that use of non-opioid drugs also declines. Not every study showed significant decreases, but most do. The Ball and Ross study showed significantly less use of all illicit drugs except for marijuana, and use of all illicit drugs decreased with increased time in treatment. Another large study, Treatment Outcome Perspective Study, (TOPS) showed a large reduction in illicit drug use within the first three months of treatment. (9) Methadone patients should receive counseling, in addition to methadone. It's probably this counseling that helps reduce use of non-opioid drugs.

Methadone treatment reduces death rate of opioid addicts

Methadone treatment reduces mortality. Patients on waiting lists for methadone clinics have a death rate three times higher than patients in treatment on methadone. Many people would say this is reason enough to support methadone clinics. What other treatments in medicine can boast of such a reduction in mortality? Another study showed a mortality rate of 1.6% per year for addicts on continuous methadone maintenance, as opposed to a mortality rate of 8.1% per year for addicts who left treatment.

However, in the first two weeks of methadone treatment, patients may have an increased risk of death from methadone overdose, underlining the need for caution with initial doses

Methadone treatment reduces HIV transmission

Methadone treatment reduces the transmission of HIV. Fortunately, this disease now is viewed as a chronic disease, rather than a death sentence, since the newer highly active HIV drugs have been available. Unfortunately, thirty percent of new diagnoses of HIV are related to injection drug use. A review of all studies of HIV transmission among methadone maintained patients versus untreated opioid addicts showed that treatment with methadone significantly reduced behaviors leading to increased HIV risk. In one study of HIV negative intravenous heroin users followed over eighteen months, twenty-two percent of *untreated* addicts converted to HIV positive. But only three and a half percent of patients converted to HIV positive who were on methadone maintenance for the entire eighteen months.

Methadone treatment reduces crime

Multiple studies have shown that opioid addicts on methadone maintenance significantly reduce their criminal activity. Both drug dealing and predatory crimes, which are usually committed to pay for their drugs, are reduced as much as ninety-four percent. (8) Most studies show an increase in rates of employment for patients on methadone, compared to similar addicts not in treatment. Even people with no concern for suffering addicts should be willing to endorse methadone maintenance, if for no other reason than to reduce the risk of getting mugged!

Methadone maintained patients can drive safely

Some members of the community, or even law enforcement, criticize opioid treatment centers because they "give patients drugs and let them drive on our roads," not knowing that a patient who is on a stable, appropriate dose of methadone, and not abusing any sedatives, isn't impaired when driving. Numerous studies show methadone patients on a stable dose have driving ability and functional capacity of age-matched controls.

However, initial doses of methadone, particularly in a person who is opioid naïve, may sedate and impair driving. If a methadone patient ingests sedatives or alcohol, they *will* be impaired, due to the synergy between methadone and these drugs. A methadone patient should *not* drive if he has consumed alcohol or sedatives.

During methadone induction in the first two weeks of treatment, patients may have some sedation as their dose is adjusted, and should drive with caution. Of course, they shouldn't drive if they feel sleepy or sedated.

Methadone for pain

As of this writing, methadone prescribed to treat pain isn't regulated, like methadone prescribed to treat opioid addiction. Any physician with a valid DEA number can prescribe methadone, as she feels is medically appropriate, so long as it isn't used to treat addiction. Only physicians working for specially licensed and regulated clinics can prescribe methadone to treat addiction.

In the last five years, doctors have been using methadone to treat pain more often. It's a strong opioid, and inexpensive. Ironically, after doctors began to realize the abuse potential of OxyContin, many stopped prescribing it and switched to methadone. However, the analgesic, or anti-pain, effect of a dose of methadone wears off after about six hours. Methadone prevents opioid withdrawal for twenty-four hours or more. This is why methadone, prescribed only for pain, is given in smaller amounts every six hours, while methadone to treat opioid addiction is dosed in one larger daily dose.

Methadone clinics don't usually treat patients with only chronic pain, but no addiction. This is because clinics dose patients only once per day. Patients with chronic pain would still have significant pain in the afternoon or evening. Methadone prescribed in pill form from a doctor's office can be taken in divided doses, and it works much better for pain control.

Patients with both pain *and* addiction are the most difficult to treat. Unable to adhere to the dosing instructions of the physician, they overuse medications prescribed a month at a time, and run out before the month's end. Opioid treatment programs usually are the best options for these patients. At least the addiction can be controlled, and often once-daily methadone brings the pain to a manageable level.

How methadone acts in and on the body

Methadone is quickly absorbed from the stomach and intestines, stored in the liver, and released into the bloodstream over time. Plasma levels peak at around two to four hours after dosing. Though stored in the liver, methadone doesn't damage the liver. Medical illnesses that affect the liver may affect the storage and metabolism of methadone, but methadone will not hasten deterioration of liver function. In fact, there are no serious, long term, adverse effects with indefinite methadone treatment. The most common side effects are sweating, constipation, weight gain, and sexual dysfunction.

Methadone causes sexual dysfunction, particularly in men. All opioids, including methadone, suppress testosterone levels. This in turn can decrease sexual desire, and limit the ability to initiate and sustain an erection. Sometimes, as the body adjusts to the presence of a steady level of opioids, testosterone levels may return to normal. If not, some male patients may need to be started on replacement testosterone.

Many patients on methadone say they crave sweets. Most people do gain weight while on methadone, but the reason isn't clear. Some of the weight gain may be due to eating more regular meals, and expending less activity to get illicit opioids.

The most common side effects include sweating and constipation. All opioids can cause both of these side effects, but methadone is more likely to cause both. Tolerance doesn't seem to build for this, so these effects usually don't improve with time.

Euphoria and drowsiness can be seen if the initial methadone dose is too high, or if the dose has been raised too quickly. Tolerance develops within two weeks to both of these symptoms, and any euphoria felt by the patient subsides. However, patients don't develop a tolerance to the blocking effects of methadone, meaning that once they get to a stable dose, they do not need to continually increase their dose in order to keep withdrawal symptoms at bay.

Methadone can cause dry mouth, but does *not* cause teeth to rot, a common myth among addicts. Most likely, many addicts in active addiction neglect dental hygiene. When they enter treatment with methadone, they're able to take note of their physical condition, see the poor condition of their teeth, and perhaps blame it on the methadone. Also, methadone does *not* get into the bones. This common myth likely comes from the severe bone and joint pain experienced during opioid withdrawal. I've heard addicts talking to each other, saying that this pain is "the methadone coming out of you." This isn't true.

Methadone has interactions with many drugs, so patients need to tell their primary care doctor, the methadone clinic doctor, and any other doctors about all medications they're taking, even over-the-counter medicines. Methadone is metabolized in the liver by several enzymes in the cytochrome P450 system, so other drugs metabolized by the same pathways are likely to cause changes in the metabolism of methadone. These changes could either increase *or* decrease the blood level of methadone and possibly the other medication.

Many medications for the treatment of HIV interact with methadone, so it's important for the doctor prescribing HIV medications to know about any methadone dose changes. Some anti-seizure medications can significantly increase the rate of the metabolism of methadone, requiring the methadone patient to need an increase in her dose. Conversely, medications like erythromycin and cimetidine (Tagamet) can significantly slow the metabolism of methadone, causing the methadone level to increase, which in turn can cause sedation and toxicity from methadone.

I remember a patient I'll call Janet, who had a history of seizure disorder, which was well-controlled on an anti-seizure medication. She entered methadone treatment and did very well. She stopped all illicit opioids, went back to work, saved money, came every day for her methadone and saw her counselor frequently. She felt normal at a dose of eighty-five milligrams.

She went to her neurologist for her seizure disorder, and he changed her medication. She forgot to tell her methadone clinic about the new medication, and she didn't tell her neurologist that she was on methadone, fearing he would judge her harshly for being an addict and being on methadone.

A few weeks later, her counselor asked me to see her again, because she began having withdrawal symptoms in the evenings, with muscle cramping and nausea, though her dose hadn't changed. She believed the dosing nurse had secretly decreased her dose, since she started feeling some withdrawal symptoms. She was upset about this.

As I talked with her, I discovered her seizure medication had changed. Her new medication induces the metabolism of methadone, meaning it was speeding the metabolism of her methadone, and decreasing her methadone levels. Her symptoms made perfect sense, and we were able to adjust her dose and eliminate her withdrawal symptoms.

This illustrates the importance of the obligation the patient has to notify their methadone clinic of any and all medication changes, even for over-the-counter medications. It also illustrates how the stigma of addiction treatment with methadone can damage patients. Many clinics have lists of over-the-counter medications that are safe, and will not affect their methadone level, and ask patients use these for minor ailments.

Methadone can cause a problem with the way electrical impulses are conducted through the heart. This condition is called prolongation of the QT interval, or "QT syndrome". The QT interval is the distance between two normal electrical events of the heart, and is easily measured by looking at a patient's electrocardiogram, or EKG. Methadone can cause changes to this interval, usually more pronounced with doses over one hundred and twenty milligrams, or in those with underlying heart disease. These changes can make it more likely the patient will have a fatal heart rhythm problem, called *torsade des pointes*.

Because of the recent increase in deaths associated with methadone, some scientists suspect that sudden cardiac death, due to this particular heart rhythm problem, is responsible for some of these deaths.

Some doctors have advocated EKG screening of all patients at the beginning of treatment, shortly after they get to their stable dose of methadone, and yearly thereafter. Other doctors say we need to screen only those patients who are at extra risk for this syndrome: patients with known heart disease, age over 50, slow resting heart rate, methadone dose above one hundred and twenty, low blood potassium level, or use of other medications that can also prolong the QT interval. These doctors say we don't have enough evidence to know if any deaths have been due to prolongation of the QT interval by methadone, and making patients get EKGs, when they're at low risk, just creates another obstacle to treatment. Most specialists are now awaiting final guidelines from ongoing studies. One study compared the QT intervals of patients on methadone, patients on buprenorphine, and people in a control group on no medications. There were no significant differences in QT interval between the groups. (10) But this was a small study, and we need larger, prospective trials to provide more information, so that evidence-based guidelines can be established about the exact nature of the risk of prolongation of the QT interval posed by methadone.

Appendix A contains references for all of the studies supporting the statements in this chapter, and a small summary is included with each reference.

Now let's look at the way an opioid treatment center actually operates day to day.

Endnotes

1. National Institute on Drug Abuse, International Program, *Methadone Research Web Guide*, (Baltimore, MD, 2006 Substance Abuse and Mental Health Services Administration). http://international.drugabuse.gov/collaboration/guide_meth adone/index.html

2. Eric C. Strain, M.D., and Maxine L. Stitzer, PhD, *The Treatment of Opioid Dependence*, (Baltimore, MD, 2006, Johns Hopkins University Press) p. 4.

3. Michael Massing, *The Fix*, (New York, Simon and Shuster, 1998) pp.88 – 134.

4. General Accounting Office, *Methadone Maintenance: Some Treatment Programs are not Effective, Need Government Oversight*, Report HRD-90-104, 1990.

5. Richard A. Rettig and Adam Yarmolinsky, eds., Institute of Medicine, *Federal Regulation of Methadone Treatment*, (Washington, D.C., National Academy Press, 1995)

6. Effective Medical Treatment of Opiate Addiction. NIH Consensus Statement, Online 1997 Nov 17-19; [accessed 2009, July, 18]; 15(6): pp. 1-38.

7. Department of Health and Human Services, , *National Survey of Substance Abuse Treatment Services*, (Rockville, MD, Substance Abuse and Mental Health Services Administration, Office of Applied Studies, 2007). http://www.oas.samhsa.gov

8. Ball JC, Ross, A, *The Effectiveness of Methadone Maintenance Treatment*, New York, NY: Springer-Verlag Inc., 1991. In: National Institute on Drug Abuse, International Program, *Methadone Research Web Guide*, (Baltimore, MD, 2006 Substance Abuse and Mental Health Services Administration). http://international.drugabuse.gov/collaboration/guide_meth adone/index.html

9. Hubbard RL, Marsden ME, Rachal JV, et. al., *Drug Abuse Treatment: A National Study of Effectiveness*. Chapel Hill: University of North Carolina Press, 1989. *In:* National Institute on Drug Abuse, International Program, *Methadone Research Web Guide*, (Baltimore, MD, 2006 Substance Abuse and Mental Health Services Administration). http://international.drugabuse.gov/collaboration/guide_meth adone/index.html

10. Athanasos P, Farquharson Al, and Compton P et. al., *Electrocardiogram characteristics of methadone and buprenorphine Maintained Subjects, Journal of Addictive Diseases* (2008) 27:3: pp. 31-35.

CHAPTER 9

How Methadone Clinics Work

How does methadone work? What makes it such a powerful treatment for opioid addiction and why the insistence on its distribution only through licensed opioid treatment clinics?

Methadone maintenance clinics are now called opioid treatment centers, because they don't prescribe only methadone, but usually buprenorphine too. Still, many people use the terms interchangeably.

When an opioid addict applies for admission to a methadone clinic, he is first assessed to see if he's appropriate for treatment. The addict must be over age eighteen, and have opioid addiction, with physical dependency of at least one year. This requirement is imposed by the federal government, because *it is difficult to taper off of methadone*. If the addict has been physically addicted less than a year, abstinence-based treatment or buprenorphine are better choices.

Since 2002, buprenorphine is an option for addicts with less than a year's addiction. Pregnant women don't have to meet the one year standard before entering methadone treatment, because of the overwhelming benefits of methadone in opioid addicted pregnant women. Opioid addicts who have been on methadone maintenance within the past two years may be re-admitted, even if not presently physically dependent, if relapse is deemed imminent.

An adolescent under eighteen years old can enter a methadone maintenance program only if she has failed two attempts at inpatient treatment, separated by at least two weeks, and written permission is given by her parent or guardian. The methadone clinic needs special licensing to admit addicts under eighteen.

After a thorough evaluation by an addictions counselor, the clinic nurse draws blood and may do an EKG, depending on the patient's medical history. The clinic nurse again explains methadone treatment, and the patient signs consent for treatment, if they haven't already done so.

The patient then sees the doctor, who will take a history and perform a physical exam, to assure the patient is appropriate for treatment, and to identify other health issues, physical and mental, which need to be addressed. The doctor makes sure the patient is appropriate for methadone treatment and knows the benefits and risks of methadone maintenance, as well as other treatment options. Based on information gleaned from the patient's history, exam, and drug screen results, the doctor decides on an appropriate starting dose.

Some clinics also treat their patients for uncomplicated physical and mental health issues, while other clinics refer patients to physicians in the community, to manage these issues. Studies have shown that methadone patients have better outcomes when these services can be provided along with addiction treatment, under the same roof. In fact, studies show that the more services offered at the opioid treatment center, the better the outcomes for their patients. Unfortunately, many methadone clinics don't treat much more than the opioid addiction.

Each patient must realize what is involved with methadone treatment, before they make a commitment to start. They need to realize that methadone is hard to get off of, possibly harder than the opioid they were using, but methadone can allow them to live a more normal life. At a good clinic, the counselor makes sure the patient understands this, the nurse reinforces it, and the doctor explains it at length. The intake process can take several hours.

Methadone is a tricky drug to start. Because each dose stays in the body for so long, each day's dose stacks atop the previous day's dose. A steady blood level isn't reached until about five days. Figure 1 shows what the blood level does when starting treatment, even with no change in the dose

In opioid treatment programs, the first two weeks of initiating and adjusting the methadone dose is called the induction phase. This is the most dangerous time for patients, for the reasons stated above. Most doctors start patients with a known opioid dependence on twenty or thirty milligrams on the first day, and increase by five to ten milligrams periodically, usually no sooner than every three days. Because of the recent increase in methadone overdose deaths, most doctors now tend to prescribe lower starting doses, and give dose increases less frequently.

Initially, we know the dose will not last for twenty-four hours; we are most interested in how the patient feels three hours after dosing. If a patient was drowsy at three hours post-dose, he may in reality need a dose decrease, even though he was in withdrawal at twenty-four hours.

Steady State Simulation - Methadone Maintenance
Steady State attained after 4-5 half-lives -1 dose every half-life

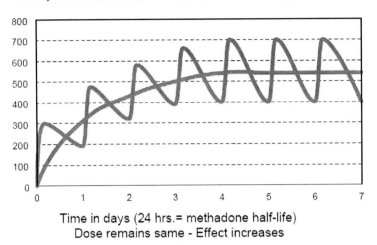

Time in days (24 hrs.= methadone half-life)
Dose remains same - Effect increases

In the graph above the wavy line represents the blood levels of methadone as well as the "effect" it has on the individual patient.

Many times, a patient who has withdrawal at the end of a twenty-four hour dosing cycle does not need more methadone but *more time at the same dose.*

This is complex and difficult to explain to patients who are feeling sick from opioid withdrawal, but it's essential information. Many addicts will continue to use illicit opioids, if the methadone dose isn't high enough. Opioid addicts are not well known for their patience, and there's a fine line between giving enough medication to prevent withdrawal, and giving too high a dose, risking a methadone overdose. It feels like trying to steer a large oil tanker between two dangerous reefs: too far one way and the patient could die of a methadone overdose; too far the other way and the patient could die of an interaction between methadone and an illicit opioid or benzodiazepine, taken because of continued withdrawal.

Because addicts don't feel high right after taking methadone, they may mistakenly think they need more to "feel it." However, since it takes up to three hours after ingestion to feel the effect of methadone, by the time they do feel an effect, they may have taken a fatal dose. This is how black market methadone causes overdoses. Methadone is active in the body for a much longer time than other opioids. If an addict takes methadone too close to the previous dose, levels build in their system, causing an overdose. Also, tolerance develops quickly to the euphoric effects of methadone, while tolerance to respiratory depression develops more slowly.

The very properties that make methadone a good replacement medication for treating addiction also make it a dangerous drug on the streets.

The methadone dispensed at a clinic is usually dosed as a liquid, taken orally, in the presence of the nurse dispensing the medication. Some methadone programs use forty milligram tablets, called discs or wafers, and water is added to them, to be taken orally. Since methadone is fairly bitter, it's sometimes mixed in some sort of juice or Kool-Aid, to make it more palatable. Methadone is not, as some mistakenly believe, injected at the clinics. There is no difference between the strength, milligram per milligram, between different forms of methadone. Liquid, discs, and pills have exactly the same effect.

According to federal and state regulations, an addict entering a methadone program must demonstrate stability for at least ninety days before that person can be granted any take home doses. In other words, the patient must come to the clinic every day of the week for their dose of methadone, though some clinics do give take home doses on Sundays and holidays, even for new patients. The take home bottles contain liquid methadone for one day only. They're usually small square bottles, filled with red liquid, and have a seal on the top, plus a child proof cap, like any medicine bottle. After a hundred and eighty days, the addict can be granted up to two take home doses. With time of proven stability, as evidenced by negative urine drug screens and participation in treatment, the number of take home doses can go up over time, to thirteen days to twenty-nine days of take home doses.

Most clinics open early in the morning, at 5 or 6am in order to be able to get their working patients dosed and off to work on time, since a return to productive living is one goal of treatment. Patients who frequently need to work out of town can't usually be treated at an opioid treatment center, because of government restrictions on take home doses. No take homes are allowed in the first three months of treatment, except under extraordinary circumstances. These patients may be able to guest dose at a clinic in the area they are traveling to, but many times this is difficult and expensive. Many clinics close at noon, though large clinics may have both morning and evening hours.

Methadone treatment can be expensive and time consuming, if the addict lives far away from the nearest clinic. At one clinic where I worked, patients often drove an hour and a half, one way, to get treatment. I once commented to one of these patients that she must have a strong desire to get treatment, to spend that much driving time, and she said yes, but she still spent less time driving to the clinic than she had driving around, looking for pain pills every day.

All methadone patients are assigned to a substance abuse counselor. The regulations say patients must meet with their counselors at least twice per month, but this is the minimum. Hopefully, most patients will agree to get counseling more often than this, because more counseling sessions show better patient outcomes. Some patients aren't interested in counseling. Counselors of those patients have to nag them to come for sessions at least twice per month, and work against patient resistance. In some clinics, patients are required to participate in group meetings at the clinic. Other clinics encourage, but do not require, attendance at group meetings.

Federal regulations say each counselor can have up to fifty active patients on their caseload. Counseling these patients can be high intensity work, so most addictions counselors find a caseload of fifty patients is challenging. In addition to the needs of the patient, there is a tremendous amount of paperwork to be done on each patient. Medicaid patients take much more of the counselor's time, due to the additional charting required by this government program. Counselors say that Medicaid paperwork is overwhelming, leaving less time for actual counseling.

Federal regulations mandate drug screening for methadone patients at least eight times per year. Most methadone clinics check random urine drug screens on the average of once per month, or more often, if a patient's behavior suggests illicit drug use. Ideally, the results of the drug tests are not used to dismiss people from methadone treatment, but to start a conversation about what drugs the patient is still using and how the counselor and clinic can be of help. Counselors should work with patients, to identify triggers for drug use and high risk situations for relapse. Positive drug screens usually mean the patient needs a higher "dose" of counseling.

I recall a patient I'll call Jill, who had repeatedly positive urine drug screens for cocaine. At the weekly meeting of counselor, program manager, nurse and the doctor, we were discussing whether Jill should stay on our methadone program or be referred for inpatient treatment, after we tapered her off methadone. During the staffing, the counselor mentioned she'd observed symptoms of depression in Jill.

Untreated depression can be a trigger for drug use, so she was referred to the local mental health clinic. She was prescribed a medication to treat her bipolar disorder and her mood improved. Her counselor worked with Jill more intensely. They discussed relapse triggers and how to handle them. She stayed off cocaine for more than a year and improved tremendously. We were able to keep her in treatment, because she improved so much, with treatment of her mental health disorder and increased counseling. Jill's case illustrates the importance of giving a patient every chance to succeed on methadone. Many times, this includes addressing untreated mental and physical health issues.

If the patient's drug screens are positive for illicit opioids, like oxycodone and heroin, the patient is not yet at a blocking dose of methadone. Continued opioid use suggests the patient is still able to feel a high, or euphoria, from illicit opioids and the dose needs to be increased.

If a methadone patient's drug screen is repeatedly positive for other illicit drugs, and no progress is made after many months, the medical doctor and the treatment team at the clinic may feel the patient would be best served by a higher level of care, which usually means inpatient treatment. Methadone clinics with abstinence-based treatment philosophies are more likely to terminate treatment if patients aren't making progress in recovery. Not many inpatient programs keep a methadone patient on their dose, while addressing addictions to other drugs, so usually the patient has to come off the methadone, as well. Understandably, most patients on methadone don't want to change to a treatment where they'll have to come off methadone and endure the difficult physical withdrawal.

On the other hand, at clinics with a harm reduction philosophy, patients are kept in treatment, even if they keep using illicit drugs. The studies show that the longer a patient is kept in treatment, the better they are likely to do. As long as the clinic's treatment improves some aspect of the patient's life, they will be kept on methadone though they don't get take home doses.

Patients entering methadone clinics need to be made aware that the methadone may be more difficult to get off of than the opioid they've been using on the street. If methadone is stopped suddenly, the acute withdrawal lasts for up to three weeks, compared to five to seven days for drugs such as oxycodone or hydrocodone. This is because of its long duration of action. When I tell addicts entering methadone treatment this fact, many ask, "So why would I want to get on methadone?" My answer is that an addict can live a relatively normal life on methadone, other than having to come to the treatment center each day for their dose.

The methadone studies show that patients have the best outcomes, when they stay on methadone indefinitely. On the other hand, many of those studies were done on IV heroin addicts and we don't yet know if data from studies done with heroin addicts applies equally well to younger patients, addicted to pharmaceutical opioids. Many addiction specialists would still say that staying on methadone is the addict's best chance for a normal life, but most patients yearn to be off methadone. The treatment can be cumbersome (due to federal, state, and local regulations), is expensive and is surrounded by stigma.

Many patients have unreasonable fears about tapering their dose, having been through an awful experience with opioid withdrawal in the past. When methadone is tapered slowly, the patient can expect low grade fatigue, anxiety, and malaise. For most people, it's unpleasant and draining. However, many patients find these symptoms manageable, especially if they know they can increase their dose again, if they need to do so. It takes patience to slowly wean off methadone and many patients think they can taper faster than recommended.

Tapering at five milligrams per week is usually the fastest any patient can tolerate. For doses lower than forty milligrams, two milligrams per week is usually the fastest tolerated. At lower doses, five milligrams is a bigger percentage of the whole. The more slowly the patient takes his dose down, the more successful he's likely to be.

Even given the tremendous difficulty in getting off methadone, it still can be the best choice for addiction treatment for a great number of opioid addicts. Methadone maintenance treatment has been proven to work, is safer than active addiction, and is legal. Also, in good clinics, counseling is a big part of the methadone program.

Governmental Regulation

Opioid treatment centers prescribing and dispensing methadone have many layers of regulations they must follow, from the local level, all the way to the federal level.

The federal government has strict rules governing the prescription of methadone for the purposes of treating addiction, which came into effect soon after Drs. Dole and Nyswander's ground-breaking work with methadone. Due to the dramatic and positive results Drs. Dole and Nyswander saw, in their studies with methadone in opioid addict patients, other physicians applied for permission to prescribe methadone as an Investigational New Drug (IND). Any other way of prescribing it was against the law, and had been since the 1914 Harrison Narcotic Act.

The permissions for use of INDs were readily granted by the FDA. Soon, around three hundred doctors had special permission to prescribe methadone, ostensibly for the purposes of conducting research. However, many physicians just used an IND permit as a way to be able to use methadone to treat opioid addicts. The FDA became alarmed at this, and the Narcotic Addiction Treatment Act of 1974 was born.

Since the passage of this act, providers who wish to treat opioid addicts with methadone must obtain special registration and permission from the Attorney General. Regulations have changed somewhat since then, but many layers of government agencies and organizations are involved in the approval of a new clinic and maintaining licensure to function.

In addition to obtaining approval and periodic re-approval from the Food and Drug Administration (FDA), an opioid treatment program must also be approved by the Drug Enforcement Administration (DEA). The DEA conducts random, unannounced audits of opioid treatment centers. The Substance Abuse and Mental Health Services Administration (SAMHSA) must approve the clinic and they do periodic inspections, through the Center for Substance Abuse Treatment (CSAT), an arm of SAMHSA. Each state has a State Methadone Authority, who must approve the clinic and approve a certificate of need, before a clinic can ever come into existence. Next, there's the state's version of SAHMSA. In North Carolina, it's called Department of Health and Human Services (DHHS), and they inspect periodically, review patient charts, and even interview patients. Then the county may have restrictions on methadone treatment which must be followed. After twelve months of clinic operation, the facility must pass inspection by the Commission on Accreditation of Rehabilitation Facilities (CARF) to become fully accredited. CARF alone has seven steps to accreditation. Of course, there are fees to be paid to many of these organizations.

In other words, for an opioid treatment center to open and stay in operation, multiple layers of regulations must be observed. Opioid treatment centers are closely observed by all these agencies.

Characteristics of effective methadone clinics

All methadone clinics are NOT created equal. Some clinics are well-run and some are poorly run. The poorly managed clinics give all methadone clinics a bad name.

In the past, clinics were funded from public sources, but in the 1980s these sources of funding were reduced, leaving a void that was filled by for-profit clinics. Methadone clinics can be incredibly profitable and most clinics in the U.S. are proprietary, or for-profit, clinics.

Some people speak derisively of for-profit clinics, but were it not for these clinics, there would be few methadone clinics and more addicts dying of active addiction. Until taxpayers feel that methadone is a treatment worth supporting, we're fortunate that clinics of any profit structure are available.

We know from research studies which clinic factors are associated with successful patient outcomes. Effective clinics have well-trained staff. This would seem obvious, yet in some states, no special training is required to become a methadone counselor, except a willingness to become certified in that state. After a counselor is hired, the counselor should receive continued training, specific for opioid addiction and treatment. (1)

Effective clinics offer more psychosocial services for their patients. This can include not just individual counseling, but also family counseling or family programs, vocational rehabilitation programs, and health care for physical and mental issues. The more services, the better the outcomes, though these services don't seem to give higher retention rates in treatment. Effective clinics also have integration of medical, counseling, and other services, so that patients have as many resources as possible available under one roof. (1)

Past studies have shown us which patient characteristics are associated with success in methadone treatment. Older age, being employed, and having a stable marriage are, not surprisingly, associated with better treatment outcomes. Chronic criminality is associated with a poor treatment outcome, as is significant mental illness, and addiction to more than two types of drugs. Less time in active addiction is associated with better treatment outcomes, as is an intact social network. (2)

We've looked at what methadone is and how it works, reviewed the history of methadone for treating opioid addiction, and how clinics work. We've examined factors that describe well-run clinics. Now let's examine the mist of controversy swirling around the use of methadone.

Endnotes

1. National Institute on Drug Abuse, International Program, *Methadone Research Web Guide*, (Baltimore, MD, 2006 Substance Abuse and Mental Health Services Administration). http://international.drugabuse.gov/collaboration/guide_methadone/index.html
2. Ward, J, Mattick, RP, Hall, W, *Methadone Maintenance Treatment and Other Opioid Replacement Therapies*, (Harwood Academic Publishers, Amsterdam, 1997).

CHAPTER 10

Methadone: the Good, the Bad, and the Ugly

For every complex problem there is an easy answer, and it is wrong. -

H.L. Mencken

Most people who are opposed to methadone aren't interested in how much good it has done for numerous addicts; they're opposed to methadone because it causes overdose deaths.

Deaths associated with methadone have risen sharply over the last ten years. The Centers for Disease Control, studying data from 1999 compared to 2005, found that methadone overdose deaths increased from seven hundred and eighty-six deaths in 1999, to four thousand, four hundred and sixty-two in 2005. (1) This was a more than five-fold increase. During this time, overdose deaths from all opioids increased, but those from methadone showed the largest relative increases.

The majority of these fatalities, at eighty percent, were classified as accidental overdoses. These disturbing statistics have prompted extensive examination of the circumstances surrounding these overdoses. Some states had markedly higher death rates than others. Maine had the highest per-capita rate in 2005, followed by Utah, Washington, Nevada, New Hampshire, Kentucky, North Carolina, and West Virginia.

Prescriptions for methadone increased over the last ten years. The DEA reports the amount of methadone sold between 1998 and 2006 increased by seven hundred percent. (2) Most overdose deaths were seen in patients who had been prescribed methadone for the treatment of pain, and many of their physicians were not specialists in pain management. It's likely these doctors were less experienced with the use of methadone.

Family practitioners were the most common prescribers of methadone in the more powerful forty milligram disc form, and nurse practitioners were among the top five types of prescribers of methadone in this form. After this study, the forty milligram tablets of methadone were restricted, available only to opioid addiction treatment programs, not community pharmacies.

Many doctors learned of OxyContin's dangers, and mistakenly thought methadone would be a better option for patients with chronic pain. Methadone is cheap, at pennies per dose, and can be an effective pain medication, when taken appropriately. Physicians switched patients to methadone and didn't always give adequate instructions to their patients about how to start the methadone. Some patients were given accurate instructions, but didn't follow them. A few physicians mistakenly prescribed methadone at too high a starting dose, because they didn't understand the pharmacology of methadone. Some patients purposely misused the pills and accidently overdosed, which is easy to do with a long acting opioid like methadone.

Most methadone clinics dose with a red liquid form of methadone, but the vast majority of overdoses have been with methadone in pill forms. The DEA states that in 2006, the liquid form of methadone, used primarily by methadone clinics, accounted for only thirty-nine percent of all methadone sold in the U.S. However, *ninety-four percent of overdose deaths occurred with the pill, rather than liquid form of methadone*, when the form of methadone ingested in the overdose could be determined. (2)

From all the information gathered and processed by the Center for Disease Control (CDC) and DEA, it is clear that most methadone overdose deaths occurred in people who were *not* patients at any methadone clinic. Because of this, governmental agencies are considering new ways to monitor the distribution, prescription, and consumption of methadone and other Schedule II controlled substances. This new program is called the Risk Evaluation and Mitigation Strategy, and will be discussed again in later chapters.

The National Association of State Alcohol and Drug Abuse Directors, with the support of SAMHSA and CSAT, released a brief focusing on methadone overdose deaths. This brief emphasized what the studies have shown: the increase in methadone overdose deaths is associated with its use for pain, not from its use by opioid treatment centers. The DEA, which tracks the location of sales of methadone, found that methadone overdose deaths were increased in areas that had higher numbers of prescriptions written for the treatment of pain, but there wasn't a correlation with opioid treatment program density. (3)

Methadone causes more overdose deaths, per exposure to the drug, for exactly the same reason it is an effective medication for opioid addiction. It has a very long duration of action. While this is desirable in a blocking medication, because it only needs to be dosed once per day, it causes problems for addicts or abusers, taking methadone illicitly, to get high. An addict may take some methadone, not "feel it," due to its delayed peak effect, and take more pills. The methadone builds in the addict's system before the addict feels high. This powerful opioid turns off the brain center responsible for telling the body to breathe when asleep. The patient falls asleep, stops breathing, and dies, when vital organs such as the brain and heart are starved for oxygen.

A patient's tolerance to the respiratory depressant effect of methadone may develop more slowly than the patient's tolerance to the analgesic, or anti-pain, effects of methadone. The patient may unwittingly take increased doses of methadone to ease their pain, but die from the respiratory depressant effect.

Not all people using methadone illicitly are trying to get high. Some addicts use illicit methadone to try to detoxify themselves, without the expense and time-consuming process of admission to a methadone clinic. One counselor interviewed for this book estimated that around ninety percent of new admissions had tried methadone on the street at least once prior to coming to the methadone clinic. Most said they were trying to detoxify themselves, or wanted to see how methadone would affect them, before they made a commitment to enroll in a methadone program.

Most people who died with methadone in their system also used other drugs in combination. As discussed in previous chapters, when methadone is combined with other sedatives, such as benzodiazepines, alcohol, or barbiturates, it takes less than expected of each medication to cause an overdose, due to synergy between the two types of medications. This information is critical. Yet again, it points to the danger of combining opioids with benzodiazepines and other drugs. One study of deaths in patients starting a methadone program showed that in ninety-two percent of the decedents, drugs other than methadone were also found. (4)

Methadone isn't the only opioid causing overdose deaths, but it was responsible for the largest relative increase in poisoning deaths. In 2005, poisoning deaths became the second most common cause of accidental deaths in the U.S., and fifty-six percent of these deaths were due to opioids. (1)

One study looked at eight hundred and ninety-three opioid over-dose deaths that occurred in Southwest Virginia, from 1997 to 2003. This study looked at all drugs found on autopsy, not just methadone. It found that few of these decedents had only one drug in their system at the time of death. The most commonly found opioid in these overdose deaths was methadone, found in twenty-eight percent of the decedents.

No information is available to know if any of the decedents were patients of methadone clinics, but there were few opioid addiction treatment clinics in that area then, so it seems unlikely that many were clinic patients. In the majority of cases, opioids were not the only drugs present. Benzodiazepines (like alprazolam or diazepam) and antide-pressants were the most common drugs found, along with an opioid. Deaths occurring in rural areas were more likely to be positive for ben-zodiazepines, in addition to opioids. Women, age thirty-five to forty-five, were over-represented among these overdose deaths. (5)

The information in this study raises questions about the safety of prescribing benzodiazepines with methadone, but also about the safety of using antidepressants with any opioid. We know benzodiazepines are dangerous when taken with opioids, but we know less about interac-tions of specific antidepressants with methadone or other opioids. Some antidepressants are metabolized by the same liver enzyme system as methadone

It's also possible the presence of antidepressants correlates with a higher incidence of psychiatric disorders in the decedents. Perhaps antidepressants didn't contribute to overdose, but were markers of patients with more severe mental illness, which in turn is associated with a higher incidence of overdose death. This information also indi-cates that with prescription medications, a relatively older, female pop-ulation may be at higher risk than we've seen in the past.

Opioid treatment programs *have* had patients die from overdoses, and even one death is too many. It's difficult to get accurate statistics of the number of methadone clinic patients who died of overdose deaths, because the pathologist may not be aware that the decedent was enrolled in a methadone clinic. This means it is *essential that all opioid treatment programs report all of their patient deaths.*

As discussed in the previous chapter, two-thirds of the patients who die of an overdose while on an opioid treatment program do so in the induction period, the first two weeks. To address this, many clinics re-considered their maximum starting doses, since higher starting doses have been correlated with increased overdose risk. Clinics are also reducing the rate of dose increases. While it's true that lower starting doses and less frequent dose increases may compel patients to use illicit opioids for longer, until their methadone dose is high enough to suppress withdrawal, methadone clinics will be able to assure themselves they didn't contribute to a patient's death, by overly aggressive dose increases.

It's hard to explain the pharmacology of methadone to an addict in withdrawal. Nearly all addicts voice concern that the initial dose won't "hold them," and that they'll be in withdrawal later in the day. It's hard to tell them that yes, the first doses won't last all day, but we still must start with lower doses, for safety reasons. Because of the very long half life of methadone in most patients, about half of today's dose will still be in the patient's system tomorrow. Many times, when a patient feels like their dose is "wearing off" they don't need an increase, just more time at the same dose, to allow the full accumulation of methadone. Addicts in withdrawal tend to be impatient, and it takes a great deal of tact and reassurance to keep them in treatment long enough to get their dose to a reasonable level, and do this safely.

At the non-profit clinic where I worked from 2001 until 2008, the number of patient deaths increased in the years 2005 until 2007. The death rates were lower than the national average, but even one death is appalling. Not all of the deaths were from overdoses. Some patients died from homicide or suicide, or unrelated medical ailments.

An analysis of data from the charts of the decedents showed that two-thirds of the overdose deaths were last dosed at the clinic on a Friday or Saturday. Because of this information, our clinic stopped approving any dose increases on weekends, and ultimately decided to stay open to dose three-hundred and sixty-five days per year. Prior to this, the clinic had been closed on Sundays and holidays, and allowed take home doses for patients on those days.

More than two-thirds of the decedents also had issues with benzodiazepine abuse and addiction. Curiously, some of the official state autopsies had drug screens that were negative for benzodiazepines, in deceased patients who had recently tested positive for a benzodiazepine at our clinic. There are forty-some different benzodiazepines. No commercially available screen detects all of them. I think the state lab missed some of the benzodiazepines that the methadone clinic was able to detect, and it's possible that the state lab tested for some benzodiazepines that our clinic didn't.

In response to this death data, we re-worded the methadone treatment consent form so that it better described the risk of death when benzodiazepines, alcohol, or other sedatives are combined with methadone. Patients signed acknowledgement that they read it, or had it read to them, and that they understood this information.

We began to postpone admissions of patients who were known to be addicted to benzodiazepines, unless/until they could stop taking benzodiazepines. We did the same with alcohol- addicted patients. These patients were referred to inpatient detoxification units. After making these two changes – more strongly worded cautions about mixing sedatives with methadone, and postponing admission for benzodiazepine addicted patients – the overdose deaths plummeted. Once we were able to screen patients on our state's controlled substance data base, even fewer deaths occurred.

Methadone clinics in this state re-considered the safety of dosing benzodiazepine-addicted patients with methadone. Some clinics dismiss these patients, due to the increased overdose risk. Many addicts use benzodiazepines, without being addicted to them, and some opioid addicts use them only occasionally to help with opioid withdrawal symptoms. But methadone clinics see a small, but worrisome, number of opioid addicted patients who either can't or won't stop taking benzodiazepines. Some addicts say they like the high they get from mixing methadone and benzodiazepines like Xanax.

It's difficult for a patient to stop taking benzodiazepines, and it cannot be done quickly, if the patient has been taking them regularly for any period of time. In fact, stopping benzodiazepines suddenly can be fatal, causing withdrawal seizures. Some patients may have to be weaned off benzodiazepines over many months. Some patients aren't able to stop as an outpatient, and need long inpatient detoxification admissions.

Physicians who work at opioid treatment programs in North Carolina, with the help of North Carolina's Governor's Institute, created an informal group to confer on such issues. We have monthly conference calls and twice yearly face to face meetings. One of our topics of discussion was the dilemma of the methadone clinic patient who is also addicted to benzodiazepines, like alprazolam (Xanax), or clonazepam (Klonipin).

North Carolina opioid treatment centers and their doctors differ in how they handle this situation. Some clinics reduce the methadone patient's dose by a set percentage with the first drug screen that's positive for benzodiazepines, followed by repeated reductions with further positive screens. In contrast, in other opioid treatment centers, the clinic doctor will prescribe benzodiazepines, when deemed necessary, either to treat psychiatric problems or to help patients wean off benzodiazepines. Some methadone clinics admit patients also addicted to benzodiazepines, and with counseling, attempt to help the patients eventually stop the benzodiazepines.

One clinic assigns patients who repeatedly used benzodiazepines to an intensive counseling program, which meets three times per week, three hours per session. If methadone patients want to stay in treatment, they have to participate in this intense counseling. The alternative is to have their methadone dose gradually decreased to zero. Then, another form of treatment for addiction is recommended.

Our group of doctors has not come to a consensus about how to handle the benzodiazepine situation, but we have profited from listening to ideas from other doctors. Exchanging ideas helps us recognize whether we're doing something drastically different from other doctors in the state.

My own decision was that some patients, addicted to or abusing benzodiazepines, are at a prohibitively high risk to be on a methadone program, and should be tapered off of it, to prevent overdose death. For patients unwilling or unable to stop benzodiazepines after a few months in treatment, methadone program enrollment is too dangerous, except under unusual circumstances. Some doctors might think my approach is unwise, because it would unduly restrict the numbers of patients able to be treated with methadone. Other doctors have a more restrictive approach. Good physicians disagree about this issue.

Who is right?

I don't know. The studies of the effectiveness and safety of methadone treatment were done on heroin addicts. Are the recent pain pill addicts different than heroin addicts? Is it possible that pain pill addicts tend to take more benzodiazepines, and thus are more likely to overdose, while on methadone maintenance treatment?

Flawed Data?

Some of the data regarding the increase in methadone-related overdose deaths may be flawed, because pathologists over-read the toxicology reports, causing a misdiagnosis of the actual cause of death. (6)

Most of the time, pathologists have no information regarding the opioid tolerance of the decedent. This information is essential, because *there is a significant overlap between what pathologists would call toxic and life-threatening, and normal, appropriate levels in a methadone-maintained patient.* (7)

In other words, the methadone level in a properly dosed methadone patient would kill a person who had never taken opioids, and had no tolerance. If the pathologist knew the decedent was enrolled in a methadone program, and was on a stable dose, it should influence the pathologist's opinion about the cause of death.

Medical examiners don't have a standard case definition of what constitutes a methadone overdose death, and criteria vary a great deal between states. Some pathologists declare methadone toxicity as the cause of death, no matter what the concentration of methadone. A standard case definition of methadone overdose death could delineate cases where methadone is clearly the cause of death, versus cases where it is a contributory factor, versus cases where methadone is present in the body, but not related to the cause of death.

In my state, the pathologists didn't appear to take the decedent's opioid tolerance into account, even when that information was available. Thus, patients of the methadone clinic were often declared to have died from methadone toxicity, even if they had been on the same stable dose for months.

Methadone is stored in the liver. After death, it leaches from the liver into large blood vessels, like the aorta and vena cava, rendering blood levels inaccurate and highly variable, depending on the amount of time between death and autopsy. (7) Post-mortem blood levels are unreliable, and samples taken from the aorta are always higher than from more peripheral vessels, like the femoral vein, since the femoral vein is farther from the liver. Liver levels are more accurate, but again, a toxic level for a non-opioid tolerant person may be therapeutic for a methadone patient. For some reason, in this state, post-mortem blood levels of methadone are still performed despite their known inaccuracy. Methadone is an easy target, and saves the pathologist from having to look any further for a cause of death, if one is not immediately apparent.

So how much of the purported increase in methadone overdose deaths is attributable to over reading of the toxicology report? Probably not much, since patients in methadone clinics accounted for a small percentage of all methadone overdose deaths anyway. Decedents with methadone in their system, who weren't patients at either an opioid treatment center or a pain clinic, may also have been tolerant of opioids. However, this would be difficult to assess, and probably couldn't be determined with certainty.

The inaccurate attribution of a death to methadone toxicity can be harmful to both the methadone clinic and the family of the decedent. For example, at a clinic where I worked, a patient, who had been on the same dose of methadone for many weeks, began having problems with his asthma. Methadone clinic nurses sent him to a nearby hospital emergency department for an evaluation.

The hospital treated and released him, but two days later, he called 911, saying he was very short of breath. An ambulance rushed to the scene, but he was dead when they arrived, and didn't respond to resuscitation efforts.

Since he was a patient at our clinic, I called the pathologist who did his autopsy. That pathologist reported classic findings of status asthmaticus, which means a prolonged and severe asthma attack. The history certainly fit that diagnosis. But when the toxicology report returned, the methadone level was slightly higher than their cutoff for "toxic" in a patient unaccustomed to opioids. Because of this, the cause of death was reported as methadone toxicity.

This report was released to his mother, who became understandably distraught, thinking the methadone clinic killed her son with too much methadone. Though I knew the cause of his death was not methadone toxicity but rather a severe asthma attack, I couldn't change what the pathologist wrote. I did all I could, by notifying the pathologist that this patient had been on a stable and unchanged dose of methadone for weeks. His only recent complaint had been shortness of breath, unrelated to his dose of methadone. He also had a recent relapse to smoking cocaine (also found at autopsy), and I still suspect the crack contributed to the asthma attack, which eventually killed him.

The risk of overdose death for patients of methadone clinics should be compared to the risk of untreated opioid addiction. Patients on waiting lists for methadone clinics die at a *three-time higher rate* than patients started on methadone, even taking into account the brief time of *increased* risk for methadone patients in the first two weeks of treatment. (8)

In 1997, one study looked at mortality in a population of five hundred and seven methadone clinic patients. (9) One hundred and ten patients left the clinic. Of those, nine were dead at one year, six from overdose with heroin. Of the three hundred and ninety-seven patients who remained in treatment, four died. *Therefore, patients in methadone treatment had a death rate of 1% per year at this clinic, while patients who left methadone treatment had a death rate of 8.2% per year.* This is a significant difference.

This study concluded that it was worthwhile to keep patients in treatment, even if they weren't doing as well as expected, given the much higher risk for death for addicts who left the clinic. Of course, there may have been other factors in play. Perhaps the sickest addicts left treatment on their own, or were asked to leave treatment, and they would be at higher risk, either in or out of treatment. Perhaps the ones who stayed in treatment had a more fervent wish to do well in recovery.

A study conducted in the late 1960's through the late 1980's showed mortality rates for heroin addicts not in any treatment was *sixty-three times that of age matched controls.* (10) This dropped to only eight times age matched controls, while these heroin addicts were enrolled in methadone maintenance treatment, which correlated to a death rate of 1.4% per year.

This study showed that methadone maintenance treatment dramatically reduced the risk of death for these opioid addicts, though even the addicts in methadone maintenance treatment still died at a higher rate than age-matched controls. This increase in death rate while in treatment was attributed to diseases contracted prior to entry into methadone treatment. Of note, HIV emerged during these years.

This data shows that methadone can help intravenous heroin addicts a great deal, just by reducing their death rates, without even considering whether they have abstained from all other drugs. Just like with OxyContin, methadone can be used for great good or great harm, depending on how it is used, and who is using it. If precautions are taken, both medications can be safe and effective. With inattentive or inexperienced prescribers, both medications can be deadly.

Methadone clinics are sometimes accused of being greedy, and people have criticized these clinics for making profit off the misery of addicts. (11) Methadone clinics can be very lucrative, and perhaps some of the criticism is deserved. But why do we expect addiction treatment centers to be non-profit?

Healthcare in the U.S. is a business, with a free market system, at least as of this writing. Many private hospitals, clinics, doctors' offices, and surgery centers are for-profit businesses, and exist to make a profit from treating disease. Until U.S. citizens vote to change the basic structure of our healthcare system, addiction treatment centers have as much right to be profit-driven as treatment centers for other diseases. I'd love to work with drug addicts in a situation where money was no object, but that's not the situation now in the U.S.

In the 1980's, federal support for methadone clinics dropped, and private clinics began opening, because there was a need for this kind of treatment. As of 2008, 558 of the 1132 clinics in this country are for-profit, or just at 49%. Around 39% are non-profit, and federal, state, and local governments operate the rest. (12) The VA operates 36 opioid treatment centers, or about 3% of the total. Considering the number of opioid addicts who need treatment (well over 1.7 million) versus the total number getting treatment in methadone clinics (approximately 268,071), we need to be grateful that for-profit clinics filled some of the void, left when federal support dropped away. Indeed, if anything, existing data show that we need more opioid treatment centers, profit or nonprofit.

The money spent on addiction treatment is money well spent. Most addicts save money, once they are in an opioid treatment center. They've been spending much more money, per day, than they're charged at an opioid treatment clinic, sometimes as much as ten times the amount. Since some opioid addicts sell drugs, in order to finance their own addiction, when addicts enter treatment, many stop selling drugs. As we saw in previous chapters, crime rates drop dramatically, when opioid addicts enter into methadone treatment.

Not only do the patients save money, but also the community saves anywhere from $4 to $13 for every $1 spent on methadone treatment. (13) Most of this savings comes to taxpayers because of the reduced financial burden of housing addicts in prisons. Multiple studies have shown the cost effectiveness of methadone treatment. (14, 15) It's a good deal for both opioid addicts and the taxpayers, and methadone treatment of opioid addiction has been shown to result in a much lower cost per quality-adjusted life year than many other treatments frequently used in medical practice today. (14, 16)

Many clinics will give financial exceptions, on a temporary basis, if the patient is doing well and not using other drugs. However, most clinics won't give free treatment to patients still using other drugs, such as cocaine, because that would be, in essence, subsidizing the patient's continued illicit drug use.

Prescription Monitoring Program

In 2007, North Carolina developed a computerized prescription monitoring program. Since July of that year, any physician who prescribes controlled substances can apply for access to this website database. The information can improve the quality of treatment at an opioid treatment center, along with challenges.

Each new patient entering an opioid treatment center should be screened on the state database for controlled substances, because many can be harmful when taken with methadone or buprenorphine. The nature of addiction induces addicts to keep secrets, lie, and manipulate to continue using drugs. Patients entering methadone treatment programs don't always tell the doctor about all of their other addictive medications.

Methadone clinics have check for "dual enrollment" for years, which is a form of prescription monitoring. Dual enrollment programs are meant to prevent a patient from receiving methadone at two or more clinics at the same time. A prescription monitoring program is similar, except it lists controlled substances prescribed by any physician in the state. However, opioid treatment centers don't report to this site, given the need for a higher level of privacy for substance abuse treatment, due to the stigma.

The database can be used to confirm the history of a patient who wants to enter a methadone treatment center. All entering patients are screened by rapid urine drug screen for opioids: morphine, codeine, oxycodone, hydrocodone, and methadone. If all are negative, the diagnosis of opioid addiction is questionable, no matter what the patient says. Frequently, a look at the database provides evidence to support a prospective patient's claim of opioid addiction, and proves that patient is appropriate for admission.

In the clinics where I worked, the prescription monitoring plan was used to identify methadone clinic patients who were getting strong opioid prescriptions from another doctor. Sometimes, patients filled their prescriptions from their community doctor, used a month's prescription in two weeks, and then came to the clinic to be on methadone for two weeks, to avoid withdrawal. When it was time for another prescription, they left treatment at the opioid treatment center, filled their prescription, used the pills too quickly...and so on.

After prescription monitoring became available, this came to an end. If the prospective patient was getting other addictive medications, the patient had to give me permission to call the other doctor. Prior to admission to our methadone clinic, the other doctor and I conferred, and decided the best way to manage the patient's medical problems. If the patient was receiving opioids long-term for treatment of chronic pain, we would work to find a non-opioid way to treat the residual pain.

The monitoring plan helped us keep our patients safe. It enabled us to know if they were prescribed a strong opioid or benzodiazepine, which could kill them if used with methadone.

I recall a patient whom I'll call Jane, who seemed to be doing well, as far as we knew. She was on a stable dose of methadone, had urine drug screens repeatedly negative for all other drugs, and had a full time job. She was doing well for so long, or so we thought, she was able to receive take home doses for up to two weeks at a time. Then when the prescription monitoring program came online, I found she had been filling prescriptions for large amounts of OxyContin, in addition to the methadone we were prescribing. She had not, of course, mentioned this to anyone at the clinic, not the dosing nurses, the program manager, her counselor, or me.

When I confronted her with what I'd found, she was outraged. She said it was none of my business what other prescriptions she had, and she would call my boss, to protest my unfair treatment of her. She claimed I was singling her out from all the other patients (I wasn't) and all the patients were using other drugs (they weren't).

I felt irritation, then fascination. Here was a lady who had entered our treatment center, professing to want treatment for her opioid addiction. Now, she not only defended her clandestine use of OxyContin, but also told me it was none of my business. She didn't understand that when she entered our treatment program and received methadone from our clinic, under my prescription, it became my business. I wasn't sure if she'd been taking the OxyContin, and somehow falsifying her observed urine drug tests, or perhaps had been giving or selling the OxyContin to someone else.

How strange this disease is! This was a smart lady, but she had no insight into her behavior at that time.

We couldn't continue to dose her with methadone, while she was furtively filling a prescription for large amounts of OxyContin, so she had to leave treatment. We recommended she re-consider her drug use, and told her she was welcome back if she changed her mind, was willing to stop getting the OxyContin prescriptions, and give me permission to contact her other doctor. She indicated she wouldn't return.

It was a shame that she left treatment, but it would have been a bigger shame if she'd died of an overdose.

Another woman at a different opioid treatment clinic, had five pages, single-spaced, of controlled substance prescriptions on the database, which she had filled over the previous six months. She lived in a small town, infamous for the staggering numbers of its citizenry taking benzodiazepines. Even taking that into account, her list was impressive. She had prescriptions for three or four different kinds of opioids, at least three different benzodiazepines, and some stimulants thrown into the mix. She was seeing at least fifteen different doctors. Obviously, local physicians were not using the prescription monitoring database.

Yet her observed urine drug screens were all negative for drugs other than methadone. When the program manager asked her about all the prescriptions, she said she sold the medication to make her house payment. She had Medicaid, so each prescription of sixty or ninety pills cost her three dollars, but she could sell each pill at anywhere from one dollar to forty dollars. She tearfully agreed to sign any releases we wanted, and she stopped getting these prescriptions. Later, she admitted to selling many of these drugs in the parking lot of the methadone clinic.

Usage of the prescription monitoring program reduced drug dealing on clinic premises. It kept patients from easily obtaining prescription medications to sell to other methadone patients. Of course, it did nothing to detect patients selling street drugs like marijuana, cocaine, and methamphetamines.

Sadly, drug dealing does occur on opioid treatment center property, despite efforts by clinic staff to stop it. Even with security guards and cameras, drug deals can still occur. This constitutes danger to patients who are trying to get well. Good clinics do everything they can to eliminate drug dealing.

Thirty-one hundred active patients were enrolled in the nonprofit methadone clinic where I worked when the state's prescription monitoring plan became functional. Of those, about twenty percent were found to be getting controlled substance prescriptions about which they hadn't informed the clinic. A rough estimate of the street value of these drugs was around a half million dollars per month.

We had clinics in eight sites, and percentages of patients with unknown prescriptions ranged from a low of seventeen percent at a rural clinic in the mountains, to a high of thirty-four percent in a mid-sized town near Charlotte, NC. This is not necessarily a reflection on the patients, but rather the prescribing habits of the doctors in the communities. The clinic with the rate of thirty-four percent was located in a community where it seemed many residents were given a monthly prescription of benzodiazepines by one or more local physicians.

It would be easy to get discouraged by the patients who get other prescriptions, or who are still using drugs, but the majority of methadone clinic patients do well. The vast majority do *not* furtively obtaining other controlled substance prescriptions. Most of the patients said they were glad we were taking measures to keep our patients safe.

Based on my experience screening methadone patients on the prescription monitoring program, it's essential to screen all methadone maintenance patients at admission and then randomly, at least several times per year. Because most of the overdose deaths of methadone clinic patients are from the synergistic interaction of other drugs with methadone, it's imperative that doctors do all we can to keep our patients safe.

The owners and administrators of an opioid treatment center contribute to the quality (or lack of quality) of their programs. The owners, in the case of a for-profit clinic, or the administrators, in the case of a non-profit clinic, help set the tone of the clinic. In an ideal world, well-educated physicians would decide medical policy regarding opioid addiction treatment with methadone. Doctors should have the ability and authority to decide if a patient is appropriate for treatment. But I know firsthand how subtle pressure can be put on doctors to admit all comers, and keep patients in treatment no matter what. For-profit clinics would be expected to be the worst at pressuring physicians to keep patients in their clinic, but I've experienced exactly the opposite.

Using the prescription monitoring plan is essential for patient safety, for reasons stated above. But every time I updated the non-profit clinic's administrator on results from accessing the state's prescription monitoring database, I was discouraged. He said things that gave me the feeling he would rather I didn't look at this database. He said he worried I was using the information to "keep patients out of treatment," which at that clinic usually meant, "cut into the money we get from methadone patients." Though this was a non-profit clinic, the money from methadone patients supported other programs, like twenty-eight day inpatient treatment. Those were great programs to fund, but not at the cost of methadone patient safety.

I tried to reassure him I wasn't making an issue of the occasional prescriptions for hydrocodone or oxycodone from a dentist or emergency room visit, but rather focused on the patients who were repeatedly getting large amounts of powerful opioids like methadone, Opana, fentanyl, and OxyContin, while they were also dosing with methadone while in our clinic. These powerful opioids, and benzodiazepines, were the drugs I was most concerned about when mixed with methadone.

I used my best medical judgment as to how to handle patients getting these prescriptions. When possible, I tried to keep patients in treatment with us, but only if I could get the patient's permission to contact the other prescribing doctor. At that time, in North Carolina, it was illegal to contact the other prescribing physician without the patient's permission. This changed in July 2009. Physicians can now contact each other without patient consent.

After I left this non-profit clinic, I worked in a for-profit clinic. When I checked their patients on the North Carolina database, only nine percent were getting dangerous amounts of other strong opioids or benzodiazepines. The management of that clinic encouraged me to check all of their patients on intake and periodically during treatment. My medical decisions were supported by both their medical director and clinic administrators. The atmosphere was markedly different at that clinic. Also, by the time I was employed at the second clinic, SAMHSA and our state methadone authority scrutinized opioid treatment centers closely, given the state's recent methadone overdose deaths. Times had changed. Plus, the for-profit clinic did not accept Medicaid as payment for admission, and the non-profit clinic did. Medicaid patients tend to have more severe diseases, both mental and physical.

HARM'D

HARM'D, which stands for Helping America Reduce Methadone Deaths, is an organization that lobbies against methadone, or at least against methadone related deaths. Though they fall short of advocating abolishment of methadone completely, they do advocate for stronger federal regulations of methadone clinics and more intensive education for the doctors working at clinics prescribing methadone. They also campaign for methadone patients to be started only as inpatients, instead of as outpatients, as is generally done at present. They would like to see a reduction in the number of take home doses allowed for stable patients, so patients on methadone would have to come to the methadone clinic more often. They promote quick detoxification from a methadone clinic, if urine drug screens are positive.

I actually agree with a small portion of what HARM'D advocates. Clearly, it would be much safer to start patients on methadone while they were hospitalized, but at what cost? These patients usually have little, if any, financial assistance available to fund hospitalizations. Besides the actual cost of the hospital admission, it would be very difficult for most of these patients, who are usually the working poor, to afford to take time off work, or to obtain adequate childcare. Requiring inpatient start of methadone would be an insurmountable barrier to treatment for many opioid addicts. They would remain in active addiction.

HARM'D discounts the many stable and successful patients on methadone. The majority of patients who start in methadone programs do extremely well, and have no further drug use. They return to their work and to their families, and become functional citizens. As I've mentioned previously, these patients are anonymous. They keep quiet about taking methadone, because they don't want to face the stigma of being a methadone patient. They know that some people in their lives would criticize them harshly for choosing this treatment option. HARM'D doesn't see these patients. Nobody sees these patients, except the staffs at their methadone clinics.

Additional training for physicians working in methadone clinics is a great idea. Perhaps doctors who work in opioid treatment clinics should be required to have American Society of Addiction Medicine (ASAM) certification or the equivalent in the field of psychiatry. If a physician who wants to work in an opioid treatment center has no previous experience with addiction and its treatment, required attendance at a comprehensive, one day training course would assure that this physician understands the pharmacology of methadone. This would increase the quality of care at opioid treatment clinics, and doesn't seem overly burdensome for physicians who desire to work in clinics.

In fact, such a course took place in North Carolina, in September of 2009, and over one hundred nurses and doctors attended. It was sponsored by CSAT, the treatment arm of the Substance Abuse and Mental Health Services Administration, and provided an excellent summary of essential information. At present, this one-day course is purely voluntary, but in the future, something akin to this may be required prior to employment at an opioid treatment center.

Listening to the videos on HARM'Ds website, and reading some comments posted by HARM'D's members, gave me the impression the organization was completely opposed to methadone. However, I emailed the organization with some questions and Ms. Melissa Zuppardi, identified as president of HARM'D's board, responded quickly.

I discovered that HARM'D doesn't want to outlaw methadone, but they want to make sure it's prescribed safely. Ms. Zuppardi outlined some of HARM'D's positions. (17)

They advocate special training and licensure for physicians who work at methadone maintenance clinics, mandatory drug testing for patients (though these are already mandated, by federal regulations for patients in opioid treatment centers). They want naloxone (brand name Narcan, a drug that reverses the sedation of an opioid overdose) to be dispensed so if a patient overdoses at home, their family can learn to inject them with Narcan and thus revive them.

HARM'D advocates the use of methadone only as a last resort, after safer drugs fail. HARM'D wants to make sure patients in pain clinics and methadone clinics are adequately informed about the dangers of methadone. They say doctors treating chronic pain patients have other drugs from which to choose. They want to eliminate take homes for patients who are still using drugs, and want clinics to be open every day of the year, for new or unstable patients. They recommend that methadone clinics have a "no benzo" policy. (17)

I was surprised at Ms. Zuppardi's cogent arguments. The little I knew about HARM'D was gleaned from extreme and inflammatory statements made on various website discussion boards. Perhaps these people, though members of the organization, do not speak for it. The statements on HARM'Ds website are fueled by grief from the deaths of loved ones, who died from methadone overdoses, and I feel empathy for the families. On their website there is a video, describing loved ones who died with methadone in their system. Most were young people, and many were not addicts, but made a bad choice and died as a result of it. Watching the video is heartbreaking.

And yet, it may not be productive to blame the drug. Methadone is not the problem. Drug abuse and drug addiction are the problems. In some cases, methadone *was* inappropriately prescribed, and doctors do need to be better trained to prescribe methadone safely. But most of the deaths described in their own video were not from doctor incompetence, though the website advertises a law firm that specializes in suing doctors for methadone overdose deaths.

To further complicate the issues, many personal injury lawyers are becoming involved in filing lawsuits on behalf of patients who have died from methadone overdose deaths and their families. In fact, on HARM'Ds home page, a law firm has a prominent advertisement trolling for cases against doctors and methadone clinics. (18) A search of the internet reveals many similar advertisements. One law firm advertised themselves as "Dangerous Drug Lawyers." This probably wasn't the best wording they could have chosen.

Thankfully, there is also an advocacy group for patients on methadone: NAMA, for National Alliance for Medication-Assisted Therapy. They have wisely asked members to take an advocacy training course, before speaking out about methadone. This is smart, because it gives NAMA more credibility. It's easy to state your position and support it with facts when you know the facts. Many members of HARM'D seem to be talking from a place of emotion, while members of NAMA focus on the facts, as revealed in forty years' worth of scientific studies and forty years' worth of outcome studies for addicts.

There is no doubt that HARMD has a point: methadone is a dangerous drug to prescribe. It's risky to prescribe methadone a month at a time, through either a pain clinic or by any community doctor, particularly if the doctor isn't experienced with this medication. As outlined at the beginning of this chapter, the data shows that most of the methadone responsible for overdose deaths came from methadone written as a prescription and then diverted to the black market, rather than from methadone clinics.

Opioid treatment centers already have many regulations they must follow. Even following all of these regulations, a small amount of methadone will inevitably spill into the black market, but this amount is small, in comparison to the amount of methadone pills diverted to the black market from pain patients. We don't need more regulations. We need to have clinics follow the ones already in place.

The U.S. has a fairly restrictive system for dispensing methadone, compared to other nations. For example, in England, about half of opioid addicts maintained on methadone are treated by general practitioners, called GP's. The other half are treated by only by an addiction specialist, or by a combination of both kinds of doctors. Many of the GPs prescribe weeks or up to a month of methadone at each visit, and there is no observed dosing. Some GP's do prescribe limited amounts, to be consumed at their pharmacy, but most patients get take home doses much more easily than the same patients would get in the U.S. In this country, we would worry about giving so much methadone as take home doses. Perhaps the English GP's do too, because they tend to under-dose their patients, giving about half of the doses currently recommended. (19)

Fifty-five countries use methadone to treat opioid addiction. Israel has the most restrictive system. It requires limits on the case load of each clinic and each physician, regular urine drug screens, limits on daily dose and limits on take home doses. Methadone can only be prescribed by addiction medicine specialists and only in specially licensed facilities. France's system is the least restrictive, requiring only monthly drug screens and limits on daily doses.

In Russia, it's illegal to use opioid replacement therapies, much as it was in the U.S. from 1920 until the 1960's. Russia also has the highest rate of heroin addiction in the world, with an estimated five million heroin users in a country with about half of the population of the U.S. (20)

In Russia, nearly all heroin comes from Afghanistan. Intravenous heroin use presently causes about eighty percent of the HIV infections in Russia, where needle exchange programs are still quite controversial. At present, around 1.1% of Russia's population is infected with HIV, compared to less than two-tenths of one percent in the U.S. (21) Russia's present opioid addiction treatment policy isn't working.

Diversion of opioid drugs doesn't only happen after they're sold to individual patients at the pharmacy. Diversion of controlled opioids can occur anywhere along the line of manufacture and distribution. By law, manufacturers and distributors of opioids keep strict records of the drugs' handling. If any controlled substances go missing or get stolen, in the time between manufacture and sale to the consumer, the manufacturers, shippers, and pharmacies must report this to the Drug Enforcement Administration (DEA). The DEA keeps a record of all stolen and lost controlled substances on their Drug Theft and Loss Database (DTL). (22)

The amount of drugs diverted before they reach the consumer has been growing. The DEA recorded over twenty-six million dosage units reported as stolen or lost in 2007, compared with only thirteen million in 2003. Some of these drugs were reported as "lost in transit," accounting for over eighteen million dosage units in 2007. Other categories of loss included armed robberies, customer theft, employee theft, or pharmacy burglaries. From this, we can see that relatively large amounts of prescription opioid get diverted before they ever reach the drug store. In 2003 alone, in twenty-two Eastern states there were thirteen thousand cases of opioid diversion before reaching the local pharmacy. (22)

Maintenance-to-Abstinence?

Most studies show that patients have the best outcomes if they remain on methadone for an indefinite time, perhaps for life. If an opioid addict is on methadone and doing well, it's not advisable to plan to taper that patient off methadone, as it will expose him to the risk of relapse, which can be fatal. Dead addicts don't recover. That's what the data show, and yet, most patients don't want to be on methadone. It's expensive, time consuming, and has a great stigma. Most patients want to taper off methadone.

At the American Society of Addiction Medicine, physicians at their 2008 conference discussed whether it makes sense to have a methadone maintenance-to-abstinence track for some patients. For example, if a patient is highly motivated to get involved in recovery and has made progress in all areas of their lives, do they really need to stay on methadone for at least one year to get the full benefit? I think most doctors would say we need to make individual decisions, based on the clinical situations.

Also, before we accept data from past studies, are opioid addicts entering opioid treatment centers today the same as those who participated in the studies of the past? Perhaps not.

Until very recently, methadone studies have been done on intravenous heroin addicts. But now, approximately half of the opioid addicts entering treatment with methadone or buprenorphine are addicted to prescription pain pills. In some areas, the majority of patients admitted are pain pill addicts, rather than heroin addicts. As we saw in previous chapters, there were several reasons why this rise in prescription opioid addiction increased. Now, we must decide if these pain pill addicts will have the same outcomes on methadone treatment as heroin addicts do.

The physical processes of opioid addiction are the same for heroin as for prescription opioids, so we have assumed the data on outcomes will be the same, but we need studies to prove our assumption. There may be very different socioeconomic factors influencing the course of addiction and recovery for both types of addicts.

For example, prescription addicts may not have fallen so far outside mainstream culture, and may be easier to reach with counseling techniques. Heroin addicts tend to endorse subculture values, and may not be interested in a more traditional lifestyle. But many of the rural addicts say the reason they want to get help is because of their families.

These addicts seem strongly motivated to do well in treatment, and have more supportive families who are still involved in their lives. Perhaps these rural prescriptions opioid addicts have different psychosocial needs and desires. Perhaps abstinence is a legitimate goal for many.

We don't know for sure if prescription opioid addicts will have the same relapse rates if they come off methadone as heroin addicts. If the addict desires to get off methadone at some point, then we need to make sure they have the best possible chance for success, and help them with advice about the rate of taper, and support their desire to be completely drug-free. We should also make it easy for a previous patient to get back on methadone, if they do relapse.

Many people have made valid criticisms aimed at methadone clinics who have sloppy or permissive attitudes towards dispensing methadone and their care of addicts overall. There is no defense for a poorly run clinic. Since methadone can be such a two-edged sword, clinics have an obligation to maintain order and do all in their power to stop drug dealing on clinic premises.

Opioid treatment centers need to screen patients, and admit only suitable candidates for this treatment, because some addicts are too sick for treatment with methadone. Opioid addicts with severe coexisting mental illness, or with sedatives or alcohol addiction may be better suited to another form of treatment, though we know those other treatments are hard to access.

The clinic needs to be a place of calm, not chaos. Addicts who want to get well should be able to come to a methadone clinic and not be inundated with offers to buy drugs. A poorly run and chaotic clinic can destroy community relations and undo any good will that otherwise could emerge. Mismanaged clinics can taint public opinion about all methadone clinics.

Just as some people fall into the error of believing methadone should never be used, methadone clinics can fall into the opposite error. They can come to believe that all opioid addicts are good candidates for opioid replacement therapies, when this is clearly not the case. Since methadone is a very potent opioid, there are some patients who don't do well with this treatment.

Methadone isn't a bad or evil medicine. It's merely a medicine, and it can do great good or great harm, like so many other medicines. It shouldn't be outlawed, but used in more responsible ways.

Most doctors working in methadone clinics are there because they love their work. Many doctors feel as I do: we see the big, positive changes in patients who are treated for addiction. I never saw people improve as quickly in primary care as I do now, in addiction treatment with replacement medications. Not only does the patient improve, but the whole family gets better. The ripple effect into the community is a delight I'm privileged to witness.

Educated and caring professionals in the addiction treatment field try very hard to do the best they can for the patient who sits in front of them. Sometimes we make errors in judgment in one direction or another. The best insurance against becoming unteachable, implacable or outside the standard of care is to stay in touch with other professionals in the field. It's essential to have frequent and free exchanges of ideas, so we stay abreast of new trends in addiction and its treatment. The next chapter explains one of these new treatments: buprenorphine for opioid addiction. So far, it doesn't have the negative stigma that methadone has persistently endured.

Endnotes:

1. Lois A. Fingerhut, National Center for Health and Statistics, *Increases in Poisonings and Methadone related deaths: United States, 1999 – 2005* Center for Disease Control, 2008.
2. Methadone Mortality Work Group, Drug Enforcement Administration, Office of Diversion Control, Department of Justice, *Methadone*, 2007.
3. Lewis Gallant, Ph.D., Director, for The National Association of State Alcohol and Drug Abuse Directors, Inc., *State Issue Brief on Methadone Overdose Deaths*, (June, 2007).
4. Zador D. & Sunjic, S. *Deaths in methadone maintenance treatment in New South Wales, Australia*, 2000, Addiction 95: p. 77-84.
5. Martha J. Wunsch, MD, et.al. "Opioid deaths in Rural Virginia: A Description of the High Prevalence of Accidental Fatalities Involving Prescribed Medications," *American Journal on Addictions*, 18, no. 1, (2009): p. 5-14.
6. Steven B. Karch, MD, *Pathology of Drug Abuse*. 4 ed. (Boca Raton, FL: CRC Press, 2009).
7. Lewis Gallant, Ph.D., Director, National Association of State Alcohol and Drug Abuse Directors, Inc., *State Issue Brief on Methadone Overdose Deaths*, p3 – 5. (June, 2007).
8. Trachtenberg, A., Cone, EJ, & Leavitt, S., *Toxicology: Selected Issues and Infrastructure Concerns*, PowerPoint presentation http://www.iom.edu/Object.File/Master/8/712/ML-Trachtenberg.pps accessed 8/13/09.
9. Zanis DA, Woody, GE, *One-year mortality rates following methadone treatment discharge*, Drug and Alcohol Dependence, 1998; 52(3): p. 257-260.
10. Gronbladh, L, Ohlund, LS, Gunne, LM, *Mortality in Heroin Addiction: Impact of Methadone Treatment*, Acta Psychiatrica Scandinavica Volume 82, issue 3, p 223-227
11. Lisa Berry, *Inside the Methadone Clinic Industry*, (Wheatmark, 2007), pp. 84-104.
12. Substance Abuse and Mental Health Services Administration, Office of Applied Studies. *National Survey of Substance Abuse Treatment Services (N-SSATS): 2008 Data on Substance Abuse Treatment Facilities*, DASIS Series: S-49, HHS Publication No. (SMA) 09-4451. Page 57. http://wwwdasis.samhsa.gov/08nssats/nssats2k8.pdf .

13. Office of Applied Studies, *National Survey of Substance Abuse Treatment Services*, (Substance Abuse and Mental Health Services Administration, Rockville, MD, 2007) http://oas.samhsa.gov .

14. California Department of Drug and Alcohol Programs, 2004, *California drug and alcohol treatment assessment (CALDATA)* California Department of Alcohol and Drug Programs. California Drug and Alcohol Treatment Assessment (CALDATA), 1991-1993 [Computer File]. ICPSR02295-v2. Ann Arbor, MI: Inter-university Consortium for Political and Social Research [distributor], 2008-10-07. doi:10.3886/ICPSR02295.

15. Harwood, Hubbard, Collins et.al., *Treatment Outcome Perspective Study*, Compulsory Treatment of Drug Abuse: Research and Clinical Practice, NIDA Research Monograph Series 86, (Rockville, MD, National Institute of Drug Abuse, 1988).

16. Barnett PG, Hui, SS, *The Cost-effectiveness of Methadone Maintenance*, Mount Sinai Journal of Medicine, 2000, 67 (5-6): 365:74.

17. Personal communication with Ms. Zuppardi via email.

18. http://harmd.org.

19. John Strong, MD, "The International Experience" lecture, ASAM Conference, New Orleans, LA, 5/09.

20. New York Times, "Russian Scorns Methadone for Heroin Addiction", July 22, 2008, accessed online at http://www.nytimes.com/2008/07/ 22/health/22meth.html on 7/5/2009.

21. USAID Russia, *HIV/AIDS Health Profile*, 9/08, accessed online at http://www.usaid.gov/our_work/global_health/aids/Countries/eande/russia_profile.pdf on 7/5/2009.

22. National Drug Intelligence Center, *National Prescription Drug Threat Assessment*, Drug Enforcement Administration, U.S. Department of Justice, 2009.

CHAPTER 11:

Buprenorphine: "It's a Miracle"

"Nobody will laugh long who deals much with opium: its pleasures even are of a grave and solemn complexion."

Thomas De Quincey

Buprenorphine, commonly known by its brand name, Suboxone, is an exciting new option for opioid addicts seeking help and for the doctors who treat them. For the first time in nearly one hundred years, people with the disease of opioid addiction can be treated in the privacy of a doctor's office. Addicts no longer have to go to special clinics to get medication for their disease. Since many opioid addicts don't live near a methadone clinic, or live near a methadone clinic that has a six month wait for admission, or wouldn't be caught dead in a methadone clinic, due to the stigma, buprenorphine is a fresh option.

Many opioid addicts who are horrified by the thought of going to a methadone clinic will consider treatment at a doctor's office. A physician's office is more private than an opioid treatment clinic. Since the patient could be seeing the doctor for any medical problem, the patient isn't branded an addict, just by walking in the door. A doctor's office usually has a healthier ambience than methadone clinics.

The truth is, not everyone in treatment at a methadone clinic is ready to get well. No matter how careful the methadone clinic is, there will be some patients engaged in furtive drug activity. A patient with opioid addiction who still has her job and family may come to a methadone clinic, see some patients who have embraced what can be politely described as a counterculture lifestyle, feel that she isn't like these other addicts, and leave in a hurry. Some, though not all, methadone clinics can be scary places for people who are not part of a drug subculture. Many prescription addicts have never used street drugs like cocaine and marijuana.

Thankfully, people in government saw that the estimated six hundred thousand to eight hundred thousand intravenous heroin addicts in the U.S. far exceeded the one hundred and fifty thousand treatment slots available at methadone clinics at that time, and began looking for a new way to help addicts into treatment. Then, as discussed previous chapters, the number of people addicted to opioid pain pills climbed at an alarming rate, adding about 1.7 million more people who needed treatment for opioid addiction. The difference between the number of patients who need treatment and the number of patients who actually receive it is called the "treatment gap." Ideally, there should be no gap. An addict should be able to get into treatment as soon as he's ready, with no waiting period. Buprenorphine is now helping to bridge the treatment gap for opioid addiction.

Congress passed the Drug Addiction Treatment Act of 2000, in order to allow addiction treatment in office-based practices, instead of the more cumbersome methadone clinics. In 2002, the FDA approved buprenorphine as the first schedule III controlled drug that could be used under the DATA 2000 Act. The drug became available in pharmacies in 2003. Thus far, buprenorphine is the only medication that's approved by the FDA to treat opioid addiction in a doctor's private office.

As we learned from previous chapters, the court's interpretation of the Harrison Drug Act of 1914 made it illegal for physicians to prescribe opioids from an office setting for the treatment of opioid addiction. DATA 2000 was significant because for the first time in more than eighty years, the government was not only granting permission for appropriately trained and licensed office-based doctors to prescribe controlled substances to treat opioid addiction, but they were actually *encouraging* it. The passage of the DATA 2000 showed a remarkable change in attitude of policy makers, and an open mindedness rare in the history of addiction treatment in the U. S. However, buprenorphine still has special restrictions on its use.

In order to prescribe buprenorphine to treat addiction, a physician must have a special DEA number, called an "X" number. To get that number, the physician must attend an eight hour training course to learn about opioid addiction and its treatment with buprenorphine. In lieu of the training course, credentials such as certification from the American Board of Addiction Medicine, or a subspecialty board certification in addiction psychiatry, are adequate to be granted the waiver, without attending a training session. After a doctor is qualified by training, she can then apply to the Substance Abuse and Mental Health

Services Administration (SAMHSA) for a waiver from the regulations of the Controlled Substances Act. If granted, this means the physician doesn't have to meet all of the conditions and regulations of traditional opioid addiction treatment centers (methadone clinics).

The doctor must certify she has the capacity to refer patients for counseling in addition to prescribing buprenorphine, and cannot treat any more than thirty patients at any one time. After SAMHSA grants the waiver, the DEA gives the doctor a special DEA number, to be used only for patients who are being treated for addiction. After one year, the doctor may apply for permission to treat up to one hundred patients at any given time.

Both addictionologists and primary care physicians were encouraged to get the required training to prescribe buprenorphine. It was hoped that many primary care doctors would become licensed to prescribe buprenorphine, and would be able to treat their own patients who developed opioid addiction, instead of referring them to specialists, or dismissing them from the practice.

SAMHSA co-sponsored many eight-hour training courses for physicians in the prescribing of buprenorphine all around the country. The manufacturer of Suboxone and Subutex, Reckitt-Benckiser, also generously sponsored training courses for physicians. Of course, the drug company had a financial incentive to train as many physicians as possible to prescribe their drug, but their sponsorship of trainings has been helpful for patients and doctors. The drug's patent recently expired, and a generic form of buprenorphine just entered the market, so the drug company stopped sponsoring courses, as of June of 2008.

Eighty percent of physicians who received training to prescribe buprenorphine did so at these eight hour training courses. Twenty percent did web-based trainings. By September of 2009, nearly 24,000 physicians were trained, but only around 19,000 of these doctors applied and received permission to prescribe buprenorphine. Only 3,685 doctors applied for permission to treat up to one hundred patients. By 2009, around 500,000 patients were receiving buprenorphine prescriptions. (1) About twenty-seven percent have been on tapering detoxification schedules and the rest, seventy-three percent, have been on a maintenance schedule. (2) Recently, there has been a trend toward using buprenorphine as a maintenance medication, rather than for a relatively quick detoxification, as studies are showing greater benefit with longer use.

Just as with methadone, the medication alone rarely is enough to get the patient into successful long term recovery. Buprenorphine is not meant to be a stand-alone treatment, but to be combined with some sort of counseling. According to the government regulations, the prescribing physician must have the capability to refer the patient for counseling, though it doesn't specify the type or intensity of the counseling.

Many people get confused about the difference between Suboxone and Subutex. They are both used sublingually (under the tongue), and are the only two brand names of the drug buprenorphine that are approved to treat addiction. Suboxone, besides containing the active drug buprenorphine, also contains a small dose of naloxone, which is an opioid antagonist, or blocker. Subutex contains only buprenorphine.

When Suboxone is taken in the proper way, dissolved under the tongue, the naloxone is not absorbed and is inactive. But if the Suboxone pill is inappropriately crushed and injected, the naloxone *will* be active and will put the addict into immediate withdrawal. If the naloxone weren't in the drug, the buprenorphine alone could still be abused, to produce a high, or euphoria. In other words, naloxone is a safety feature, to discourage injection of the medication. The naloxone will not affect patients, if Suboxone is used correctly.

In the U.S, doctors are encouraged to prescribe Suboxone, rather than Subutex, because it's safer. In some European countries where buprenorphine was used to treat opioid addiction, it was commonly misused by injection, and turned into a major drug of abuse. In Europe, a Suboxone-type medication with both buprenorphine and naloxone wasn't available.

Buprenorphine is also marketed under one other brand name in the U.S., Buprenex. This liquid brand contains only buprenorphine (no naloxone) and is intended solely for intravenous or intramuscular injection. This form of the drug is *not* approved for the treatment of opioid addiction, but only for treatment of acute pain. Buprenex has been used in the U.S. for relief of acute pain since the 1980s. Relative to morphine, it is a fairly good analgesic. There hasn't been much diversion of this drug to the black market in the U.S., though other countries, such as Scotland, have had large numbers of intravenous buprenorhpine addicts in the past.

Doctors are now conducting studies on other delivery forms of buprenorphine. Probuphine is a brand name of buprenorphine, which is contained in small cylindrical pellets, a little less than an inch long. These pellets can be implanted just under the skin, to release buprenorphine over time, in a similar way Norplant delivers its medication for birth control. Around four pellets are implanted, and the medication is delivered in continuous low levels for up to six months.

Studies have shown that Probuphine is more effective than placebo, but the real question is how it compares to standard therapy with sublingual buprenorphine tablets. The big advantage of implantable pellets is compliance, since the patient is obviously getting the medication if the pellets are in place. In this form, it's highly unlikely to be diverted.

Buprenorphine is also marketed overseas in a patch form, for pain, but at present it isn't marketed or approved in the U.S.

Because Suboxone and Subutex are brand names, and other brand names may enter the market once the drug is off patent, I'll use the generic name for the drug, buprenorphine (b-you-pren-OR-feen) for the rest of this book.

The U.S. is not on the cutting edge of opioid addiction treatment. Buprenorphine has been used in Europe for the treatment of opioid addiction for several decades. France approved it for use in 1995, for opioid addiction treatment, and the United Kingdom approved its use in 2001. Scotland was slower to approve buprenorphine to treat addiction, because that country had a bad experience in the late 1970's and 1980's with rampant intravenous buprenorphine addiction, for the reasons described above. Physicians in Scotland have been cautious about prescribing it again.

Buprenorphine *is* an opioid. If it's stopped suddenly, a typical opioid withdrawal will begin within several days. Addicts (and their doctors and families) want a pill that cures opioid addiction, but has no withdrawal symptoms if stopped, but that's *not* how this medication works.

Buprenorphine treats the physical symptoms for as long as the drug is taken, and reduces mental obsession for opioids. Most patients say buprenorphine withdrawal is somewhat milder than withdrawal from other opioids, but a small number say it's worse. A few patients have said they felt no withdrawal after stopping it. If a patient wishes to be taken off buprenorphine, the dose should be reduced gradually, as some patients tolerate a faster taper than others. Patients vary widely in their ability to tolerate buprenorphine taper.

Buprenorphine works because of its unique pharmacology. Buprenorphine, like methadone, is a long-acting opioid. This means both drugs prevent withdrawal for at least twenty-four hours, which makes them ideal to use as opioid replacement medications.

Buprenorphine is a partial opioid agonist. This means that while it activates the opioid receptors in the body, it does so less vigorously than full agonists like morphine, methadone, or oxycodone. People usually experience it as an opioid, but in those already addicted to opioids, it doesn't cause a high or euphoria. If someone has never taken opioids, buprenorphine will cause a high, but tolerance develops quickly to that effect.

Buprenorphine has great affinity for the receptors, which means it sticks to them like glue. If any other opioids are in the body, buprenorphine will kick them off the opioid receptors. Because it's a weaker opioid, this can put the patient into relative withdrawal. *Therefore, to start buprenorphine successfully, it's important for the patient to be in at least moderate opioid withdrawal.* This is very important, for if an opioid addict takes buprenorphine while he is taking another opioid, he will suddenly feel terrible, and have what is called precipitated withdrawal, the sudden onset of opioid withdrawal symptoms. Most addicts want to avoid that awful feeling at all costs.

Changing from methadone to buprenorphine is trickier than from other opioids, because of methadone's long duration of action. Patients need to stop the methadone at least seventy-two hours before starting buprenorphine. Since methadone is also a much stronger opioid, the patient should be stable on methadone forty milligrams per day or less. Otherwise, dropping from a higher dose of methadone to buprenorphine often leaves the patient with feelings of low-grade withdrawal for the first few weeks of buprenorphine.

Because buprenorphine is a partial opioid agonist, there's a ceiling on its effects. This is why it's now permitted to be prescribed through a doctor's office, without all the regulations that methadone clinics have. After the buprenorphine dose reaches twenty-four or thirty-two milligrams per day, further increases in the dose have no additional effects. This makes the drug much more resistant to overdoses. However, if mixed with sedatives like benzodiazepines (Xanax, Valium) or alcohol, it can still be fatal. Methadone is a full opioid agonist, which means as the dose is raised, the effect on the body is more pronounced, with no ceiling. This is represented pictorially below:

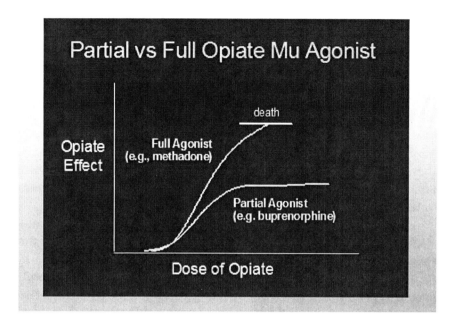

Most patients say they "just feel normal," after taking buprenorphine. When the drug works, many patients have returned to my office on the second visit saying, "It's a miracle!" They say they feel just like they did before they got addicted. They don't think about pain pills, don't feel withdrawal, and don't feel like they're medicated. Patients who have been on both methadone and buprenorphine say the methadone is heavier, and they feel medicated, but on buprenorphine they feel lighter.

A dose of buprenorphine can stimulate opioid receptors anywhere from twenty-four to sixty hours, so some patients feel stable when they dose only every other day. There is no impairment of thought processes or motor function in patients on a stable dose of buprenorphine. These patients can drive, work, and play with no limitations.

I try to temper patients from being overly enthusiastic about buprenorphine. Sometimes patients feel so good on this medication, they don't realize how much psychological work needs to be done before they can taper and stay off of buprenorphine. Patients feel so good, they minimize their addiction, and are reluctant to get the counseling they need. As the doctor interviewed in this chapter said, the drug's main problem is that it works so well.

Buprenorphine is ideal for patients with opioid addiction who have lower tolerances, who have relatively stable lives, or who have been using for shorter lengths of time. Buprenorphine is a better drug than methadone for patients who have been addicted less than one year, because methadone is more difficult to stop, once it's started.

Buprenorphine has the same side effects as other opioids: constipation, sweating, decreased libido (sex drive), and possible weight gain. Usually, these side effects are much less pronounced in patients taking buprenorphine than in patients taking methadone. Unlike methadone, there is no increased risk for fatal heart rhythms, because it doesn't affect the QT interval. Most patients do complain about the bad taste of the sublingual tablets.

Buprenorphine is metabolized in the liver by the cytochrome P450 system, just as methadone is, so all drugs also metabolized by that specific system theoretically could influence the dosing.

Buprenorphine doesn't seem to cause lasting damage to the body, even if it's continued indefinitely, though elevated liver function tests can be seen in some patients. Liver function blood tests should be checked periodically in patients who are infected with hepatitis C or B.

Buprenorphine can be fatal if taken by children. It can also be fatal in adolescents or adults not accustomed to opioids. Patients should always store their medication safely out of reach, and with a child proof cap. Since buprenorphine is absorbed through the oral mucosa, if a child puts a tablet in his mouth, some can be absorbed, even if the pill is retrieved fairly quickly. Any handling of a Suboxone pill by a child should be viewed as a possible overdose, and the child must be taken to the hospital emergency room immediately.

The following is an interview with one of the first prescribers of Suboxone in Charlotte, North Carolina. Dr. George Hall is an experienced physician, board certified in both Family Practice and Addiction Medicine, who has worked in both fields for many years and helped countless addicts and their families:

JB: What have your experiences been, treating opioid addiction with buprenorphine, or Suboxone?

GH: It's been pretty incredible from day one.......watching people, and the difference it's made in their lives, when they come on buprenorphine.

JB: Of the patients you've started on buprenorphine, what percentage would you say improved on it?

GH: Ninety-plus percent, I would think. You'll have the occasional patient who doesn't come back, and an occasional patient who can't afford it, but there's not many that stand out in my mind through the years [who have done poorly with buprenorphine].

JB: Can you describe how you decide to do a detoxification with a patient on buprenorphine, versus keeping the patients on it for longer, and what your experiences have been?

GH: The people I detox on buprenorphine are the ones who have to come off of it in a short period of time. They say, "I want off by one month or two months or three," and generally those people actually change their mind over a period of time, as they see their life getting better.

So, most of the time, it's patient-driven. As you know, the data for opiate dependency shows that this population just doesn't seem to do very well. Perhaps that's the reason I have such a positive feeling about buprenorphine. We've used it for maintenance, since day one, in a lot of patients, and those are the people whose lives you see continue to change over a long period of time.

JB: Are there any problems that you've seen with buprenorphine?

GH: I think the problem with buprenorphine is similar to the problem with methadone ...we see these people getting extremely well. They don't get euphoric, but they're not ill any longer. They're able to function, they're able to sleep. It's a long-acting medication that allows them to have a normal day. When they're out on the street or they're buying from the internet or they're going to multiple doctors, they just don't have normal days.

So is that a problem? Only if you define any sort of recovery as abstinence-based. But, if you're defining recovery as improvement in quality of life, not using other substances, able to hold jobs, able to have families and interact with families, treat their depression, then these people do extremely well.

But...I think the problem for me is.....once they begin to do so well, it's just like with anything else, whether it's an alcoholic or a cocaine addict or a marijuana addict that's been in recovery for a period of time. The acuity of the disease drops in the patient's mind, and it seems like they think, "I'm cured," and "I'm just normal now so I don't need to do other things. I don't need to go to NA meetings. I don't need counseling. Why do you keep pushing me to do this, because I haven't used in two years? I'm doing great." Whether this is the disease talking to them or it's just part of life...

And that's what I see with any addiction...the disease itself says you don't have a disease, whether it's alcohol dependency or opiate dependency, and perhaps we see that even more with opiate dependency. We see that on maintenance therapy.

JB: If you had an opiate addicted patient who had unlimited money, time, willingness, and resources, what treatment would you recommend first? If they were addicted only to opiates?

GH: When I think about that question, I think about gold standards of treatment. The people who have the highest recovery rates are professionals. Physicians in North Carolina have over a ninety percent recovery rate at five years. It's not because they're physicians, it's not because they're brilliant, it's because they're made to do a lot of stuff to help convince them they have an illness, and to treat it as an illness on an ongoing basis. They are made to do at least twenty-eight days, to three months, to six months of inpatient treatment, most of them from the beginning. If we had an IV opiate-addicted anesthesiologist, [he would get] probably at least twelve weeks of inpatient treatment, monitoring, and perhaps even a job change. So [addicted doctors] do extremely well. Not that they have unlimited funds, but if they want to remain a physician, they have to do certain things.

So that kind of brings me around to what you're asking. If money were no object, I would think fairly long term – two to four months of inpatient treatment, with a slow detox with something such as buprenorphine, which is a very soft detox compared to some of the ones we've used in the past – followed up by intensive group therapy, and then getting them involved in 12-step recovery programs. And after we bring them out of inpatient treatment, [they would get] some sort of follow up over a period of one to two years if we are looking at unlimited funds, and the willingness to do that. Which isn't practical in the general population.

JB: Because of the expense and time?

GH: Because of the expense and the time we have.

It's ironic that buprenorphine works so well, patients forget they have the disease of addiction. With addiction, it's important to address the psychological portion of the disease. When patients feel good, or normal, it can actually interfere with treatment.

Many patients argue, with legitimate reasoning, that if they can be made normal with this medication, why do they need counseling at all? If the medication cures them, why not just stay on the medication? If you look at the outcomes of clinical trials done with buprenorphine, it's hard to argue with their logic, if they're willing to stay on Suboxone indefinitely,

Subutex and Suboxone come in doses of 2 and 8 milligram pills, and patients may require as much as 32 milligrams, or four of the 8 milligram pills. Most patients stabilize on 8 to 16 milligrams per day. Each 8 milligram pill can have a retail cost of anywhere from six to twelve dollars. For a month of treatment, the expense adds up quickly. Some addicts have insurance to help with the cost, but many opioid addicts have few financial resources and have long ago lost health insurance.

Suboxone and Subutex just came off patent in late 2009. So far, there is no generic equivalent for Suboxone, only for Subutex. This creates a dilemma for physicians and their patients. From the European experience, we know the buprenorphine alone, without naloxone, has appeal as a street drug, so doctors in this country would rather not prescribe it. But many patients have no insurance, can't afford the name brand Suboxone, and demand the cheaper generic. This creates a tug-of-war of sorts. The patient is pulling to get a cheaper version of this very expensive and potentially life-saving drug, while the doctor often is pulling back from prescribing the generic, knowing it's more likely to be diverted to the street for intravenous use.

Thus far, the generics available aren't much cheaper than the name brand Suboxone. I agreed to prescribe generic buprenorphine for one patient, but she was so displeased with the generic, she switched back to the name brand. The generic wasn't all that cheap, tasted horrible, and took a long time to dissolve under the tongue. She brought the pills to show me, and they were compact hard pills, thicker than the brand Suboxone. Hopefully, the price of generics will decrease with time.

At present, even generic buprenorphine is more expensive than methadone maintenance. In methadone clinics, all services are usually bundled into one daily charge. The methadone, counseling, drug screens, visits to the clinic doctor, and lab tests are all included at fees around eight to fifteen dollars per day. Addicts can pay as they go. Most addicts can manage that, as they're used to getting money for their daily fix.

In contrast, many buprenorphine programs demand a sum of money be paid at the first visit. This can range anywhere from several hundred dollars to several thousand. The higher amounts usually include medication and counseling for some period of time, but many addicts just can't afford to pay that much at one time. Addiction demands all of the addict's time and energy, leaving little reserve to plan for future needs.

Many medical insurance companies pay for buprenorphine treatment. Charges for doctors' visits vary widely. Usually, the first visit runs anywhere from two hundred to four hundred dollars, though in some areas, prices are reported to run as high as twenty-five hundred dollars just for a first visit. Follow-up visits can range from seventy-five to one hundred and fifty dollars.

A two-tiered system of opioid addiction treatment is emerging. Patients with little money, who want medication-assisted treatment, have to go to the methadone clinic. Patients with money and/or health insurance can to go to private doctors who prescribe buprenorphine.

In the future, methadone will probably be regarded as a second line drug. With the increased safety and tolerability, buprenorphine will likely become the first-line drug to treat opioid addiction. Methadone will be saved for those patients who fail treatment with buprenorphine. Some addicts with higher opioid tolerances won't feel well on buprenorphine and will need the stronger methadone. Some patients may be allergic to buprenorphine or do poorly on it for other reasons, so methadone will still be needed for some patients.

Summit meetings for doctors, researchers, and other interested parties have been held periodically, since buprenorphine's approval in 2002. The latest trends and research about buprenorphine are discussed. At the last summit meeting of experts for which information is available, data was presented, showing from 2002 until 2007, the number of prescriptions written for buprenorphine have increased exponentially. The states with the highest per capita buprenorphine prescriptions have been the states experiencing the highest rates of opioid addition: the spine of the Appalachians, plus Utah, Montana, and varied other states. It appears buprenorphine is being used in the areas where it's needed the most. (3)

About one third of the doctors who took the training and are licensed to prescribe buprenorphine don't prescribe it. A survey of these doctors compared attitudes of novice prescribers, non-prescribers, and experienced prescribers. (4) This study found that non-prescribing doctors were most concerned about a lack of access to behavioral health support and drug counseling, staff training issues, and inadequate time for the care of these patients. Other studies have shown that these physicians feel they're too busy, don't feel they have adequate experience, or aren't interested in treating drug addicts. Some physicians felt they couldn't manage the frequent co-existing medical problems, like chronic hepatitis C, HIV, and mood disorders. Primary care doctors often don't feel they have the resources they need to prescribe. Many indicate they don't have the nursing staff or the time to treat these patients safely.

Physicians who are experienced prescribers of buprenorphine were asked about the biggest problems they encounter in their practice. They identified patients' resistance to counseling, patients' abuse of other drugs, compliance with treatment, and retention in treatment as the most concerning problems. (5). Of the doctors who do prescribe, most have just a few patients. The bulk of the buprenorphine prescriptions are written by a minority of doctors.

Any time an opioid drug is prescribed, some diversion is inevitable. Diversion means the medication gets diverted from the person for whom it was prescribed, into the hands of someone else, usually for the purpose of getting high. Scotland's experience in the 1980's clearly shows us that some people do use buprenorphine to get high. However, in the U.S., doctors have tried to minimize the risk, by prescribing mainly the combination drug Suboxone, because it will cause withdrawal if injected. There have been some reports of patients crushing and snorting Suboxone and feeling high, but thus far it doesn't seem common.

The patients I've talked to who have used buprenorphine illicitly, without a prescription, said they did it in order to see how they feel with the buprenorphine. Most were considering enrollment in a buprenorphine treatment program, but wanted to make sure the drug worked before they committed time and money to a treatment program. This aligns with what SAMHSA found in a study on the diversion and abuse of buprenorphine. The drug has been diverted, but at a lower rate than other opioids, and most cases involved addicts who didn't have access to a physician who could prescribe buprenorphine. Better access to treatment may actually reduce illicit use of buprenorphine.

A fellow addictionologist wondered why we should be concerned about diversion of buprenorphine. He accurately pointed out it is the safest opioid, and if addicts are using this, then they aren't using something more deadly. He makes an excellent point.

If buprenorphine were available to all opioid addicts, would the state of opioid addiction in this country be better or worse? I'm not sure, but it was a leap of progress for our government to allow treatment of opioid addiction from doctors' offices. Any diversion endangers the program. People opposed to buprenorphine can point to diversion, and say the system doesn't work. If buprenorphine is diverted in noticeable amounts, it gives the anti-medication people ammunition to say the program should be shut down.

Shutting down the buprenorphine program would be tragic. For many opioid addicts, it has been a wonderful treatment, giving them their life back. In the following chapter, a patient tells his story about life before and after buprenorphine.

Endnotes:

1. Clark, H. Westley, M.D., J.D., MPH, CAS, FASAM, Director of Center for Substance Abuse Treatment and Mental Health Services Administration, Keynote address, component Session 6, American Society of Addiction Medicine's Course on the State of the Art in Addiction Medicine, Washington, D.C., October 24, 2009.
2. John Renner, MD, "Educational Status Report" lecture at American Society of Addiction Medicine, component session IV 905, New Orleans, LA, May 1, 2009.
3. Denise Curry, J.D., "Drug Enforcement Administration", Buprenorphine Summit, Washington, D.C., February 21, 2008.
4. Neverland, J, et al., "Factors affecting willingness to provide buprenorphine treatment." *Journal of Substance Abuse Treatment* 2008, Vol 36, Issue 3, pp. 244-251.
5. Fiellin, David A, "The First Three Years of Buprenorphine in the Unites States: Experience to Date and Future Directions, *Journal of Addiction Medicine*, 2007, 1(2): pp. 62-67, June, 2007.

CHAPTER 12

A Patient's Success with Suboxone

I know many patients who have done very well in recovery with buprenorphine, and felt one of them could best describe their journey through addiction and recovery.

Following is an interview with Patient XYZ, who has done very well on buprenorphine. He started it with the intent to taper off it at some point, but now says his life has improved so much, he decided not to take the chance of a relapse by attempting a taper. During my interview with XYZ, he shared his journey through addiction, and his search for help. He described his trials, triumphs, and relapses. He also showed how important it is to have support in recovery, from doctors, from family, from counselors, and 12-step groups. This individual struggled through approaches that didn't work, and through his ideas he could recover alone. He was able to find the perfect mix of recovery tools.

JB: Please tell me about your experience with pain pill addiction and your experiences with buprenorphine (Suboxone).

XYZ: For me, my opiate addiction got so bad, I was taking two hundred and forty to three hundred and twenty milligrams of OxyContin per day, just to stay normal. It had gotten really, really bad. And it started out with a reason. I had kidney stones, and I was in all this pain, but then it got to the point where it solved some other problems in my life and it got out of hand. I tried a lot of different things. I went to detox, and they helped me, but it was...it was almost like I never came out of withdrawal.

JB: How long were you off pain pills?

XYZ: Even after being clean for thirty or sixty days, I would still feel bad. Bowels, stomach...really all the time.

JB: Did it feel like acute withdrawal or just low grade withdrawal?

XYZ: No, it depended on the point...I'd try to fix it myself, sometimes, and I would just put myself back where I was. It got to the point where I was making myself sicker and sicker and sicker. And then I got off of it, and stayed off of it for a hundred and twenty days, I guess...but still just sick. Just miserable, and not feeling right. I was miserable. I wouldn't eat, I was losing weight...

It [buprenorphine] gave me something that replaced whatever was going on in my head physically, with the receptors. It took that [prolonged withdrawal] away, to the point that I felt well. All that energy I would spend getting pills...and I was going to the doctors almost daily. Because taking that much medicine, nobody would write me for that much, so I had to doctor shop.

JB: Did you go to the internet [to order pain pills]?

XYZ: I did. But on the internet, the only things that I found were hydrocodone, so it would take a lot of those. I was concerned about my liver, from the Tylenol in them.

My only life was going to the doctors, figuring out what pharmacy I could use. I had a whole system of how many days it could be between prescriptions, what pharmacy to go to. It was sick. I was just trying to not get sick.

JB: And you were working during that time?

XYZ: Yeah! I was working, if you want to call it that. I wasn't a very good employee, but I held a job. I was a regional vice president for "X" company. I traveled a lot, so I had new states where I could see new doctors. That was bad. When I came off the road, I owed $50,000 in credit card bills.

JB: And your wife didn't know about it?

XYZ: No. It all came tumbling down. And I had gotten into trouble, because they were company credit cards, and they wanted the money back! So, all of the sudden my wife found out that not only do I have a pain pill problem, but we're $50,000 short, and I wasn't very ethical in the way I got the money, because it really wasn't my credit, it was my company's credit card.

JB: So addiction made you do things you wouldn't do otherwise?

XYZ: Absolutely. I lied to people, I took money from people, I ran up credit cards tens of thousands of dollars, and really put my family in serious jeopardy at that time. But buprenorphine took away that whole obsessive-compulsive need for pills, made me feel better, and took away all the withdrawal symptoms at the same time. I didn't worry about it.

To be honest, I was such a hypochondriac before. I haven't been sick in years now. I haven't had a backache or headache that ibuprofen didn't cure [since starting recovery]. I was fortunate it was all in my head. I would milk any little thing. I had two knee operations that probably could have been healed through physical therapy, but I was all for surgery, because I knew I'd get pain pills.

JB: That's the power of addiction!

XYZ: I did some research about this [meaning buprenorphine].

JB: How did you do your research?

XYZ: Online. Actually, I had some good family members, who did some research and brought it to me, because they were concerned for me, and they brought it to me and said, "Hey, there's a medicine that can help. Call this number," and I found places out there that would do it [meaning Suboxone], but my concern was the speed that a lot of them were doing it. A lot of them said, OK come in, and we can evaluate you, and after a week you'll be down to this, and after a month you'll be down to this.

This was in 2005. And when I asked them what their success rate is, it wasn't very high. It was something like twenty percent of the people who were doing it [succeeded]. So when I'd finally gotten a hold of "X," [receptionist for Dr. Hall], she saved my life over the phone. Because she said, you can come tomorrow, and she said that whatever it takes, they'll work with you. And I felt good about going to a place where it wasn't already determined how long it would take. Because I already knew how I was feeling after I would come off of opiates. I didn't want to do that again.

I saw Dr. Hall and felt better within twenty-four hours, although it took a little while to get the dosage right. I think we started off at a lower dose, then we went up on the dose and it kept me so level. I had no symptoms. It cured my worst withdrawal symptoms, my stomach and my bowels.

There's always a kind of stigma in the rooms [12-step recovery meetings] because I'd been in NA for a little bit of time then [he's speaking of stigma against medication-assisted treatment]. You realize who [among addicts in NA] is die-hard, one way to do recovery, and who is willing to be educated about some things and understand that there's more than one way to skin a cat.

And I was fortunate that I had a sponsor at that time, and still do, who was willing to learn about what exactly it was, and not make me feel guilty about it. It wasn't necessarily the way he would do it, but he was a cocaine addict, so he didn't understand that whole part of it.

He said, "Your family's involved, you've got a doctor that's involved, your doctor knows your history. If all these people, who are intelligent, think this is an OK thing, then who am I to say it's not going to work?" He was open-minded. And there are not a lot of people I would trust right off the bat [in recovery], that I would tell them. [that he's taking Suboxone]. I've shared it with some people who've had a similar problem, and told them, here's something that might help you. I always preface it with, [don't do] one thing or another, you've got to do them together. You have to have a recovery program *and* take this medicine, because together it will work. Look at me. I'm a pretty good success story.

One of my best friends in Florida called me, and I got him to go see a doctor down there, and he's doing well now. He's been on it almost eleven months now and no relapses.

To me, it takes away the whole mental part of it, because you don't feel bad. For me, it was the feeling bad that drove me back to taking something [opioids] again. Obviously, when you're physically feeling bad, you're mentally feeling bad, too. It makes you depressed, and all of that, so you avoid doing fun things, because you don't feel good.

Once I trained myself with NA, how to get that portion of my life together, to use those tools, not having any kind of physical problems made it that much easier to not obsess.

JB: So, how has your life improved, as a result of being on buprenorphine?

XYZ: Well, the most important thing for me is that I've regained the trust of my family. I was the best liar and manipulator there was. I'd like to think of myself as a pretty ethical and honest person, in every aspect of my life, other than when it came to taking pills.

JB: So, you regained the trust of your family, felt physically better...

XYZ: I gained my life back! Fortunately, I had enough of a brain left to know it had to stop. Once I started on buprenorphine, it gave me back sixteen hours a day that I was wasting. That's when I decided I really don't want to jeopardize my recovery, by going out and looking for a job again [he means a job in corporate America, like he had in the past], because I've got this thing, this stigma...they're going to check a reference and I'm screwed. I'm not going to get a job doing what I was doing for the same amount of money.

My brother had enough faith in me that it was worth the risk of starting this business [that he has now] together. I spent hours setting up a "Z" company in a ten foot by twenty foot room above my house. My wife and I started on EBay, making and selling "Z," and slowly grew it to the point that, three years later, I'm going to do over two million dollars in sales this year, I've got [large company] as a client, I've got [large company] as a client, I'm doing stuff locally, in the community now, and can actually give things back to the community.

JB: And you employ people in recovery?

XYZ: Oh, yeah. I employ other addicts I know I can trust. I've helped some people out who have been very, very successful and have stayed clean, and I've helped some people out who came and went, but at the same time, I gave them a chance. You can only do so much for somebody. They have to kind of want to do it themselves too, right?

JB: Have you ever had any bad experiences in the rooms of Narcotics Anonymous, as far as being on Suboxone, or do you just not talk to anybody about it?

XYZ: To be honest, I don't broadcast it, obviously, and the only other people I would talk to about it would be somebody else who was an opioid addict, who was struggling, who was in utter misery. The whole withdrawal process...not only does it take a little while, but all that depression, the body [feels bad]. So I've shared with those I've known fairly well. I share my experience with them. I won't necessarily tell people I don't know well that I'm taking buprenorphine, but I will let them know about the medication. Even though the information is on the internet, a lot of it is contradictory.

It's been great [speaking of Suboxone] for someone like me, who's been able to put a life back together in recovery. I'd tell anybody, who's even considering taking Suboxone, if they're a true opioid pill addict, (I don't know about heroin, I haven't been there), once you get to the right level [meaning dose], it took away all of that withdrawal. And if you combine it with going to meetings, you'll fix your head at the same time. Really. I didn't have a job, unemployable, my family was...for a white collar guy, I was about as low as I could go, without being on the street.

Fortunately I came from a family that probably wouldn't let that happen, at that point, but who knows, down the road... I had gotten to my low. And that's about it, that's about as much as I could have taken.

It [Suboxone] truly and honestly gave me my entire life back, because it took that away.

JB: What do you say to treatment centers that say, if you're still taking methadone or Suboxone, you're not in "real" recovery? What would you say to those people?

XYZ: To me, I look at taking Suboxone like I look at taking high blood pressure medicine, OK? It's not mind altering, it's not giving me a buzz, it's not making...it's simply fixing something I broke in my body, by abusing the hell out of it, by taking all those pain pills.

I know it's hard for an average person, who thinks about addicts, "You did it to yourself, too bad, you shouldn't have done that in the first place," to be open minded. But you would think the treatment centers, by now, have seen enough damage that people have done to themselves to say, "Here's something that we have proof that works....."

I function normally. I get up early in the morning. I have a relationship with my wife now, after all of this, and she trusts me again. Financially, I've fixed all my problems, and have gotten better. I have a relationship with my kids. My wife and I were talking about it the other day. If I had to do it all over again, would I do it the way I did it? And the answer is, absolutely yes. As much as it sucked and as bad as it was, I would have still been a nine to five drone out there in corporate America, and never had the chance to do what I do. I go to work...this is dressy for me [indicating that he's dressed in shorts and a tee shirt]

JB: So life is better now than it was before the addiction?

XYZ: It really is. Tenfold! I'm home for my kids. I wouldn't have had the courage to have left a hundred thousand dollar a year job to start up a "Z" business. I had to do something. Fortunately, I was feeling good enough because of it [Suboxone], to work really hard at it, like I would have if I started it as a kid. At forty years old, to go out and do something like that...

JB: Like a second career.

XYZ: It's almost like two lives for me. And if you're happy, nothing else matters. I would have been a miserable, full time manager, out there working for other people and reaping the benefits for them and getting my little paycheck every week and traveling, and not seeing my wife and kids, and not living as well as I do now.

I joke, and say that I work part time now, because when I don't want to work, I don't have to work. And when I want to work, I do work. And there are weeks that I do a lot. But then, on Saturday, we're going to the beach. I rented a beach house Monday through Saturday, with just me and my wife and our two kids. I can spend all my time with them. I could never have taken a vacation with them like that before.

JB: Do you have anything you'd like to tell the people who make drug addiction treatment policy decisions in this nation? Anything you want them to know?

XYZ: I think it's a really good thing they increased the amount of patients you [meaning doctors prescribing Suboxone] can take on. I'd tell the people who make the laws to find out from the doctors...how did you come up with the one hundred patient limit? What should that number be? And get it to that number, so it could help more people. And if there's a way to get it cheaper, because the average person can't afford it.

The main thing I'd tell them is I know it works. I'm pretty proud of what I've achieved. And I wouldn't have been able to do that, had I not had the help of Suboxone. It took me a little while to get over thinking it was a crutch. But at this point, knowing that I've got everybody in my corner, they're understanding what's going on...it's a non-issue. It's like I said, it's like getting up and taking a high blood pressure medicine.

This patient obviously has a healthy recovery on buprenorphine, and plans to continue his present recovery program. He goes regularly to Narcotics Anonymous meetings, has a sponsor, works the twelve steps of recovery, and contributes to NA by sponsoring people and doing other service work. He had such a good outcome, because he didn't neglect the psychological aspect of his recovery, even after Suboxone took away the physical withdrawal symptoms.

For the patients I treat with buprenorphine, the most challenging part is coaxing, coercing, and cajoling patients to get some sort of counseling. Whether they go to an individual counselor, pastoral counselor, or to 12-step meetings doesn't matter to me. I'd love to be able to send them to local intensive outpatient treatment centers, but as will be discussed later, most of these centers require the patient be off buprenorphine completely before they can enter treatment, which can create a curious circle of relapse. Fortunately, I know good counselors, knowledgeable about addiction and its treatments, willing to see my buprenorphine patients. They markedly benefit from this individual counseling, though group settings can give patients insights they won't get any other way.

When buprenorphine was first released, the addiction treatment community and opioid addicts had very high hopes for this medication. Many patients say, "It's a miracle," on their second visit, after they've started the medication. Most patients are surprised they don't feel high, and don't have any withdrawal symptoms.

However, it's really not a miracle drug. It's still an opioid, and though it's weaker than other opioids, some patients have extreme difficulty when they try to taper off of this medication. One can read postings on internet message boards that describe the difficulty some patients have.

In my own practice, I've had some patients who stopped buprenorphine suddenly, and claim they had no opioid withdrawal symptoms. At the other extreme, I've had patients who wean to one milligram of buprenorphine per day and say they get a terrible withdrawal if they go a day without even this one milligram. I've had many patients who gradually cut their dose on their own, until they take the medication every other day, and gradually stop it.

Patients appear to differ widely in their abilities to taper off buprenorphine. Some patients are dismayed to discover it's just as hard to taper off of Suboxone, and stay off opioids, as it is to taper off methadone and stay off opioids.

If it's appropriate to consider tapering a patient off of buprenorphine, best results are seen if the taper is done slowly. In the past, I have informed patients who wished to taper completely off buprenorphine that addiction counseling improves outcomes, and reduces relapse rates, but this may not be true.

Information presented at the American Psychiatric Association's 2010 conference calls that advice into question. In a study of over six hundred prescription opioid addicts, relapse rates were remarkably high when patients were tapered over the course of one month, after two months of stabilization. (2) The addition of fairly intensive addiction counseling didn't improve relapse rates. In the treatment as usual group, prescription opioid addicts met weekly with their doctors and after their taper, ninety-three percent had relapsed within four weeks. Even in the group getting doctor visits plus twice- weekly one hour counseling sessions, ninety-four percent relapsed within the first four weeks after buprenorphine was tapered. This was the largest study done so far specifically focused on prescription opioid addicts, as opposed to heroin addicts. The overall message from initial results of this study seems to be that adding fairly intense drug counseling doesn't improve patient outcomes, if the buprenorphine is tapered off within the first three to four months.

Once a patient is on buprenorphine and doing well, he or she often becomes very reluctant to participate in counseling, or even 12-step meetings. As Dr. Hall insightfully observed, once patients feel physically back to normal, they begin to minimize the severity of their addiction, and don't think they need any counseling.

Some patients admit they need counseling, but say they can't afford it. This is a valid excuse, because counseling sessions can cost around a hundred dollars each. Private counselors usually like to see their patients weekly, so that's an additional four hundred dollars per month that patients need to pay. Even patients with insurance are allowed only a limited number of sessions. Those without insurance have great difficulty affording counselor fees on top of all the other expenses, like doctors' visits, drug screens, and medication. Patients have fewer valid excuses for not participating in Narcotics Anonymous or Alcoholics Anonymous, since they're free, and located in nearly every city or town.

If a patient for whom I've prescribed buprenorphine is doing well, but refuses to go to counseling, should I stop prescribing buprenorphine? Particularly in view of the recent data showing high relapse rates after taper from buprenorphine, I usually don't stop prescribing. If that patient has returned to a productive life, isn't using opioids, and not at risk for an overdose with buprenorphine, I prefer the patient stay on buprenorphine. Given the misery of active addiction and the increased death rate of untreated opioid addiction, it would be unethical to stop a medication that at least reduces the amount of harm from addiction. Once again, I think of the saying, "Dead addicts don't recover." If there's something I can do to keep an addict alive, on or off medication, I think I should do it. That addict may or may not decide to transition to a fully opioid-abstinent recovery later, but at least he'll be alive to make the decision.

Some good clinicians disagree with me. They would say that I'm only exchanging one opioid for another, and that the patient is still physically addicted. They'd say that even though these patients have improved, they've missed an opportunity to have a drug-free recovery. They may say that the good is the enemy of the best, just as it is for methadone.

As discussed previously, one person's harm reduction is another person's enabling.

Buprenorphine patients who are *not* doing well may have to be referred to another form of treatment, usually a local methadone clinic. Fortunately, in my location, there are three clinics who can quickly accept a patient. This referral is appropriate for patients who continue to use illicit opioids, despite an adequate dose of buprenorphine, or patients who have continued in a chaotic lifestyle, with multiple drug use and criminality. These patients usually do better with the increased structure of an opioid treatment center, or an inpatient treatment program, if possible.

Just like with methadone, benzodiazepines are risky with buprenorphine. The few patients for whom I've stopped prescribing buprenorphine couldn't stop using benzodiazepines. I've also stopped prescribing for patients who continue to get opioid prescriptions from other doctors, and are not improving on buprenorhpine.

In the practice where I work, we use our state's prescription monitoring database. Each day before seeing patients, I consult the database, to see if that day's patients are getting any unknown controlled substance prescriptions. If they are, we discuss it at their appointment that day. I've had a few patients who either could not, or would not, stop getting opioids or benzodiazepines from other doctors. I was unwilling to prescribe buprenorphine in those situations. Because they still take other opioids, it's unlikely they're taking much of the buprenorphine, and may be diverting one or both of the prescriptions.

Random pill counts can help assure a patient isn't diverting buprenorphine. In my practice, we've called patients, and asked them to go to their pharmacy, so the pharmacist can count the leftover pills, and call me back. That way, if the pills are being sold, or otherwise diverted to someone else, we'll see that the patient has fewer pills than he should.

In summary, buprenorphine is a great new tool for the treatment of opioid addiction, mainly because it's safer than methadone and can be prescribed in a doctor's office. In the future, buprenorphine will likely become the first line drug for opioid addiction, saving methadone for more severely addicted individuals. Once the drug goes off patent and generic forms enter the market, the price will hopefully drop, and more people can afford buprenorphine as a treatment option.

However, buprenorphine is not a panacea, and doesn't work for every opioid addict. It seems to be as difficult to taper as methadone, for some patients. Thus far, studies show that patients do better if they stay on buprenorphine for more than four months.

A list of all prescribing doctors and more information about buprenorphine can be found either at the Department of Health and Human Services website at http://buprenorphine.samhsa.gov or through the drug manufacturer's website: www.suboxone.com .

Endnotes:

1. Amass L, Bickel WK, "A preliminary investigation of outcome following gradual or rapid buprenorphine detoxification" *Journal of Addictive Disease*, 1994; 13: pp. 33-45.
2. Weiss RD, The American Psychiatric Association 2010 Annual Meeting: Symposium 36, presentation 4. Information from the National Drug Abuse Treatment Clinical Trials Network Prescription Opioid Addiction Treatment Study, May 23, 2010, New Orleans, LA.

CHAPTER 13

Trudging the Road of Happy Destiny: Recovery in 12-step groups (and others)

"Religion is for people who are afraid they'll go to hell. Spirituality is for people who have been there."

– Anonymous 12-step group member

A great uncounted population of recovering opioid addicts can be found in the 12-step programs of Narcotics Anonymous and Alcoholics Anonymous. Very few of these addicts take replacement opioid medications. Because of the anonymous nature of this program, it's difficult, if not impossible, to calculate the number of people who are recovering in this and other 12- step groups. Many of these people don't want anyone to know they're recovering addicts, due to stigma. Even addiction professionals may never see this population of recovering people.

Most of these recovering opioid addicts say they don't need replacement medications to stay clean. When NA members use the term "clean," they mean abstinence from all addicting drugs and alcohol. From the addiction medicine literature and addiction medicine conferences, it would seem rare that anyone stays in abstinent, non-medication-assisted recovery from pain pills or heroin for any length of time. Yet in a meeting of fifteen or so members of Narcotics Anonymous, one can usually encounter at least four or five who say opioids, either pain pills or heroin, were their main drugs of destruction. It's obvious they had been "real" addicts, because many used opioids intravenously and in large amounts. Many used heroin for years before finding recovery in Narcotics Anonymous.

If there are large numbers of opioid addicts recovering with no medication-assisted therapies, perhaps 12-step recovery is one way that a newly abstinent opioid addict can get through the uncomfortable and prolonged post-acute withdrawal period. In NA, a recovering person can access help from other recovering addicts anytime of the day or night. Perhaps it is this support, particularly from another person recovering from the same malady, that helps members of NA get through periods of cravings.

Since Alcoholics Anonymous had its first meeting in 1935, other groups dealing with other addictions have adapted the steps for use with their addictions. Narcotics Anonymous and Alanon (for friends and family members of alcoholics) are the next largest 12-step groups. Others include Overeaters Anonymous, Naranon (for friends and families of drug addicts) Sex and Love Addicts Anonymous, Cocaine Anonymous, Methadone Anonymous, and Gamblers Anonymous. Worldwide, there are ninety-four separate twelve step groups. (1)

Methadone Anonymous would seem like the most useful place to refer opioid addicts in treatment on methadone. In some parts of the country, this may be true. Where I work, there are few MA meetings available. In fact, according to the Methadone Anonymous website, there are no MA meetings in my state of North Carolina.

Our treatment center encouraged patients to form their own groups. This happened in a few clinics, but the groups eventually collapsed. It may be that this group didn't have enough stable members dedicated to keeping it going. I know that in other areas, MA is a strong resource for patients on methadone, but in our area, Narcotics Anonymous and Alcoholics Anonymous are the most accessible group meetings outside of the opioid treatment center.

Methadone Anonymous started in 1991, and many meetings are held on an opioid treatment center's premises, though the recovering addicts conduct the meeting, not treatment center staff.

Patients prescribed methadone and buprenorphine sometimes have problems fitting into 12- step recovery. If these patients share in the group about being on medication, they may be chided about "still using." People in meetings may not even understand what methadone and buprenorphine are, or why they are used.

It can be harmful to the prospective NA member on medication-assisted therapy, who feels like he or she is being judged by the whole group, rather than being accepted as a fellow sufferer from addiction. I advise new patients to go to NA or AA, but not to share about any medications. I advise them to try different groups, and keep going to the groups where they feel most comfortable. Like the patient on buprenorphine interviewed in Chapter 12, some addicts on medication just don't mention them at meetings, and continue to get the benefits from 12-step recovery.

Anyone who works in the addiction treatment field should become familiar with both Narcotics Anonymous and Alcoholics Anonymous. Anyone can go to an *open* meeting of either fellowship. Family members, counselors, and therapists are welcome. However, no one but people seeking recovery for their own addiction should go to a *closed* meeting.

Obviously, since 12-step meetings insist on anonymity, gathering information about these groups has been challenging. However, from member surveys taken at their world conventions, both Alcoholics Anonymous and Narcotics Anonymous have compiled information from their members. In AA, 65% of its members are male, while in NA, 55% are male. In AA, only 1.5% of their members are under age twenty-one, while in NA, 3% of its members under age twenty-one. In NA, the forty-one to fifty year old age group is the largest, making up 40% of the total members, but in AA, the largest age group is over age fifty-one, making up 39% of AA's membership.

In NA, 30% are non-white, while in AA, around 10% of the members are non-white. NA has a higher percentage of employed members, at 81%, and AA has 71% employed, probably because 14% of AA members are retired, compared to only 3% of NA members. The average length of time in continuous abstinence was eight years for AA and seven and a half years for NA. (1)

This data should be interpreted with some caution. Since these surveys were taken at their world conventions, the respondents to the survey may not represent typical members of these fellowships. It's likely that the most enthusiastic members of AA and NA attend these conventions.

Twelve step recovery meetings differ from recovery group meetings held in treatment centers and therapists' offices. In 12- step meetings, participants do not "cross talk." This means directing something in the group toward a specific member of the group. Members of NA usually do not give advice, feedback, or criticism to other members. Instead, members share from their own experiences, so all who are present can benefit.

By contrast, in group therapy meetings, participants are often asked to give feedback to each other. Some treatment centers believe that alcoholics and addicts must be confronted, so that denial can be broken through. Twelve-step meetings don't take this stance. Instead, members offer their own experience, freely and without expectations.

Individual 12-step recovery meetings vary in many ways. Some are serious, and some are more lighthearted. Some meetings have hundreds of members in attendance, and some meetings may have only two or three. Some meetings are loud and boisterous, and others may be quiet, with few people sharing.

Meetings are held in slightly different ways in different areas of the country. In some places, meetings range from fifty minutes to an hour and a half. At speaker meetings, one person tells their story of addiction and recovery for the whole hour, traditionally telling "what it was like, what happened, and what it's like now." At other types of meetings, all persons present are offered a chance to share or pass to the next person. In some meetings, members who wish to share raise their hands and are called on by the meeting chairperson.

At meetings, members rarely talk about the possessions or money they have – or don't have – but are encouraged to talk about what they want to do about their problem of addiction and how the group can help.

No record of attendance is kept. A person is considered to be a member of Narcotics Anonymous when that person says they are a member. The only requirement for membership is a *desire* to stop using drugs. Most groups insist on paying rent, even at the churches and community centers that would be willing to host them for free. This is because of one of the traditions of NA, which states, "Every NA group ought to be fully self-supporting...." (2) This tradition encourages both the groups and addicts in the group to begin the process of becoming financially responsible.

Most of the patients I see at opioid treatment centers or in my own office have been reluctant to attend NA, or AA. Patients offer an endless and often contradictory litany of reasons why they cannot go to meetings: meetings conflict with the hours they work, childcare responsibilities, fear of seeing someone they know, fear of not knowing anyone, fear of being "brainwashed," not wanting to use meetings as a crutch, and so on.

Many times, these excuses veil a reluctance to attend a meeting of any kind, because to attend means to admit an inability to control drugs and alcohol. Most addicts have to summon an enormous amount of courage to tell a doctor about their problem with addiction, and recoil at the thought of announcing their dependence to unfamiliar people, even if those people have the same problem. It's more comfortable to remain behind a façade of self sufficiency, but it's also a terrible and exhausting burden. It takes a great deal of courage to go to these meetings, and to keep going to recovery meetings, even when it's not comfortable or convenient, but the benefits are enormous, for the people who are willing to do this hard work of recovery. There are legitimate reasons why meeting attendance can be difficult, but these are usually solvable problems. If the addict expends the same energy to get to a recovery meeting as he did to get drugs, meeting attendance isn't a problem.

Twelve step groups don't endorse a single religion, and in fact, mention of a specific religion at a meeting is discouraged, because addicts of a different religion may feel excluded. All 12-step groups strongly endorse spiritual principles, including honesty, open-mindedness, and willingness. The twelve steps offer a pattern and a structure for living that some addicted people have never had in the past. The twelve steps help the addict admit loss of control over drug use, seek help from other recovering people and a power greater than one's self, make an inventory of wrongs done to others and make amends for these wrongs.

Some patients say they object to the "cult" atmosphere of AA or NA. From my own observation, 12-step groups bear little resemblance to cults. Cults have a charismatic leader, who wants all of its members' money, and he or she attempts to control the lives of cult members.

But in NA, there is no leader. Every recovering person is considered an equal in the group, regardless of the amount of clean time. There is no "Head Addict" or "Head Alcoholic." Responsibilities for chairing meetings, making coffee, and setting up the meeting rooms are shared by the whole group. The people who lead meetings are considered "trusted servants."

Twelve step groups don't ask for all your money, like cults do. In fact, it's optional to place a dollar in the basket that goes around at most meetings, which is collected to pay for coffee, supplies, and rent. Some groups pointedly ask newcomers and visitors NOT to put any money in the basket.

Every addict is treated with respect, and newcomers are told that they are the most important people at the meetings. It's through helping new addicts that the members of NA stay clean themselves, and contact with new members prevents older members from getting complacent about their disease. Recovering addicts in NA don't give advice, but rather share their own experience, strength, and hope with the expectation that this will help other recovering addicts, struggling with similar issues.

Alcoholics Anonymous and Narcotics Anonymous do not recruit members, as cults do. No one forces membership upon anyone. In fact, one of their traditions prohibits this. "Our public relations policy is based on attraction rather than promotion..." (3)

Recently, drug courts and professional licensing boards have commanded alcoholics and addicts to attend 12-step meetings as part of their ordered treatment. This has been successfully challenged in court, and it was ruled that these people should be given the option of attending secular support groups, instead of 12 step groups. Twelve step groups take no official stance on this matter, but say that anyone is welcome at an open meeting, though closed meetings are reserved for people who are members or prospective members of AA or NA.

Twelve step programs all have sponsorship in common. A sponsor in a 12-step program helps a newer member work the twelve steps of recovery. The person being sponsored is called the sponsee, or sponsoree. The sponsor usually is of the same sex, to prevent romantic feelings from interfering with the work to be done, but if the newcomer is homosexual, the sponsor may need to be of the opposite sex.

A special relationship usually develops between the sponsor and sponsee. A sponsee often calls his sponsor when experiencing an urge to use drugs or act out in other harmful ways. The sponsor can help the sponsee to think through all of the consequences and often provides suggestions about ways to handle negative emotions. This is a purely voluntary service on behalf of the sponsor, and no money is exchanged for the help provided. It's expected that when the newcomer has significant time in recovery, she will, in turn, help newer members. Many twelve step group members say that sponsorship is a critical part of their recovery.

Sponsorship provides a way, 24-hours a day, for a newly recovering member to have access to a more experienced recovering addict, who can help during times of extreme drug cravings. This valuable service may be one of the key ways that 12-step recovery works.

In summary, people usually find what they are looking for at 12-step meetings. If they are looking for a romantic hook-up, they may find it. If they are looking for drugs, they may even find that. And if they look for recovery, they will certainly find it.

Considerable objective evidence proves 12- step recovery groups work. For this reason, most respectable addiction treatment centers recommend ongoing 12-step meetings for their patients. *This is an evidence-based recommendation.* Since addiction follows the pattern of a chronic disease, it makes sense to continue some sort of recovery program after the patient leaves professional treatment.

Millions of people have been helped by 12-step recovery, with drug, alcohol, gambling, and overeating, to name the main addictions. Also, 12-step recovery is free and widely available. The only cost is the time involved in attending the meetings, and addicts usually spend more than an hour using drugs, recuperating from using drugs, and getting more drugs. Alcoholics Anonymous and Narcotics Anonymous do help addicts who are willing to attend.

I was more fortunate than most medical students, because my medical school, Ohio State University College of Medicine, had a teaching module on alcoholism, which required each student to attend an AA meeting by themselves. Back then, I thought this was a waste of my time, but I went as directed.

Back in the class room, the professor asked us how we felt as we entered the meeting. Some students said they felt awkward, fearful, out of place, under scrutiny, among other things. I know I felt very awkward and I thought about how embarrassed I would be, if someone saw me going into an AA meeting.

Our professor told us to remember two things: always consider referring an alcoholic to AA, and remember how difficult it was for us to go to a meeting, even as students without, presumably, a drinking problem. I didn't know it at the time, but this course was one of the most practical and useful of my four years in medical school.

Going to an AA meeting is the best way to get a feel for what happens at a meeting. Over the years, I've gone to many open meetings of AA, NA, Alanon, and Naranon. The meetings gave me a more thorough understanding of addiction, and the shame and stigma that can accompany it. I also got a better understanding of recovery, possible obstacles to treatment, and the workings of 12-step groups.

Bill W. and Bob S, founders of Alcoholics Anonymous, were not particularly religious people, though AA did start as a branch from a Christian organization called the Oxford Group. Alcoholics Anonymous soon severed ties with all religious groups, so they could maintain their focus on helping other alcoholics. Many meetings are held in churches, but also in synagogues, libraries, and community centers. AA has no association with any of these organizations, but does pays rent for use of their facilities.

Studies of AA's effectiveness have been conducted since 1945. A metanalysis of thirty-three studies, done from 1945 until 1990, shows a positive association between the frequency of AA meetings attended by an alcoholic and increased abstinence from alcohol. In other words, an overall summary of these studies shows that the more AA meetings attended, the more likely the alcoholic stayed sober. (4) However, there were two of the thirty-three studies that showed a negative association, meaning that more AA meetings was associated with less time of sobriety. At times, organizations that oppose Alcoholics Anonymous quote one of these two studies and give no information about the other twenty- nine studies.

Of course, it may be that alcoholics who are more motivated to stay sober go to more AA meetings, and the number of meetings attended was thus a marker of commitment to sobriety. Was it the degree of motivation of the person, rather than the AA program, that produced the better outcomes? Later studies done in the 1990s controlled for the degree of personal motivation and still showed a positive correlation between number of meetings attended and sobriety. (5)

Later studies looked not at the number of AA meetings attended, but rather the degree of involvement of alcoholics in the AA program. Several studies showed that the degree of involvement was a more important determinant of length of time of abstinence from alcohol than just the number of meetings attended. Multiple studies, looking at outcomes other than abstinence from alcohol, have found that AA attendance was also associated with emotional well-being, serenity, and finding purpose in life. (4)

AA doesn't claim to have all the answers or solutions. (6) Strangely, most alternatives to 12-step recovery use as their main selling point, "Not like Alcoholics Anonymous." (7) I have read books authored by people who seem quite bitter that AA did not "fix" them, as if AA had some obligation to do so. As pointed out above, 12-step recovery programs don't force membership on anyone. In fact, the only way to become a member is to say you want to be a member.

Before I attended my first Narcotics Anonymous meeting, I thought "Narcotics" meant only people addicted to opioids would be there. However, NA makes it clear that any addicting drug is included in their program, and they don't separate alcohol from other drugs, despite its legality. So in meetings of Narcotics Anonymous, one can find people addicted to cocaine, pain pills, heroin, methamphetamine, diet pills, alcohol, marijuana, nerve pills, and all combinations of the above.

Since meetings focus on the process of recovery from addiction, rather than on the past use of an individual drug, it's actually hard to know what drug the NA members were addicted to. Mention of specific drugs is discouraged at meetings, because this may cause drug craving for a newcomer, or may prevent some addicts from identifying with what's being said, if they never used that particular drug. But before and after meetings, recovering addicts are usually quite willing to talk about their drug use history in some detail.

Various addiction treatment centers refer addicts to Alcoholics Anonymous rather than Narcotics Anonymous because some treatment professionals believe that the NA program is less stable than the AA program. In some areas, this may be true. Also, especially in rural areas, AA meetings can far outnumber NA meetings, making them more available. Many addicts do find acceptance and recovery in AA. However, because one of AA's twelve traditions states that their primary purpose is to help alcoholics stop drinking, some AA groups ask that members don't share about drugs other than alcohol. In these groups, addicts may not feel welcome.

NA started much later than AA. A group of recovering drug addicts, inmates at the Federal Narcotics Farm in Lexington, Kentucky, held weekly meetings for twenty years, calling the group, "Narco." This group, which used the twelve steps of AA, was one of the precursors of Narcotics Anonymous.

Thanks to the persistent efforts of Jimmy K. and others, Narcotics Anonymous was finally formed in Southern California in 1953, and over the years, began to grow in size and stability. Many of the first members of NA had been members of AA, who already had experience with 12- step recovery. Fortunately, AA granted permission for NA to use their twelve steps and twelve traditions. NA meetings were more difficult to start and keep going. In some states, such as New York, with its Rockefeller laws, it was illegal for addicts to meet together. It was difficult for the addicts to find a place to meet each week, so many times the meetings were held in members' homes. (8)

Despite its wobbly start, Narcotics Anonymous has grown considerably in the last twenty years. As of 2007, the date of their last membership survey, NA had over 25,000 groups in a hundred and twenty-seven countries, and the Basic Text of Narcotics Anonymous has been translated into fifty languages. As of 2007, NA had a total census of around 185,000 members, while membership of AA is around 1,190,600. (1) (9)

Some patients refuse to return to NA, reporting they saw a drug deal occur at an NA meeting. I asked a member of NA about this. He's been going to meetings for over twenty years, and estimates he's been to about four thousand meetings of NA. He saw a drug deal once, when a person was selling marijuana in the parking lot of the meeting place. He said members of NA called the police and that was the end of the drug dealing. This recovering addict said that at meetings where patients from inpatient treatment facilities are brought, to familiarize them with NA, one may "see anything," but most meetings consist only of people who want to be there, to get clean and stay off drugs.

Members of 12-step groups are not perfectly well-behaved. Bad behavior does occur at meetings, as one would expect from addicts at different stages in their recovery. Some addicts may be fairly cultured and hail from an upper or middle class, but others may have spent much of their lives homeless and penniless, and have to learn or re-learn social skills. A visitor may hear some foul language at an NA meeting, but most of the meetings are surprisingly free from curse words. As time in recovery lengthens, old ways of thinking and behaving undergo change.

The "the thirteenth step," is a term for a special kind of bad behavior sometimes encountered at a 12-step meeting. This term refers to a situation where newcomers to recovery meetings are approached by members of the group with multiple years of recovery, whose intent is not to help the new person with their recovery, but rather to start a romantic relationship. This is generally frowned on by members of Narcotics Anonymous, because this can cause a newly recovering addict to lose focus. A new romantic partner can become the focus of the newcomer, rather than growing in recovery. Also, it's easier to take advantage of a newcomer, particularly if they're rather fragile.

Though nearly all of the studies have been done on Alcoholics Anonymous, it is likely that Narcotics Anonymous works in the same way. This is a big assumption, but one based on observation of addicts attending NA.

Besides the twelve steps that both Alcoholics Anonymous and Narcotics Anonymous follow, both groups also follow the same twelve traditions. These traditions are ingenious. They have prevented the kinds of controversies which cause most human organizations to collapse.

For example, one tradition states that NA has one primary purpose – to help addicts to stop using drugs. Due to this tradition, NA keeps its focus, doing one thing well, rather than trying to be all things to all people. Another tradition states that NA shouldn't be associated with any other organization. This keeps NA from associating with any treatment center, whose practices may not be acceptable to some NA members, and to keep NA from getting into arguments over "money, property, and prestige." (2)

Another tradition states that NA has no opinion on outside issues. This means NA neither condemns nor endorses other types of recovery programs, including inpatient treatment centers, secular recovery groups or the like. It also means that the political issues of the day are not discussed at meetings. That's not the purpose of the meetings. An NA member may be interrupted, if she strays from topics directly relating to recovery. This tradition prevents groups from being split regarding controversial issues, and ensures the focus is kept on recovery from addiction. (2)

Anonymity is obviously an important tradition, but not just for obvious reasons. I thought anonymity protected members from being revealed as an addict, protecting them from potential prejudice. The eleventh tradition does that, but much more. NA asks its members to remain anonymous at the level of press, radio, and film, because breaking one's anonymity can lead to pride ("Look at me, I recovered from addiction in NA!") and to the relapse and downfall of the addict. Also, if the addict who proclaims membership in NA relapses, that can hurt the reputation of NA as a whole.

Oddly, very religious people seem to have as much trouble accepting AA or NA as do atheists. The words, "God" or "Higher Power," are mentioned in six of the twelve steps and are scattered throughout the literature of AA and NA. The concept of this Higher Power is an essential component of their programs. Some atheists and agnostics have difficulties with these concepts, but many prefer to think of their higher power as the healing power of the group, or think of God as Good Orderly Direction. But some patients with strong religious beliefs vehemently object to the vagueness of spirituality in 12-step meetings. Highly religious people can be offended that the twelve steps refer to

God in the broadest sense, without preference for their own religion. For this reason, recovery groups, specific for a particular religion, have sprung up in the U.S. Overcomers Outreach, and Celebrate Recovery are designed for the Christian religion, and Jewish Alcoholics, Chemically Dependent Persons, and Significant Others (JACS) for the Jewish religion, to name but a few.

Many of my patients refuse to go to 12-step meetings. Clearly, 12-step recovery groups don't work for everyone. For these patients, I recommend some other sort of counseling, or secular recovery groups. Group settings can teach addicts things they can't learn in any other way. We can see ourselves in other people, and learn from them in a way that can't be done in individual counseling. For patients who don't do well with NA or AA, these secular groups may be helpful.

Life Ring Secular Recovery is a non-profit recovery group that was formed in 1997. (10) This organization split from another non-twelve step group, called Sober Organizations for Sobriety. Life Ring meetings are run by volunteer members, called "convenors." Life Ring does endorse complete abstinence from alcohol and all addicting drugs, and doesn't encourage belief in a higher power. This group publishes, "How Was Your Week," as a guide to be used in meetings, and also publishes a larger workbook titled, "Recovery by Choice." Though Life Ring doesn't have sponsorship, like 12-step programs, it does encourage members to help each other. In the group setting, members are encouraged to give feedback to each other.

Though Life Ring does have meetings in the U.S., Canada, Asia, and Europe, their website only lists twenty-four meetings in the U.S., outside of California, where this group originated. Unless the addict lives in California, meetings will be hard to find. Of note, this organization states they also have online meetings.

SOS, which stands for both Secular Organizations for Sobriety, and for Saving Ourselves, says on its website that it's an "abstinence based self-empowerment program." It was formed in 1986 by James Christopher, a recovering alcoholic who felt uncomfortable with AA's approach. Judging from their website, there seem to be more meetings of this group than in Life Ring. In North Carolina, ten meetings per week are listed. The founder has written four books, which members are encouraged to read, in addition to attending meetings.

Rational Recovery (RR), a for-profit organization, has no meetings now, though it did have them in the past. Rational Recovery employs the same concepts as Cognitive-Behavioral Therapy, and Rational-Emotive Behavioral Therapy. Rational Recovery believes that addiction is not a disease, but a voluntary behavior, which can be overcome with one's own efforts. In 1999, the founder, Jack Trimpey, announced that recovery meetings were not helpful, and in fact were harmful, and declared all RR meetings closed. Rational Recovery does have a two-day seminar one can attend for $2600, or a VHS tape containing the same material for $449 advertised for sale on the Rational Recovery website (7). He has written a small book, titled *Rational Recovery* which can be purchased at most bookstores.

There have been few, if any, objective studies of these secular recovery programs. One study was done of RR back in 1993, when it still held meetings, and found frequency of RR meeting attendance to be associated with abstinence. (11)

Women For Sobriety (WFS), formed in 1976 by Jean Kirkpatrick, Ph.D., is a secular recovery group for women only, as the name implies. (12) This group has a thirteen step program, which encourages emotional and spiritual growth, through both meetings and literature. This group believes that female alcoholics require a different treatment approach than men. It is self-supporting, through members' contributions. Information about meeting location is available only after contact with the group is made by email. After sending a request, I was sent a meeting list of eight meetings per week, scattered throughout my state of North Carolina. They also have online meetings available.

Since some addicts have a strong aversion to 12-step programs, the secular recovery meetings described in this chapter should be considered, and presented as an option for these patients. Few independent studies have examined the effectiveness of these groups, but it seems likely they will be helpful for some people. The main limitation of these groups is their scarcity.

Following is an interview with a recovering addict. His history demonstrates how NA can help an addict, and illustrates some of the main tenants of 12-step recovery.

JB: What kinds of drugs did you use?
ML: Everything. I shot cocaine, Dilaudids, heroin, quarter-grain morphine tablets, and always alcohol. Alcohol and marijuana were

just a given. They were daily.

JB: Can opioid addicts get clean just using NA?

ML: Yeah. My sponsor did, and other people [have].

JB: What percentage of people in NA used opioids?

ML: Back in1982, when I entered recovery, it seemed like seventy-five percent of people in NA used opiates. Then in the 1980s, more people addicted to crack came into NA, so now I'd estimate about fifty percent or less. But there's no numbers [statistics kept by NA].

JB: How else has NA changed?

ML: Back in the early days of NA, most addicts hit a low bottom, before coming to NA, but now, with the growth of treatment centers, drug courts, information on the internet...when my father told me I had to leave the house unless I got help, I looked in the phone book and there were only two numbers to call for help. I called the Council on Alcoholism and got directed to AA. There's been such a growth in [addiction treatment resources]. Every family has had experience with some kind of addiction. There's more acceptance and knowledge now. People get to NA before they hit the kind of bottom that I did. That's a good thing.

JB: How effective is NA? Some people say that only two percent of people who go to a twelve step meeting stay clean. What do you say to that?

ML: (laughs) I'd like to know where they got their numbers.

A lot of people get their start in NA and find other means to recover...other fellowships, churchs,...it's an individual thing. It depends on what kind of living situation the individual is in, how willing the individual is [to get clean], and what kind of recovery the people at those [NA] meetings have. It depends on how deeply they get involved in that fellowship [NA].

In my case, I went to meetings for more than a year, but I didn't work any steps. But I stayed clean, by going to meetings and getting support from the people at the meetings. Then I moved away and didn't have that support. It didn't take long for me to relapse. I was around old friends I used with, old sights and sounds...It takes more than just going to meetings to be successful. There are always exceptions, though. Some people have stayed clean for years that way.

In my case, the seed was planted. I wasn't at a point where I could honestly look at my situation. So after I skinned my ass up [experienced consequences from using drugs], I went to inpatient treatment and then a halfway house. Plus meetings [Narcotics Anonymous and Alcoholics Anonymous]. I had a little more honesty, a little more willingness. But that second time, I didn't work all the steps. I had three and a half years clean, got to the fourth step, and I relapsed. That relapse happened when my priorities shifted from going to meetings five or six times per week to relationships, working twelve hour days, hunting and fishing. Looking back, being surrounded by people in recovery was carrying me along.

It wasn't long. I hadn't experienced the change that comes from working all of the steps. It was only a matter of time before the self-deception set in. How in the hell could I talk myself into thinking I could sell dope, without using it? I was dissatisfied with my job, went traveling, and met "X." He knew I'd hauled dope out of Florida in the past, for my brother in law. He asked about my connections and asked if I could help him move some kilos. I told him I still knew a few people, but I can't be handling the stuff. I talked myself into believing I could sell that stuff and not use it. Insane.

That led to two and a half years in state prison. This put me in a controlled environment. I knew enough about recovery and the twelve steps and the change that can happen. I'd heard enough about it that I reached out and asked people I knew in NA to get me some [recovery reading] material. That was in 1988. They didn't have as many 12-step meetings or substance abuse programs [in jail] then like they have now. I had to reach out and ask for help. I paid "Y" [an inmate] a candy bar so he would allow me to have an NA meeting in his cell, because it was the biggest. I paid a candy bar to him each meeting. He'd never been to a meeting in his life. This was in the county jail.

When we both got to state prison, they had NA meetings there. He got real involved. He got clean and is still clean today! He has twenty-one years in recovery, works in construction, and travels the world. I went to an AA meeting a few years ago, when I was visiting a town in Alabama, and it turned out he was speaking that night. He pointed to me and said, "That man is one of the reasons I'm here." (At this point, ML tears up and takes a pause).

I had regular correspondence with friends, who sent me recovery literature. There was a "black market" step working guide. I used it and that's the first time I did a "fearless and searching moral inventory" of myself. I didn't have anyone to do my fifth step with [this is the step where the addict admits to God, himself, and another human being the exact nature of his wrongs].

At this point, I was in the county jail, about to go to state prison. This guy from Minnesota was in jail for thirty days for old warrants. It turns out he had a few years of recovery. He heard my fifth step and guided me through step seven. He mentioned his dad got [was sentenced to] forty years for murder. In the late 1970's, when I was bringing cocaine out of Miami, the guy who set me up with the Columbians was named "Z". I would meet him in a field [to exchange drugs] and he had a young boy with him. The guy who heard my fifth step was his son!

I'd been going in the front door of this state prison for six years, as an NA member, bringing meetings to the prisoners. Now I was in that prison. I progressed on through the steps, and experienced a change in my being...a real deep change that I can't put into words. I recognized it was the beginning of a change that would continue to occur over a lifetime.

I relapsed once more, after nearly ten years clean. I got away from people in recovery, quit doing all the things I'd done on a regular basis, like prayer and meditation, meetings, contact with people in recovery. That relapse lasted a year. I was rescued by the Macon County Sheriff's Office. I knew I was going to die. I was waiting for the overdose, the gunshot, whatever. I had no hope.

An addict always has the potential for relapse. I don't care who they are, where they are, how long they've been clean or whatever. But once I experienced change on a deep level, mentally, emotionally, spiritually, and then used drugs again...you're not the same addict. You don't have the hustle. You can't be as thoughtless, selfish, and solely self-focused as you were, before you experienced that change. I knew I couldn't use drugs successfully, and I knew it was going to kill me. But when I lost that support, when I pushed away that foundation, that God of my understanding...That allows self-deception. It might be only momentarily, but you forget. You forget who you are, and if you're where substances are available, you're deceived.

JB: How's your recovery now?

ML: Awesome. If you'd asked me in 1999 how I'd be doing now, I wouldn't have gotten close. My life today is better than it's ever been. I'm extremely blessed and grateful to be where I'm at today. I'm blessed to have the work, the people, a wonderful fiancée ... I'm blessed to be able to share my life with the people I have in my life.

JB: What kind of work do you do?

ML: I work as a counselor. I work in a jail's substance abuse treatment program. Looking at what they have available in jails now...fully staffed treatment programs, right in the county jail! From having to pay a candy bar to hold a meeting to where they have whole dorms in the county jail to treat addiction...the change has been awesome to see.

This addict, ML, now has over ten years of continuous abstinence from drugs, but has been in and out of recovery for twenty-seven years. He described how his recovery progressed over time, and how he had setbacks and relapses. Obviously, given the morbidity and mortality of active addiction, treatment professionals and addicts prefer relapse-free recovery, but for many, relapse is part of the recovery process. Many fortunate addicts are able to get back into recovery, before catastrophe occurs.

ML is also a good example of how 12-step recovery meetings can help. Addiction treatment professionals should always inform addicts seeking recovery about these meetings, and encourage addicts to go to several meetings, before deciding if 12-step recovery is right for them or not.

There are many recovering opioid addicts who used 12-step resources or other counseling to become completely opioid free and were able to get through both the acute physical opioid withdrawal and the more prolonged post-acute opioid withdrawal. Therefore, it does appear that drug-free recovery may be a reasonable goal for some opioid addicts who are motivated to do the work of recovery. For addicts who find the spiritual theme of 12-step recovery unacceptable, secular recovery groups are available.

12-step recovery is free, widely available, and proven to work. It's still the best deal in town.

Endnotes:

1. Lauded, Alexander B., "The Impact of Alcoholics Anonymous of Other Substance Abuse –Related Twelve Step Programs," *Recent Developments in Alcoholism, Volume 18,* (Humana Press, Totowa, NJ, 2008) p 81.

2. *NA Basic Text, 6th ed.,* (Narcotics Anonymous World Service Office, Van Nuys, California, 2008) p 70.

3. *Ibid.* p 75.

4. Tonigan, J. Scott, "Alcoholics Anonymous Outcomes and Benefits," in *Recent Developments in Alcoholics, Volume 18, Research on Alcoholics Anonymous and Spirituality in Addiction Recovery,* edited by Marc Galanter and Lee Ann Kaskutas, pp. 357-372.

5. McKeller J, Stewart E., Humphreys k, "Alcoholics Anonymous and positive alcohol-related outcomes: cause, consequence, or just a correlate?" *Journal of Clinical Psychology,* 2003, April, 71 (2) pp. 302-308.

6. *Alcoholics Anonymous, 4th ed.,* (often called the "Big Book of Alcoholics Anonymous") Alcoholics Anonymous World Services Inc., New York City, 2001, p 164.

7. http://rationalrecovery.com

8. *Miracles Happen: the birth of Narcotics Anonymous in words and pictures,* Narcotics Anonymous World Services, Inc., Chatsworth, California, 2002.

9. Narcotics Anonymous website, http://www.na.org

10. http://www.unhooked.com/ life Ring

11. Galanter, M, Egelko, S, Edwards, H., "Rational Recovery: Alternative to AA for Addiction?" *The American Journal of Drug and Alcohol Abuse,* 1993, vol 19, no 4, pp. 499 – 510.

12. http://www.womenforsobriety.org/

CHAPTER 14

Politics and Stigma

"Prejudices, it is well known, are most difficult to eradicate from the heart whose soil has never been loosened or fertilized by education; they grow there, firm as weeds among stones."
Charlotte Bronte

We've reviewed numerous treatment options and recovery programs available to opioid addicts, and we know which treatments work the best, and are the most acceptable to most opioid addicts. Years of research studies prove the efficacy of medication-assisted treatment with methadone or buprenorphine. Why then do we still have hundreds of thousands of individuals addicted to prescription pain pills who aren't getting the help they need? Why is there such opposition to treatments which have been proven to work?

Much of it is due to the lack of knowledge about treatments which use replacement medications. The public lacks knowledge about opioid addiction and available treatments with methadone and buprenorphine. Sadly, many medical professionals have little knowledge about the relative success rates of the different treatments. Even many workers in the addiction treatment field lack knowledge about replacement medications. They prefer to say they don't "believe" in methadone, rather than looking at objective data.

When trying to find a publisher for this book, I approached a friend, the medical director of a well-known treatment center. This center has a publishing division, and I asked my friend if he thought they may be interested in a book that explains medication-assisted treatment for opioid addiction. He said he didn't think his treatment center would want to publish a book about "intoxicant-based therapies." It was an incredible statement, particularly since he is an addiction psychiatrist.

During the time I spent working at a methadone clinic, I admitted thousands of opioid addicts into treatment with methadone. For the first few years, I frequently questioned myself. Was I doing more harm than good?

It was easy to become discouraged. Our clinic was the target of frequent criticism from many sources, including local newspapers, state government, families of addicts, and other healthcare professionals. Every time I got discouraged, I recalled the faces of addicts who did find recovery through methadone, and the dramatic changes that were possible, not just for them, but for their entire families. It's an honor to be able to witness the miracle of positive change, and it does happen at methadone clinics.

I read summaries, based on forty years of scientific studies, regarding methadone's effectiveness, and knew that methadone treatment saves lives. Mountains of evidence, from multiple studies, show that outcomes for opioid addicts are much better when they are maintained on methadone. So why did our clinics meet such opposition?

I don't want to get to the end of my career and see that I've based my practice of medicine on inaccurate data, or worse, been blinded by my own prejudice. I often thought of the television clip of the tobacco executives, all in a row, hands raised as they swore to tell the truth, and they all said they didn't think tobacco was addictive. Why did they do that? Didn't they feel ridiculous swearing to something that everyone knew wasn't true? Or worse, did they actually believe what they were saying? Maybe they became so blinded by ideology and economic interests, they believed their own rhetoric.

I don't wish to make that mistake. I recognize how easy it is to be closed minded to treatment approaches that differ from one's own. I listened closely to the opinions, both for and against medication assisted treatments for opioid addiction.

The people opposed to the use of methadone, and presumably buprenorphine, didn't have facts to back their position, at least not about methadone prescribed under accepted guidelines, with appropriate controls against diversion. Most people who opposed methadone and buprenorphine said it wasn't "real" recovery, and they didn't "believe" in it, as if it were some mythical beast, like a unicorn. Addiction specialists who supported medication assisted recovery had evidence-based proof that it worked, and that many addicts could lead healthier and more productive lives.

Family

An addict, doing well in his recovery on methadone or on buprenorphine, can experience censure from both expected and unexpected sources. Ironically, family can be a huge obstacle to successful recovery with medications. Family members hear negative publicity about methadone and demand their loved one "Get off that stuff." Countless patients have told me their mother, father, or spouse pressured them into stopping the methadone. For some patients, that may be a reasonable long term goal, but if they try to stop methadone before making needed changes, their risk of relapse is high. Relapse back to active drug use damages the addict's self-esteem. Worst of all, it can be fatal.

Family members may lack even a basic understanding of methadone. When dosed properly, their loved one should look and act completely normal. A patient on an appropriate dose of methadone is able to drive and do any other activity they need to do. Families worry the addict will be asleep or sedated on methadone, but they shouldn't be, unless the dose is too high or the addict is using other drugs, and blaming the methadone for his sedation.

Sedation in a methadone patient is cause for grave concern. The family should notify the opioid treatment center if the patient ever appears sedated. The methadone treatment center isn't able to release information to the family without the patient's consent, but they can always receive information. If the clinic gets a report of sedation in a patient, it's easy to investigate. The clinic can have the patient come back about three hours after dosing, when the methadone is at its peak level, to re-assess the patient.

But even patients who are doing well on methadone get pressured to stop taking it as quickly as possible. Recently, I talked to a young man who entered methadone treatment, after using pain pills off the black market for four years. He had been able to find a better job since starting methadone at the opioid treatment center, and was able to spend time with his family, because he wasn't "out chasing pills," as he worded it. He was no longer engaged in any illegal activities. Yet, his wife wanted him to stop taking methadone, because she had read negative comments about it on the internet, including that it killed people and rotted their bones. She also objected to the money he had to spend on his treatment, three hundred dollars per month.

What she didn't know, and what our patient didn't want to tell her, was that before starting treatment at the methadone clinic, he spent at least thirty to fifty dollars per day for the pain pills he had been taking. He was very frustrated, because she was nagging him to quit the very thing that allowed such improvements in both his life and his family's.

Many opioid-addicted pregnant women get bad advice from family and friends. Forty years of studies teach us that sudden withdrawal from all opioids during pregnancy increases the risk of complications to both mother and fetus. Yet many families, with the best intentions, demand that a pregnant woman stop taking methadone, even if she is stable and doing well. These family members mean well, but they don't know the information about risks to the fetus from withdrawal.

At the time of this writing, methadone is still the best treatment for any opioid-addicted pregnant woman, though buprenorphine may become the treatment of choice very soon. Methadone should be continued through the time of delivery. This is because methadone prevents swings from intoxication to withdrawal and both the mother and fetus get a steady level of opioid. Opioid withdrawal is usually not fatal in a healthy adult, but can kill a developing fetus. Short-acting opioids like heroin give a quick high, and are preferred by addicts in active addiction. They give the addict and the fetus periods of intense highs followed by intense lows. The fetus is depleted of oxygen during the times of withdrawal, and this makes miscarriage and fetal death more likely. Other possible complications from opioid withdrawal include low birth weight, preterm labor, and obstetric complications. (1)

Sadly, new mothers often report shabby treatment from the obstetric nurses at the hospitals where they give birth. These nurses, and other hospital personnel, may judge these women harshly, not realizing that the moms are doing what is best for the baby by staying on methadone throughout pregnancy.

The newborns of mothers maintained on methadone can show physical evidence of opioid withdrawal after delivery. This is called neonatal abstinence syndrome, or NAS. Even with the disturbing and stressful complication of NAS, outcomes are better than the alternatives. Relapse rates are very high if the mother is slowly tapered off methadone, and in that case the baby would *still* be born with opioid withdrawal. The addicted mom is more likely to get prenatal care and more likely to give birth to a healthy baby with an appropriate birth weight if she remains on methadone treatment at a clinic. Both mother and child have lower complication rates around the time of delivery, if the mother is enrolled in a methadone clinic and treated with an appropriate methadone dose. (1)

In the future, buprenorphine may replace methadone as the treatment of choice for opioid-addicted pregnant women. A large study, funded by the National Institute on Drug Abuse, (NIDA) called the MOTHER (Maternal Opioid Treatment: Human Experimental Research) Trial is now underway, to compare the outcomes of pregnant patients dosing with methadone and their newborns to that of pregnant patients prescribed buprenorphine and their newborns. Early data appears to show a lower rate of neonatal abstinence syndrome in the babies of mothers on buprenorphine compared to methadone, but final data won't be available until late 2010.

Medical Community

Not many physicians in our communities are familiar with what methadone clinics do or how they work. Some physicians criticize their patients on methadone, even if the patients are doing well and are in stable recovery. Some physicians are unyielding in their opposition to methadone treatment, even though they know little about it.

When given an opportunity, I try gently to educate these doctors, and offer them information. Sometimes the doctors are open minded and receptive to information, and sometimes not. I've felt frustrated by these doctors, but I need to remember that before I knew much about methadone, I opposed it too. Back then, it just seemed wrong to give an addict methadone. I didn't have any reason for my belief, not being familiar with actual data. I try to remember my past lack of information, and have compassion for other doctors, who probably know as little about it as I did, before I worked at an opioid treatment center.

A doctor does *not* work at methadone clinics because of the professional prestige. If subspecialty prestige were a totem pole, and cardiovascular surgeons and neurosurgeons were at the top, then addiction medicine doctors would be the part of the totem pole that is underground.

Our colleagues know little about what we do, and tend to think of us as on the fringes of "legitimate" medicine, even though, as I've said before, we have more evidence-based data to support what we do than perhaps any other specialty.

For example, there exists much more data to support dosing a heroin addict with methadone than performing back surgery to remove a herniated disc. A recent study, comparing conservative treatment without surgery, to surgical removal of a herniated lumbar disc, showed that one-year rates of perceived recovery from pain were the same in both groups. (2)

When methadone maintained patients have an acute pain issue, like a broken bone, or need surgery, it's best to maintain the same dose of methadone, and let the physician treating the pain problem or doing surgery prescribe short-acting opioids for a limited time. The maintenance dose of methadone doesn't help much with pain, and can even block some of the anti-pain effect of other opioids. It's often necessary to use higher doses than usual, to treat acute pain under these circumstances. Usually, I call the other doctor involved and explain the standard and accepted way of managing this situation. I also encourage the recovering addict to find a dependable non-addict to hold his pill bottle, and dispense it as directed.

Occasionally, I encounter a physician who refuses to take care of a patient who is prescribed methadone by a treatment center. One doctor, a bariatric (weight loss) surgeon, told a patient who was doing well on methadone that she would have to taper off of methadone before he would schedule her weight loss surgery. At the patient's request, I called the surgeon. I tried to advocate for my patient, and explain that methadone patients can, and do, undergo all sorts of surgeries without difficulties. I explained the usual method of maintaining the same methadone dose while in the hospital, and giving short-acting opioids for management of pain after surgery, but this surgeon didn't relent. He didn't give me a reason for his decision, and since this was elective surgery, he had the right to refuse to do the operation.

The patient, eager to have this surgery, tapered off her methadone. It took months, and I don't know what happened to her after surgery. I do know she was at high risk for a relapse back into active addiction, particularly since she would need prescription opioids during the post-operative period. I hope she did well.

Recently, a prescription pain pill addict, also being treated for an anxiety disorder, entered treatment at the methadone treatment center where I presently work. She was seeing a psychiatrist who, in addition to counseling this patient, was prescribing alprazolam (Xanax) for anxiety. The patient hadn't told the psychiatrist about the pain pill addiction, due to shame and embarrassment. When she started methadone, I asked her permission to contact her psychiatrist, so that we could coordinate our treatments. When I spoke to this psychiatrist, she said this patient would be kicked out of her practice. The psychiatrist said, "Going on methadone goes against what I've been trying to do for her." I pressed about what she meant by this remarkable statement, but she wouldn't, or maybe couldn't, elaborate. Because this patient entered treatment for opioid addiction, she had to find a new psychiatrist.

Recently another patient went to the emergency room for a problem unrelated to her addiction. While she was there, the emergency room doctor ignorantly bawled out to her from across the treatment area saying, she needed to "get off that stuff." Then, in a double-play of incompetency, he gave her a prescription that shouldn't be given with methadone.

These are extreme examples. Many doctors don't know much about methadone, having never been taught about addiction or its treatment. After becoming more informed, many doctors are willing to work with, and not against, the opioid treatment center helping their patient.

Twelve step groups

Twelve step recovery group members often don't support an addict on methadone with their recovery. In some Narcotics Anonymous groups, methadone patients are told they're still using drugs, and they can't count the time on methadone as time in recovery. They're told they shouldn't pick up anniversary chips, until they are off of methadone. Some patients are told they can't share in meetings, because they're still using drugs.

However, Narcotics Anonymous' own literature, in their fifth tradition, states, "The only requirement for membership [in Narcotics Anonymous] is a desire to stop using." If a patient on methadone has made the effort to go to a Narcotics Anonymous meeting, that's good evidence of a desire to stop using drugs. NA publishes a booklet, "In Times of Illness," which contains information to help addicts, struggling with their choices of all types of medication use, while in recovery.

Some addicts find Alcoholics Anonymous more supportive. Even though they may not have had problems specifically with alcohol, these addicts go because they're made to feel welcome. Most Alcoholics Anonymous meetings don't discuss drugs other than alcohol. Addicts seeking recovery can apply what they learn about the twelve steps to their own drug or drugs of addiction, which may or may not include alcohol.

To avoid the feeling of ostracism that many addicts describe, I tell methadone patients not to tell people at NA meetings about prescription medication they're taking, unless they want to hear opinions of the group members. I also tell them NA meetings can be a huge benefit to them, especially if their goal is to taper off methadone and stay off all opioids.

This is the dilemma for an addict trying to recover, while on methadone or buprenorphine. If they don't tell anyone they're on medication, they feel as if they're not being honest. If they do tell, they can be ostracized for not being in "real" recovery. If addicts maintained on methadone or Suboxone are discouraged or shamed by group members, it's unlikely they'll return to NA meetings, once they're off all medication.

I suspect there are successfully recovering people on methadone or buprenorphine in Narcotics Anonymous meetings, but they don't mention their medications, and are able to get as much benefit from the meetings as any other recovering addict.

Law enforcement, legal community

Many law enforcement personnel and members of the legal community resist medication-assisted treatments. They seem to have difficulty letting go of their idea that addiction is a choice that deserves blame, and have a punitive stance towards addicts. I find it difficult to work with these professionals. They have low opinions of addicts who are using drugs, but often have no better opinion of a recovering addict who has sought treatment and is doing well on replacement medications, like methadone or buprenorphine. Law enforcement personnel have ways of letting methadone patients know they are regarded as if they're still using drugs.

When I worked at a methadone clinic in the mountains of North Carolina, we had a Tennessee resident, a pregnant woman, who committed a crime before she sought treatment at our methadone clinic. By the time she was sentenced to three months of incarceration, she was seven months pregnant. She asked to begin her sentence after delivering her child and her request was denied by the judge. He said he would cure her addiction by placing her in jail and then, at least, the baby wouldn't be born addicted to methadone. He had been informed she was in treatment at a methadone clinic in North Carolina.

The patient contacted her counselor at the methadone clinic, in a panic, because she knew she could miscarry if denied methadone. Opioid withdrawal could even kill her fetus. Her counselor called me and related all of the details.

I was surprised that a judge would make a medical decision like that, and if he did, it was only because he didn't have information about methadone. I called the judge's office, but couldn't get through to him. I explained everything to his clerk, and believed the patient would either be given methadone in jail or have her sentence postponed.

The next day the patient called, and said she was still going to start her sentence in two days, and that the judge hadn't changed his mind. I called the judge again, and was told the judge wasn't going to come to the phone to speak with me, the clerk had relayed the message, the mother was going to jail and no, she would not be given methadone.

Now irritated and worried, I composed a letter, detailing the possible medical complications that could occur, as a result of the judge's uninformed and ill-advised decision, and told him this was a medical decision that should be made by doctors. I described the preterm labor that could occur, if the mother was allowed to go into withdrawal. The fetus may not be able to survive if born at seven months' gestation. I ended with a plea that no matter what he thought of the mother, the baby at least should be given the best chance for survival. I faxed a copy to the judge and a copy to the patient's lawyer. Later, I heard she was allowed to deliver a healthy baby boy, prior to beginning her three month sentence.

Recently, I was asked to speak at an addictions conference, in the heart of the Blue Ridge Mountains, about methadone and its use in the treatment of opioid addiction. The speaker who gave a presentation after me was a lawyer with the local drug court. He explained how drug court got addicts, who committed crimes related to drug use, to participate in treatment, rather than just sending them to jail.

During the question and answer session, he was asked if patients on methadone could participate in the drug court program. He said no. When asked why this was, he said that to participate, the addicts must be completely drug free. Another member of the audience asked why this was the case, if methadone was a legitimate treatment and it had been started by a physician.

The lawyer did not give a clear answer, but turned to the program director of a local outpatient treatment center, sitting in the audience. The drug court contracts with this outpatient treatment center, to provide the counseling needed for the addicts participating in drug court. This program director said that addicts on methadone couldn't come to the counseling his center provided because they "would give their methadone to other patients and nod off in treatment sessions."

This was a clear example of the biases methadone patients face. I had just completed a lecture about methadone and had explained how opioid treatment center patients don't receive take home doses for at least the first three months, and how patients on the right dose are not sedated, unless they use nerve pills or other sedatives. In the above case, both the court and the treatment program were opposed to methadone, and they didn't have a clear policy on buprenorphine.

That said, at present, the majority of drug courts don't allow participants to be on methadone, though methadone has been shown to be very cost effective as well as beneficial to opioid addicts.

At Rikers Island, in New York City, opioid-addicted prisoners charged with misdemeanors or low grade felonies can be enrolled in a program known as KEEP (Key Extended Entry Program). This program treats opioid addicts with methadone and counseling. Upon release from Rikers Island, these patients are referred to methadone treatment centers in the community. Seventy-six percent have followed through with their treatment, post-release. The results of this program show *significant reduction in reincarceration and significant reduction in criminal activity*.

Drug courts would be well-advised to look at the Rikers Island program, for an example of the effectiveness of methadone maintenance. They should also consider the amount of money it can save the community. Studies have shown a cost savings of at least four dollars for every one dollar spent on methadone treatment. This money is saved because methadone patients require fewer days of hospitalization and other healthcare costs, and also because of reduction in criminal activity and incarceration costs. (3)

Many jails will not dispense methadone to prisoners who are patients in at a methadone clinic, even if they are doing well and on a stable dose. Many times, these patients are allowed to go through a terrible withdrawal. Patients tell me they have been taunted for being ill from withdrawal from methadone, and refused access to medical care. This refusal to treat an illness with an accepted and effective medication has been costly to at least one county in Florida.

In 1997, an Orange county jail inmate died after being denied her usual dose of methadone. She spent twelve days in withdrawal, before she was found dead in her cell. The family sued the county and won a three million dollar settlement. (4) Then in 2000, a second person died in the very same Orange county jail, under nearly identical circumstances. (5) She had been a patient at a methadone clinic for about five months, before entering the jail. She was denied her medication, and was found unconscious three days later, from an apparent seizure. She was then taken to a hospital, and her family removed her from life support five days later.

In 2001, Orange County decided to offer methadone to patients who were already established at a methadone clinic, and continue their dosing. They've worked out arrangements with a local methadone clinic to provide the necessary methadone. Opioid addicts who are not established in any kind of treatment are treated with a standard opioid withdrawal protocol. Soon, Orange County may begin to use buprenorphine in this jail setting. More jail facilities would be wise to heed the experience of Orange County.

In Cook County, Illinois, a man serving a ten day traffic violation died of methadone withdrawal on his sixth day of imprisonment. He was an established patient of a methadone clinic, but the jail refused to provide his methadone medication. He made repeated requests for medical attention, but was denied care, despite his obvious physical suffering, witnessed by at least three jail employees. (6) He died of a ruptured cerebral aneurysm, as a result of opioid withdrawal. His wife and estate sued the county, for failing to provide timely medical treatment, charging them with deliberate indifference to the suffering of the prisoner.

I'm glad to see these lawsuits. I've heard appalling stories from many methadone patients, who were denied their medication while incarcerated. I've heard tales of jailers taunting these prisoners, when they became sick. There is no defense for such cruelty.

On a positive note, more jails and prisons across the U.S. are beginning to offer access to medication assisted therapies, with both methadone and buprenorphine. Colorado has several counties that coordinate care with local treatment centers. A clinic within Albuquerque's city detention center offers treatment with methadone. Rhode Island's department of corrections contracts with a local treatment center, to treat opioid addiction. The jail in Seattle-King County, Washington, plans to offer both methadone and buprenorphine soon.

Community opposition – NIMBY (Not In My Backyard)

Local people judge methadone clinics by how their sickest patients are doing. Most methadone patients have great success, and become reunited with their families. They find jobs, go to work, and become drug free while maintained on methadone. But no one recognizes these thriving patients as addicts maintained on methadone, because they quietly go about their life. They work, raise children, and function like anyone else, except they take a daily dose of methadone. Some will taper off methadone, and some plan to stay on it indefinitely. They know better than to tell friends and neighbors they go to the methadone clinic, since they know the kind of negative comments they're likely to hear.

The few patients who aren't doing well can rile the whole community against a clinic. In some clinics, benzodiazepine (drugs like Xanax and Valium) use is rampant. Even one patient, high on a combination of nerve pills and methadone, can cause a great deal of consternation in the community. People of the community then think all patients on methadone behave this way. However, most patients on methadone treatment have improvement in many areas of their lives.

Meanwhile, communities across the nation start petitions, to prevent methadone clinics from opening in their town, saying it will bring addicts and their crime with them.

From the Kingsport, Tennessee Times-News, 3/18/09,

> "The Church Hill Board of Mayor and Aldermen unanimously approved the first reading Tuesday of an ordinance which, in essence, makes it almost impossible for a methadone clinic to locate within the city limits.
>
> Earlier this month, the Planning Commission recommended the ordinance, which restricts methadone clinics and drug treatment facilities to areas of the city that are zoned M-1 (manufacturing). Without the ordinance, methadone clinics and drug

treatment facilities would be permitted in any area of the city zoned to allow medical uses."

"I think we're all in the consensus that we don't want it any-where," the alderman said (name deleted). (7)

Kingsport is located in the far Eastern portion of Tennessee, one of the handfuls of areas in the U.S. with the very highest rates of opioid addiction. Yet *no* new drug treatment facility *of any type* will be allowed within their city limits.

Many citizens object to the presence of a methadone clinic in their community, because they fear a clinic will bring drug dealing and increased crime. They fear a clinic will attract addicts to their city.

In reality, we know where the opioid addicts are. Large national studies give us that information, as well as the patterns of prescription opioid distribution. Addicts don't usually all gather together in one group, or advertise their presence, so most people are unaware of their existence in the community. We can again refer to a map of rates of opioid addiction.

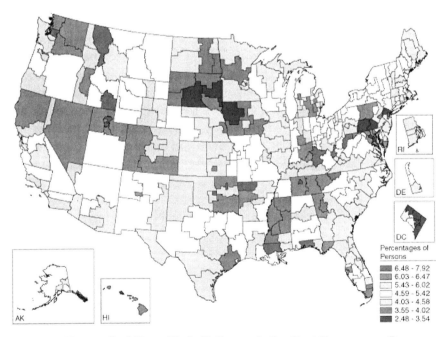

Figure 1. Nonmedical Use of Pain Relievers in the Past Year among Persons Aged 12 or Older, by Substate Region*: Percentages, Annual Averages Based on 2004, 2005, and 2006 National Survey of Drug Use in Households

As described in previous chapters, a well-run clinic reduces crime. Even if the citizens of Kingsport, Tennessee don't care about the human suffering of addiction, a methadone clinic would at least keep their possessions safer from theft.

But if a clinic is poorly run, there *can* be negative effects on nearby businesses. Besides attention to security, clinics probably should limit the number of patients at any one clinic site. When a methadone clinic exceeds two hundred and fifty people, chaos—which negatively impacts the community—is more likely to occur. If more than two hundred and fifty patients in the community need methadone treatment, then perhaps that clinic should open a second site. Sloppily run methadone clinics sometimes deserve their bad reputations in communities.

Methadone clinics shouldn't be in residential areas, to keep possible bad behavior from rogue patients at a minimum, and to maintain community goodwill. Clinics should be located in industrial areas or in medical parks. Most patients attending an opioid treatment center are serious about getting help, and they do very well, but there will always be a few patients with problem behaviors.

Patients

Patients sometimes feel ambivalent or reluctant towards methadone, too. Patients tell me they don't want to take a pill to cure a problem that pills caused in the first place. Addicts often used prescription medications in ways they were not intended, but in medication-assisted treatment, medications are used as medications, not like drugs. In recovery, it's often helpful, and even necessary, to use medication.

Many patients enter the clinic and say they don't want to be on methadone very long, just a couple of weeks. They think they'll taper off methadone quickly and be fine. I tell them that methadone clinics are for patients who aren't ready to completely stop opioids, for whatever reason. If the patient's goal is to get off opioids as quickly as possible, methadone maintenance isn't the treatment of choice. This patient should consider if it's possible to go into an inpatient treatment program. It takes months, sometimes years, to stabilize, get counseling, and taper off methadone, if that's what the patient desires.

Some patients overestimate their ability to withstand withdrawal, both physical and psychological, and ask to come off methadone too fast or too soon. Staff can talk to the patient and give them our recommendations, but in the end, if a patient wants to lower their dose, the clinic must do so, after making sure the patient is given the best recommendations by the clinic.

Methadone maintenance costs significant time and money for patients. Even though the cost and time are almost always less than addicts spent in active addiction, it's still a burden for many addicts and their families. Vacations must be planned carefully, to allow methadone patients to continue their daily dose of medication when they travel out of town. This may involve "guest dosing." When a patient who doesn't have take home doses, either because he hasn't been with the clinic long enough, or because of continued drug use, wants to travel out of town, he can get his usual dose at an opioid treatment center in that town. The home clinic faxes information to the out of town clinic, and he gets his dose from that clinic.

This is usually more expensive than dosing at a home clinic. Some opioid treatment centers charge as much as twenty-five dollars per day for out-of-town "guest dosers." Some clinics also charge a fee the first time they guest dose a patient from out of town. A patient may need to travel to an area that doesn't have any treatment centers. In that case, the government can be petitioned for extra take home doses. However, state and federal governments rarely approve more than one extra dose, above the usual number of take homes that the patient gets per week.

Patients who frequently work out of town usually can't get treatment at a methadone clinic, because of the state and federal regulations. They are better candidates for buprenorphine treatment, as it can be prescribed for weeks at a time, even for addiction treatment, so long as the patient is doing well.

At times, doctors in the field of addiction medicine underestimate the emotional burden addicts feel, from depending on a clinic or physician to supply them with methadone or buprenorphine. Some clinics may use the methadone dose as a way of punishing patients for bad behavior, an unethical policy, which causes an adversarial relationship between the clinic personnel and the patient. Patients fear the medication they need to function may be changed at the clinic's whim.

Sadly, clinic personnel occasionally behave badly towards patients. Addiction treatment professionals have let personal feelings toward some addicts color their decisions. They can play favorites, or even worse, punish a patient, because of their own feelings toward an addict.

Seeing this, it's no wonder some patients may, at times, feel their dose or take home schedule can be changed at the whim of the clinic's counselor, doctor, or program manager.

Clinics *must* watch closely for such unprofessional behavior among all staff. One system of checks and balances can come at case staffing meetings. This is when all parties who have a role in an addict's treatment come together to discuss how the patient is doing. At these meetings, members of the treatment team need to watch each other for indications of bad feelings towards individual patients. The counselors, doctors, and nurses who work at methadone clinics are only human, and dealing with addiction can be draining. The disease of addiction can create behavior that could make a saint swear like a sailor, but treatment personnel must learn not to personalize the behavior of addicts, and deliver professional care.

I wish people could see the changes that medication assisted treatment brings. I've seen so many good people, who became addicted to opioids and it nearly ruined their lives, so they enrolled in a methadone treatment center. Then, they began to feel better, look better, find jobs, spend time with their families, and in general began to lead normal lives, because the obsession with drugs and the compulsion to use drugs abated with methadone. The only thing they need to do is take a daily dose of medication, either at the methadone clinic or at home once a day. These are the patients for whom methadone or buprenorphine is literally live saving.

However, I've seen patients admitted multiple times to the same opioid treatment program, who continued to use other drugs. If they used alcohol or other sedatives, they risked their own lives and those around them, particularly if they drove while impaired. Counselors attempted to intensify sessions, required group meetings and pursued other measures, all to no avail. These patients shouldn't be on methadone, because it is too risky.

There are good doctors who would disagree with both of the above statements. Even some addictionologists are so rabidly anti-methadone, they won't consider the heaps of statistics that show methadone's benefits. By the same token, there are doctors and clinics, so sure they're doing the right thing by retaining their patients in methadone treatment at all costs, they don't heed the dangers.

Methadone, like so many other medical treatments, can work very well in some patients, but it's not the best option for all opioid addicted patients. No one treatment works for every addict. Methadone is not a panacea, just as therapeutic communities or buprenorphine are not panaceas.

Addiction Treatment Field

Some of the most vehement objections to methadone come, ironically, from the addiction treatment field. Methadone is, by its very nature, a harm reduction endeavor. Harm reduction refers to a form of treatment, or an intervention, that doesn't stop all drug use, but reduces the harm done to the individual by his or her addiction. Needle exchange programs are examples of harm reduction. Used needles are brought to needle exchange programs by intravenous drug addicts and, in exchange, they're given new, clean needles. This markedly reduces the spread of HIV and other communicable illness, and at times, can provide an opportunity to talk about drug addiction treatment with these addicts. However, needle exchange doesn't keep addicts from using, and some critics say it promotes drug use.

One person's harm reduction is another person's enabling.

Uttering the phrase, "harm reduction," can produce results akin to waving a red cape in front of a bull, if said in front of people with anti-medication mindsets. These treatment professionals advocate complete abstinence from all drugs as the only worthwhile goal of addiction treatment. They argue that, while harm reduction is good as far as it goes, it cheats the patient out of the full benefits of complete drug free recovery. They claim the good (medicating opioid addicts with methadone or buprenorphine) becomes the enemy of the best (complete abstinence from all drugs).

On the other side, many treatment professionals recognize that harm reduction has a legitimate place in addiction treatment. Many addicts entering treatment aren't yet ready to give up all drugs. Studies clearly show that the longer these addicts are retained in treatment, the better their outcomes will be. They would argue that no patient, with the disease of addiction, should be required to leave an addiction treatment program due to drug use, because drug use is a symptom of their disease. Internationally, most countries have more of a harm reduction approach to addiction treatment. Our foreign colleagues view the abstinence-only treatment approach with puzzlement.

Treatment professionals who back harm reduction policies point out that "Dead addicts don't recover." In other words, anything we can do to keep addicts alive and safer, while using drugs, makes it possible for addicts to survive long enough to enter a "better" treatment, later in their lives, whether that better treatment is abstinence based or medication assisted.

The addiction treatment field has been reluctant to accept the use of medication-assisted therapies of all sorts, but particularly resistant to the use of methadone and buprenorphine. When I first started seeing patients on buprenorphine, part of my job was to get them involved in counseling, and I recommended an intensive outpatient program in the city for my first few patients. I was shocked, when my patients reported they were turned down for admission to the outpatient program, because "they were still on drugs," and told to come back once they were off the Suboxone.

I called the director of this treatment center. I tried to explain that these patients will not be impaired in any way, and they need counseling, to obtain the tools of recovery to either get off opioids completely, as was the goal of some of the patients, or learn to stay in good recovery, while on buprenorphine. The director did listen to me, but insisted that any entering patient must undergo a taper off of the buprenorphine within six weeks, meaning the taper would end at the same time their intensive treatment ended.

However, studies show that six weeks is usually not long enough for stabilization, and a predetermined time limit may set patients up for failure.

This private treatment center certainly has the right to turn down patients, or accept them only with their own imposed conditions, but where does that leave opioid addicts, who are on medication-assisted therapies? The goal of the DATA 2000 law was to allow opioid addicts to get medication from their primary care or addiction medicine doctors, and be referred for counseling. But the very treatment centers we hoped would provide counseling for them refuse to see them.

Essentially, physicians prescribing buprenorphine are being forced to set up their own outpatient programs, if they can't find an existing treatment center to accept these patients. Most physicians lack counseling experience, particularly in group settings, which can be so helpful in the treatment of addiction. The physicians I know, who prescribe buprenorphine, have had to either look for therapists who are willing to work with patients on medication, try to do it themselves, or refer to 12-step groups like Narcotics Anonymous or Alcoholics Anonymous.

The treatment center mentioned above is a good facility, run by diligent clinicians. They honestly believe their way is the best, and they may have success with opioid addicts who have a strong desire to be completely drug free. The attitude of their personnel is not unusual; rather, it is common. Treatment centers seem to fear that patients on medications will contaminate the treatment setting, and somehow taint all of their "good" patients.

But this belief is on shaky ground, if you consider the science of addiction. The science of opioid addiction shows that there are changes in the biology and structure of the brain that may never return to normal, even with prolonged abstinence. Many opioid addicts don't do well with abstinence-based treatment, and continue to have relapses back to opioid addiction.

Workers in the field of addiction treatment are no different from other humans. It's difficult for humans to change our ways of thinking, when we're confronted with new information. The irony is that changing one's thinking is exactly what treatment centers try to teach their patients.

I met a skilled drug addiction counselor, previously addicted to heroin, who became abstinent from all drugs, by going to meetings of Narcotics Anonymous. She had been a patient of methadone clinics off and on for many years, prior to getting clean. I met her after she had more than ten years of completely abstinent recovery, yet she happily works at a methadone clinic, helping opioid addicts. I interviewed her because of her personal experience and her striking open-mindedness to different approaches to the treatment of addiction. Here is what she had to say about her experiences with methadone, and her perspective:

JB: Can you please tell me your personal experience of opioid addiction?

RJ: Well, my personal experience began at the age of...probably eighteen....and I was introduced by some people I was hanging out with. I was basically very ignorant about those kinds of things. I wasn't aware of that kind of stuff going on, 'cause I was raised in this real small town and just didn't know this kind of stuff happened.

My first experience was with a Dilaudid. Somebody said we had to go somewhere else to do it, and I really didn't understand that, because I certainly didn't know that it would be injected. That was my first experience with a narcotic, with opiates, and....I fell in love!

I loved it. I injected it, and the feeling was.....like none I had ever felt. And even though I did get sick, I thought it was what I was looking for. It was the best feeling in the world.

Obviously, they didn't tell me about getting sick, [meaning opioid withdrawal] and that after doing it for some days consecutively, when you didn't have any, you'd get sick. I never will forget the first time I was sick from not having any.

And that lead to a habit that lasted twenty-some years. My experience and my path led me down many roads... with addiction, going back and forth to prison, because I obviously didn't make enough money to purchase these drugs that I needed to have in my body, to keep from being sick. This lasted for twenty four years. I ended up doing heroin and I liked it, because it tended to be stronger. Morphine I liked a lot, but it wasn't easily accessible, so I switched over to heroin at some point. Which I liked a lot.

JB: What role did methadone play in your recovery?

RJ: I've been in numerous methadone clinics. I typically would get on methadone when I got a charge [meaning legal problems] and I wanted to call myself being in treatment. I never ever got on methadone with any expectations, hopes, or thoughts of changing my life. I got on because it kept me from being sick. And it kept me off the street for a period of time. If I had a charge, I was in treatment and I always thought that would help me in my journeys with the legal systems. That was the part methadone played in my life, it was just to help me get through it.

JB: Did it help you?

RJ: At the time, it did. My problem with methadone was, when I would get on methadone, I would tend to do cocaine, because I could feel the cocaine, and I wasn't about changing anything. I just wanted temporary fixes in my life. I'd switch to cocaine while I was on methadone. And it [methadone] worked for a time. I never got any take homes, because I continued to test positive for other substances while I was on methadone, but I thought I was doing better, 'cause I was not doing narcotics. In that aspect it did help.

JB: And you've been in recovery from addiction now for how long?

RJ: It will be fifteen years in June.

JB: Wonderful!

KS: Yes, it is wonderful.

JB: And tell me where you work now.

RJ: I work at a methadone treatment facility.

JB: How long have you been working there?

RJ: I've been there for almost fourteen years and in this [satellite] clinic for a little over two years, and I've been in methadone [as a counselor] for five years.

JB: How do you feel about methadone and what role it should play in the treatment of opioid addiction?

RJ: I believe in methadone. Our [her clinic's] philosophy certainly is not harm reduction but I believe that's what it's about. And I do believe that those people on methadone, and are doing well, have a home, have a life, I think that's all they aspire to. For them that's enough, you know, they're not out ripping and running the roads, they're not looking for drugs on a daily basis. They come and get their methadone, they go to work, they have a life, they have a family, they have a home, and for them that's good enough.

JB: Do you think it keeps them from getting completely clean [I purposely chose to use her language to differentiate being in recovery on methadone from being in recovery and completely off all opioids]?

RJ: No. I think they know they have a choice.

JB: OK

RJ: I really believe that a lot of them don't think that they can ever do anything differently, and I know from personal experience that can be very true. I think that you just get so bogged down in your disease that you don't see any way out. I think if you can find a place where you can get something legally and you're not using the street drugs, and you're not out copping [buying drugs] and you're working and basically having a life, then that becomes OK, and that becomes good enough.

And addicts by nature are scared of change, and they get in that role and they get comfortable and that's good enough for them. So I don't believe they think that they can do any better.

JB: What percentages of your patients have already used street methadone by the time they get to the clinic?

RJ: I'd say seventy-five percent. Very rarely do I do an assessment [on a new patient] that somebody hasn't already used methadone on the street. Very rarely.

JB: What are your biggest challenges where you work?

RJ: Actually my biggest challenges where I work are internal challenges. Fighting that uphill battle of no consequences for clients. There's no consequences. We allow them to do basically what they want to do. [She is speaking of her methadone clinic's style of interaction with patients].

JB: Do you think patients did better when there were a few consequences?

RJ: Oh yeah. Yeah. I mean, when certain clients can continue to have the same behaviors, like use benzos [meaning benzodiazepines like Valium and Xanax] and there are no consequences, certainly they are going to continue doing those behaviors. And those are the things that are challenges now, for us, for me.

I can't enforce any consequences because we're not allowed to, because it's called punishment. The powers that be, they see it as punishment, where I work. Being that I come from living a life of doing the wrong thing always, I'm a big believer in consequences. And I believe that if you don't have any, you continue to do those things. That's the kind of stuff, the inadequacies where I work at.

JB: What do you like most about your job?

RJ: (pause) The light…. in somebody's eyes every now and again. It might not happen much, but now and again the light comes on, and you have that "ah ha" moment. They have it, and you're like, yes! Or when somebody comes and tells you they have that little spark of hope. Yep. That's what I like most about my job.

JB: If you could make changes in how opioid addiction is treated, what would you do? If you could tell the people who make the drug laws, what would you recommend? How would you change the system, or would you?

RJ: I don't know that I would change the system. I think the system works. I think it's individual facilities that don't work sometimes. Yeah. I think – methadone's been around a long time – I mean, obviously it's worked for a lot of years or it wouldn't still be in existence. I think methadone maintenance programs work, but each individual facility maybe needs to make changes. You know, that's just my opinion.

JB: If you were the boss of a methadone treatment center, how would you handle benzodiazepine use by patients?

RJ: They wouldn't be tolerated. At all.

JB: Why is that?

RJ: Because I think they kill people. I know they kill people.

JB: How about alcohol?

RJ: Alcohol wouldn't be tolerated either. I mean, obviously you would be given a chance to straighten it and rectify it and clean it up, with help, if you need it. But that would be it. You would get that opportunity and then [if the patient couldn't stop using alcohol] you would be detoxed from that program. I believe that's the route to go. We've had too many deaths. And there's nothing to say that it's not going to continue to happen…so, yeah, if I had a facility it would not be tolerated. There would be zero tolerance, period. There just wouldn't be any.

JB: What do you say to people that say that's keeping people out of treatment?

RJ: There are other types of treatment; maybe you need a different level of care. Maybe methadone's not the answer.

JB: So you don't think methadone's the answer for every opioid addict?

RJ: No. No I don't.

JB: What do you think about people on methadone coming to Narcotics Anonymous?

RJ: I think they have a right to come to Narcotics Anonymous.

JB: Do you think they should share?

RJ: I wish they could share, but I know, there again from personal experience, how methadone is viewed by people in Narcotics Anonymous. And I think that if that person does share [that they are on methadone], they are treated differently.

JB: Do you tell your patients to go to NA?

RJ: I do.

JB: What do you tell them about picking up chips?

RJ: That's their personal call, because I feel like it is. But then I don't view methadone as using. See, I look at it as treatment, and somebody taking medication because they're sick, and trying to get better. So I don't view that as getting up and doing dope. Therefore if I were on methadone and going to meetings, I'd pick up chips.

JB: Can you think of anything else [you'd like to say]?

RJ: I believe in methadone. I really do. I just believe that it works. I know people who have been on our program for twenty years, and granted, those people will never get off methadone, but they have a life today. And twenty years ago they didn't have one. They're not perfect but I'm not either, you know, just 'cause I don't use dope any more. But they're still suffering addicts, just like I am. So I just believe that methadone works, and if you want to make changes in your life, that there are people at every facility who are willing to help you make those changes.

Treatment professionals can also make the mistake of dismissing non-medication treatment of opioid addiction as ineffective, when clearly this is not true. Though treatment with methadone and buprenorphine can provide enormous benefit, so can the other medication-free forms of treatment. And as we have seen, methadone can cause great harm when used inappropriately, and some opioid addicts don't do well on methadone.

There's no one best treatment path for every addict. Every evidence-based treatment helps some addicts.

Endnotes

1. Helmbrecht, GD, MD, FACOG, and Thiagarajah, S, MD, FACOG, "Management of Addiction Disorders in Pregnancy, *Journal of Addiction Medicine*, 2 (March, 2008), pp. 1 – 16.
2. Peul, WC, et.al., *Surgery Versus Prolonged Conservative Treatment for Sciatica*, New England Journal of Medicine, Vol. 356: pp. 2245 – 2256, May 31, 2007.
3. California Department of Drug and Alcohol Programs, 2004, *California drug and alcohol treatment assessment (CALDATA)* California Department of Alcohol and Drug Programs. California Drug and Alcohol Treatment Assessment (CALDATA), 1991-1993 [Computer File]. ICPSR02295-v2. Ann Arbor, MI: Inter-university Consortium for Political and Social Research [distributor], 2008-10-07. doi:10.3886/ICPSR02295
4. "Outrageous: the death of Susan Bennett raises serious questions about the competence and quality of the jail's nursing staff" Orlando Sentinel, editorial, March 27, 1998.
5. Doris Bloodsworth, "Inmate begged for methadone" Orlando Sentinel July 12, 2001.
6. Davis vs Carter, #05-1695 US Court of Appeals, Seventh Circuit http://openjurist.org/452/f3d/686/davis-v-carter
7. Jeff Bobo, "Church Hill Commission Moves to Prevent Methadone Clinic" Kingsport Times-News, 3/2/09.

CHAPTER 15

What now? Prescription for Hope

I will lift up mine eyes unto the pills. Almost everyone takes them, from the humble aspirin to the multi-coloured, king-sized three deckers, which put you to sleep, wake you up, stimulate and soothe you all in one. It is an age of pills.

~Malcolm Muggeridge

Now that we've examined the problem of pain pill addiction in the United States, and the treatments available, what should we do? How can we better prevent and treat this addiction?

We need to pay attention to the lessons learned in the past century and the last two decades, as outlined earlier in the book. We need to open our minds and the minds of government officials, law enforcement, medical practitioners, and individuals. We need to understand how opioids work, and we need to accept addiction as a chronic disease, which can be treated, if the addict is willing to recover.

The following pages provide guidelines to accomplish this, based on the material and research contained in earlier chapters of the book. This chapter is a comprehensive summary of methods to avoid opioid addiction, and to provide treatments that work for those who are already addicted. This chapter outlines the necessary steps that need to be taken at the individual local, state, and federal levels.

Before anything else, we need to stop creating more addiction.

Fortunately, pain management doctors have already recognized that overzealous prescribing of opioids creates addiction in susceptible patients. These pain patients then develop a second disease — prescription pain pill addiction — in addition to chronic pain. Instead of a one percent incidence, as estimated by pain medicine specialists in the past, it appears that from eighteen to forty-five percent of patients, maintained long-term on opioids, develop opioid addiction. (1)

The American Academy of Pain Medicine recently updated their published guidelines regarding the prescribing of opioids for non-cancer pain. These guidelines describe the precautions that pain management physicians should take, and ways to screen patients being considered for long-term opioid treatment. (2) The physician assesses the risk, and then informs the patient of this risk. Studies show that a personal past history of addiction is the strongest predictor of future problems with addiction, as may be expected. A family history of addiction increases the risk of addiction, as do serious psychiatric illnesses, like mood disorders and anxiety disorders. (2)

If the physician and patient decide the potential benefits of long-term opioid treatment outweigh the risks, the physician should use precautions, like monitoring agreements between the patient and the doctor. These agreements explicitly state what the physician expects from a patient for whom she prescribes opioids, such as avoidance of alcohol and any illicit drugs, and the need for random urine drug testing. Written agreements reduce the risk of misunderstandings.

Physicians may ask patients to have random pill counts done at their pharmacy. People who sell their prescriptions will have fewer pills remaining in their bottle than they should. Physicians can also use pill counts to detect patients with addiction who binge on medication, take pills too quickly, and then run out of medication early. Pill counts help identify patients with addiction, and also identify "patients" who want to divert their prescribed medication to the black market. Pill counts are an inconvenience for pain patients who don't have addiction, but may help keep opioids available for patients who need them.

Physicians should consider non-opioid methods to treat chronic pain in high risk patients. Granted, these methods are usually less effective, and aren't as easy as taking an opioid pill, but may bring pain to a manageable level without opioids.

Physical methods, like massage, physical therapy, heat/cold treatments, and TENS units can help some patients with some types of pain. Neuropathic pain may be improved with anti-seizure medications. Other prescription medications, like anti-inflammatory analgesics (ibuprofen, naproxen) or muscle relaxants, can be considered. Some patients prefer alternative treatments, like guided imagery, relaxation techniques, and acupuncture, but it's harder to find skilled practitioners for these methods. Also, they may not be covered by insurance.

There are other methods to treat chronic pain, though they tend to cost more, and require more time to produce results than prescription opioids.

Physicians and patients should be aware of the phenomenon of hyperesthesia. This is a condition of decreased pain tolerance, seen in some patients who take opioids for more than three months. With hyperesthesia, patients actually become *more* sensitive to painful stimuli of all kinds. We think this condition is caused by the changes the body makes when patients are on opioids for a long period of time. Thus, some patients taking opioid pain medications ironically end up having *more* pain because of their medication. Methadone-maintained patients may have hyperesthesia.

Both physicians and patients need to be aware of the lack of studies showing benefits for long-term (more than three months) opioid prescription. Guidelines for the treatment of chronic, non-cancer pain changed, to reflect this awareness that prolonged opioid prescription may have risks that outweigh the benefits.

Physicians need better education about how to prescribe opioids to treat pain, and better education about identifying and treating addiction. Medical students will treat many patients with pain, addiction, or both, throughout their careers. They need specific training for these medical issues. Doctors entering training in residency programs need to be taught, and re-taught, about pain, prescription of opioids, addiction, and addiction treatment options

Primary care specialties, like Family Medicine, Internal Medicine, OB/GYN, Emergency Medicine, and even Pediatrics need extra training in identifying and treating addiction, since primary care doctors are usually the first medical professionals to encounter patients addicted to drugs, including alcohol.

Many secondary medical issues spring from drug and alcohol addiction. Physicians should know at least as much about recognition and treatment of addiction as we do about the illnesses, like pancreatitis and endocarditis, that spring directly from addiction. Primary care physicians should develop good working relationships with addiction medicine specialists and treatment centers in their area.

As we saw in previous chapters, most U.S. physicians aren't skilled at identifying, much less treating, addictive disorders. Physicians already in practice obviously need specific education about opioids, pain, and addiction. The government recently began to consider if they need to require more intense training for physicians who want to prescribe the potentially highly addicting schedule II medications, including methadone and other powerful opioids.

Doctors who prescribe these strong medications need to be able to diagnose the complication of addictive diseases in their patients. Currently, no special training is required to prescribe these strong medications, other than a DEA license. The training would be a refresher course for some physicians, and new material for others, who weren't taught these subjects in their medical education.

In 2008, ASAM (American Society of Addiction Medicine) received a three-year, 1.5 million dollar grant from SAMHSA, to organize programs that help educate physicians about the best ways to prescribe methadone. This program is called the Physician Clinical Support System. Physicians with little experience prescribing methadone can access information and help – on the phone, via email, and sometimes even in person – from doctors who are experienced and adept at prescribing methadone. This is a free mentoring program, for physicians beginning to prescribe methadone. A similar program is in place for physicians starting to prescribe buprenorphine.

Besides SAMHSA's grant to ASAM, other government agencies have enacted plans to reduce opioid addiction. In 2009, The FDA started the Risk Evaluation and Management Strategy program, or REMS, to identify and manage risks of potentially harmful medications. Under the REMS program, manufacturers of strong opioids may be required to have a plan to monitor and manage the risks of that drug. The REMS plan has not yet been required of older opioids, but this may happen in the future.

One of the first drugs to have a REMS in place was Onsolis, a new form of the powerful opioid fentanyl. The fentanyl is contained in a film that dissolves in the mouth, making it suitable for patients in severe pain who are unable to swallow liquids. Because of the high risk of overdose death for patients unaccustomed to such a powerful opioid, and because of the desirability of fentanyl to opioid addicts, the drug will be available only through a restricted distribution program. Physicians and pharmacists have to register with the drug's manufacturer before they can prescribe and dispense Onsolis. Patients prescribed Onsolis also have to register with the drug manufacturer. With such scrutiny, diversion to the black market is much less likely to occur.

Some physicians and patients are concerned the REMS program will require more time and documentation from already busy physicians, making them less willing to prescribe drugs with REMS regulations. This may mean that non-addicted pain patients who require strong opioids will have difficulty finding a doctor willing to prescribe them. Some physicians predict that if the schedule II opioids fall under REMS programs, physicians will switch to the less potent Schedule III drugs, like hydrocodone and immediate release oxycodone. These drugs would be less trouble for the physician to prescribe, but they contain acetaminophen (Tylenol). If addicts take enough of these milder opioids to achieve the same results as the Schedule II drugs, they can develop liver failure from acetaminophen poisoning.

As of this date, not enough is known about future REMS programs. The FDA is hoping to have ways to reduce the risk of some dangerous drugs, without unduly restricting access. Depending on how the REMS programs are executed, they could be helpful, lifesaving strategies, or ineffective red tape, barring appropriate prescribing, and creating unintended consequences.

REMS may make it more difficult for people to share their prescription opioids with friends and family members. As discussed in previous chapters, sharing prescription medication, even controlled substances, seems to be a cultural norm in the U.S. Over half of the people abusing opioids said they initially got them for free from friends and family. Around seventy percent of the pain pills that are abused were obtained from friends and family. It is important to help people realize how harmful this can be, and change this cultural norm. (4)

SAMHSA has started to sponsor conferences to help physicians learn more about the safe treatment of pain with opioids, and the proper use of methadone in opioid treatment centers. In September of 2009, North Carolina hosted a SAMHSA conference meant to teach doctors and nurses who work in opioid treatment centers how to use methadone safely. It was titled "OTP Clinical Staff Education: Appropriate Use of Methadone in the OTP." This pilot project will be presented in a limited number of states, probably the states with the highest methadone mortality rates. The results will be evaluated, and in the future, such a course may be required for doctors who wish to work in opioid treatment centers.

The course covered all of the basic facts all doctors and nurses working in opioid treatment centers should already know. However, the course presenters didn't take definitive stands on controversial issues, like benzodiazepine use in methadone patients, EKG screening, and how or if pain pill addicts differ from heroin addicts. They also didn't say much about whether a maintenance- to abstinence plan is appropriate for some patients.

To be fair, most of these questions don't have enough data for definitive answers. Studies are ongoing with pain pill addicts, to see if their outcomes mirror that of heroin addicts. Studies of the true incidence of QT prolongation from methadone are ongoing, which hopefully will provide information to guide decisions about who needs EKG screenings, and how often. Treatment of the benzodiazepine addicted patient enrolled in a methadone clinic is perhaps more art than science, given the drastic differences in how clinics in my state handle this issue.

SAMHSA's one-day methadone training program is a marvelous idea for anyone who is relatively inexperienced at prescribing methadone. It's reasonable to require such training for doctors before they begin work at an opioid treatment center. After all, buprenorphine, a schedule III drug which is weaker and safer than methadone, requires eight hours of training before physicians can prescribe it to treat addiction. It makes sense to require at least as much training for a more powerful drug, like methadone. With the new REMS program, it's possible that in the future the FDA will require doctors to prove competence before being allowed to prescribe stronger opioids.

Doctors need to use the prescription monitoring plans in their states, to screen all patients for whom they prescribe scheduled and potentially addicting drugs. This helps to ensure there are no patients putting themselves at risk, by seeing multiple doctors for the same or similar drugs.

It's disheartening that relatively few physicians use this wonderful tool. Physicians don't use the monitoring websites because of lack of time, lack of information, and in some cases, lack of computer abilities. Hopefully, state programs will strive to make the sites easier for physicians to access and use.

Some doctors don't use the website because they're afraid they *will* discover a patient getting multiple prescriptions. This would require a difficult, time consuming, and probably unpleasant conversation with their patient. Most doctors prefer to avoid direct confrontation with patients, because it's emotionally trying and time consuming. However, this conversation can be life-saving. With so much at stake, it's worth the trouble

When discussing data found on the prescription monitoring program, the doctor should emphasize concern for the patient, and emphasize that addiction is a disease, which can be treated. If the doctor maintains an attitude of non-judgmental concern, the patient is more likely to respond positively and consider addiction treatment. Even if the patient rejects treatment, the seed may be planted for future change. At the very worst, the patient will probably tell any friends who doctor-shop for prescription medications to stay away from that doctor's office. Most physicians would consider this a good thing.

Ideally, individual state monitoring plans will be linked into a national program. Patients living close to bordering states often cross state lines for controlled substance prescriptions. At present, the physician has to get authorization to use each state's data base and it takes extra time to check two or three states, rather than one national database.

The White House has strongly encouraged the use of prescription monitoring plans. (7) That recommendation could be strengthened, if Washington D.C. set a good example, and had a prescription monitoring plan for itself, or tagged on to a nearby state's plan, like Virginia. There are still five states, as of early 2010, that have no plans to implement a prescription monitoring program: Montana, Nebraska, Missouri, Arkansas, and Maryland. (5)

In May 2009, someone hacked into Virginia's prescription monitoring program and demanded ten million dollars as a ransom in exchange for 8 million patient records. To date, the extent of the breach and patient damages from it can't be determined. Certainly this is cause for grave concern, and security measures must be re-examined and strengthened if these programs are to survive.

What of the doctors so full of avarice that they run "pill mills"? Ever since doctors have existed, a minority have disgraced our profession with their actions. Though we may never be rid of these predators completely, they need to be prosecuted. Other doctors need to notify their state medical boards of their presence among us. Emergency room doctors, addiction medicine doctors, and treatment center personnel know who they are. Certainly the prescription opioid addicts know who they are. Let's ask the medical boards to investigate these doctors, to determine if they are careless, extremely gullible, uninformed, or criminals.

The public needs to be better informed about the risks of prescription drug addiction. New public service announcements have already been broadcast, to warn citizens of the risk of prescription drug misuse and addiction. Hopefully, this will help change the perception that prescription drugs are safer than street drugs. New White House drug policy has endorsed the National Youth Anti-Drug Media Campaign's efforts to inform parents about the risks of prescription medication. The ONDCP (Office of National Drug Control Policy), along with SAMHSA (Substance Abuse and Mental Health Services Administration), have promoted the development of continuing medical education courses, to help educate doctors about the dangers of opioids, and methods to help avoid addiction.

Treatment options for those already addicted

Our government organizations took the above actions to help reduce the number of new addicts, but what about the people who are already addicted?

With any kind of illness, medical professionals, celebrities, and wealthy individuals usually get the gold standard of care. Opioid addiction is no different. *For an addict's first time in treatment, the gold standard is inpatient medical detoxification, using buprenorphine, in tapering doses, to ease withdrawal symptoms. This needs to be followed by an inpatient, opioid-free residential treatment program of ninety to one hundred and eighty days.*

Some addictionologists would argue that because treatments using methadone and buprenorphine have higher success rates, recommending drug-free treatment is careless. Those doctors might say that all opioid addicts should be started on replacement medications, given the better success rates.

But we already have addicts who are required to enter opioid-free treatment of their addiction. Licensed professionals (nurses, doctors, pilots, pharmacists) are forced to go to abstinence-based treatment, because their licensing boards hold their licenses to practice hostage, unless they comply. These boards have the professionals sign monitoring contracts for three to five years, committing to a treatment plan. These plans usually involve random drug testing, regular counseling, and three to five 12-step or other group meetings per week, for the first five years of recovery.

With this intense treatment and scrutiny, success rates for monitored professionals are excellent. In a study of physicians participating in North Carolina's Physician Health Program, ninety percent of physicians addicted to opioids had either a "good" or "good with complications" outcome. (8). This success rate is much higher than for any other group.

Another study of addicted doctors across the country shows seventy-nine percent of the doctors who participated in physician health programs were licensed and working at five years. (9) These are excellent results, proving that abstinence-based treatment *can* work, if it is long enough, and intense enough. As Dr. Hall said in Chapter 11, doctors have a better recovery rate, not because of intelligence, but rather because of availability of prolonged inpatient treatment, monitoring for five years after inpatient treatment, and severe consequences for relapse (loss of professional license).

Since opioid-free treatment works for these addicts, it can work for other opioid addicts. However, under our present healthcare system, this kind of intense treatment isn't available for most opioid addicts. Most addicts don't have these kinds of motivating factors. Most opioid addicts in this country can't, or won't, go away to inpatient treatment, and have no one to monitor them or threaten significant consequences if they don't participate in treatment. In fact, most addicts have no health insurance to pay for such intense treatment, or they can't miss work for even a month and financially survive. Mothers of young children often don't have a reliable caregiver, and won't leave them in someone else's care for three months.

According to data from the Treatment Episode Data Study (TEDS), in 2007, around fifty-five percent of patients admitted for treatment of opioid addiction had no insurance. Around twenty-one percent had Medicaid, and only fourteen percent had any kind of private insurance or were covered by an HMO. (10) Often, even those with insurance to cover the cost of admission to an inpatient program say they can't afford to take that much time off work. With no income, or significantly reduced income, they say they would lose their house and car. In some cases, that may be an excuse to avoid inpatient treatment, but in many cases, it's probably true.

Even patients with insurance or Medicaid are granted less than a month's inpatient treatment before their benefits are exhausted. We know that with opioid addiction, longer inpatient treatment produces better results. As we saw in previous chapters, seven to ten days of inpatient withdrawal management (detox) alone has over a ninety percent relapse rate, which usually occurs in the first month. So patients have to decide either to continue treatment and self-pay, or leave before getting optimal treatment.

We learned in previous chapters that therapeutic communities are effective, but are time-consuming. Most TCs consists of at least six months of treatment, and sometimes as much as eighteen to twenty-four months. This form of treatment is not appealing or practical for most opioid addicts. TCs present the same problem for the working poor addict: affording treatment and taking time off work is difficult. Besides, existing therapeutic communities can only treat three or four thousand opioid addicts per year, while we have a little over two million opioid addicts in this country when we combine pain pill addicts, estimated at around 1.7 million people, and heroin addicts, estimated at 600,000 to 1 million people.

Thus, the gold standard of treatment for opioid addiction is simply not available to most addicts. Adequate inpatient treatment is not available for most opioid addicts.

It's tempting to veer into a discussion of health care reform. For all people with opioid addiction to get the gold standard treatment, our healthcare system would need total overhaul. Perhaps that will happen someday. Until then, we must be realistic, and use what is currently available to the average addict. If the gold standard isn't available, then let's move on to an effective treatment that is available and affordable.

Medication-assisted treatment

Medication assisted treatments are affordable and cost effective. Forty years of data, reviewed in Appendix A, prove this statement. Nonetheless, many treatment professionals, who work in abstinence-based treatment programs, hold negative attitudes about using medication-assisted therapies with methadone or buprenorphine. These professionals may be unacquainted with the outcome studies using these medications, and commit the error of contempt prior to investigation, as I did. Treatment professionals opposed to these medications can also be so blinded by their own ideology that no amount of information can convince them there are valid options besides their own brand of treatment.

Many opioid addicts seeking treatment for their addiction aren't willing or ready to go through opioid withdrawal. They're not ready to face life without opioids, though they do want addiction to stop ruining their lives. Many have tried, and failed, to stop on their own. For them, medication-assisted treatment with methadone or buprenorphine can be life-saving. These patients may transition to a drug-free recovery at some point, or stay on medication indefinitely. Either way, their death rate goes down, and their quality of life usually goes up on medication.

Only two medications, methadone and buprenorphine, are currently approved by the FDA as replacement therapy of opioid addiction. The other two medications approved to treat opioid addiction, naltrexone and clonidine, have limited efficacy, and are described in more detail in Appendix B.

Ideally, buprenorphine should be the first-line medication for treatment of opioid addiction.

Buprenorphine is a milder opioid, and certainly safer than methadone. Fatal overdose *is* still possible, but nowhere near as likely as with methadone. It's probably easier, though still not easy, to taper off of buprenorphine than methadone, if appropriate at some point. At present, the expense of buprenorphine prevents its use by many opioid treatment programs, although a few opioid treatment programs have begun to offer it. In the future, buprenorphine as a first-line drug will likely become the standard of care.

Methadone should be saved for patients who do not do well on buprenorphine. There will always be some addicts for whom only methadone is effective, usually those with higher tolerances to opioids.

More family doctors need to be able to prescribe buprenorphine for uncomplicated opioid addicts, to treat them in a mainstream medical setting. However, this treatment setting isn't appropriate for all opioid addicts. Patients with more severe addiction, or other mental health issues, may need the structure of more frequent contact with counselors in an addiction treatment setting, rather than in a primary care setting.

This is similar to treatment methods of other chronic diseases. For example, family doctors do a great job at treating mild to moderate asthma, but for severe asthma, they often refer patients to a pulmonologist, or lung specialist. We could have a similar model for opioid addicted patients on buprenorphine, with the sicker patients referred to addictionologists.

Since buprenorphine is still more expensive than methadone, the people who need it most can't afford it. Buprenorphine treatment costs about twice what methadone treatment costs, if patients without insurance or Medicaid have to pay out of pocket for the medication. The drug is now available in a generic form, but the price hasn't dropped much. This higher price has been an obstacle to opioid treatment centers that want to offer buprenorphine, because these clinics have to charge higher prices to cover this medication. As mentioned before, methadone costs pennies. The money paid by patients at methadone clinics goes to the salaries of clinic personnel: counselors, nurses, clinical director, and doctor.

In some regions of the country, physicians who prescribe Suboxone have charged exorbitant prices for office-based buprenorphine treatment. Some patients told me that they've paid twenty-five hundred dollars on the initial visit. Of course, this may have included medication and counseling, so it's still hard to know what to make of this information. Hopefully, as more physicians become licensed to prescribe Suboxone, fewer doctors will indulge in price gouging. Again, healthcare is still a business, as of this writing, and providers make profits under this system, but there's a difference between legitimate profit and outrageous profiteering.

Methadone treatment at an opioid treatment center is the most affordable option for opioid addicts, at least as of early 2010. Until it's financially practical to prescribe buprenorphine as a first-line treatment for opioid addiction, we'll need to continue to use methadone.

Addiction treatment professionals can learn from each other, but only if we remain teachable. After all, we're asking our patients to become open-minded to a new option – life without drugs – so perhaps we can model open-mindedness in our interactions with other treatment professionals.

Sadly, many treatment programs in the U.S. are vehemently abstinence- based and unwilling to consider other options to help patients. Even while mouthing agreement that they believe addiction is a disease, they take an attitude that patients use medications, like buprenorphine or methadone, are weak or unwilling. One can detect echoes of judgmentalism, even in treatment professionals. Ideology still battles with science.

Even addiction professionals fall into this error. Dr. Drew Pinsky, of VH1's "Celebrity Rehab," states in his book, When Painkillers Become Dangerous:

> "Some patients elect to take the road of harm avoidance through what is called maintenance therapy, such as a methadone program…But the possibility of emotional change necessary to recovery is closed to these patients. The replacement drug, such as methadone, blocks many of the brain mechanisms that must be set in motion for emotional growth and the development of recovery. These patients are committed to a chronic state of affairs. Though harm-avoidance may be lifesaving for some patients, abstinence-based recovery offers a richer alternative." P 9

I challenge Dr. Drew Pinsky to produce evidence that supports this remarkable statement. I don't know of any evidence showing methadone or buprenorphine maintenance prevents the psychological and spiritual aspects of an individual's recovery from proceeding. In fact, most evidence points to the opposite conclusion. Patients assisted with methadone or buprenorphine do regain their lives, particularly the relationships with loved ones and the larger community. Most people would see this as proof of emotional growth and development, necessary ingredients of the spirituality of recovery.

If patients on medications don't access the 12-step programs that emphasize spiritual recovery, perhaps it's because they will be ostracized. Many methadone patients feel they're lying, by not revealing that they're on methadone, but know they may receive harsh criticism if they do. Some patients do successfully combine maintenance medication with 12-step recovery (see interview of Patient XYZ in Chapter 12) and reap the full benefit of both, experiencing rich recovery. Many patients on maintenance medications with methadone and buprenorphine attend churches or other spiritual venues, and have flourishing spiritual lives.

Some opioid-addicted patients have tried abstinence-based recovery programs of adequate duration and have still relapsed, sometimes multiple times. Ethically, medication-assisted treatment options must be discussed with such patients. For that portion of opioid addicts who have prolonged post-acute withdrawal symptoms, causing multiple relapses, both buprenorphine and methadone can be life-saving.

Certainly, both patients and doctors see drug free recovery as the ideal. In fact, patients and their doctors prefer to manage any disease without medication, if possible. Patients with high blood pressure often say they don't want to stay on the medications forever, and ask me if they can ever stop their medication. I explain that I don't know, because there are too many variables involved. Some patients, who lose weight and exercise, *can* stop their blood pressure medications. Some patients lose weight and exercise and still need blood pressure medication. Some patients never lose weight or exercise, and have to stay on medication. Are the last two types of patients "bad" for needing medication? Do we judge patients with diabetes for their lack of willpower to lose weight and exercise?

Some people do judge such patients. There is a movement afoot to hold patients accountable for their own behavior in the treatment of their illnesses. Some doctors are now paid on a "pay for performance" plan. This means the doctor gets paid more, if their patients achieve certain goals, like good control of their diabetes or blood pressure. While this has the benefit of encouraging doctors to discuss the importance of compliance with their treatment, it has had an unexpected consequence. Some doctors have started terminating the patients who aren't compliant with treatment, because keeping these poorly motivated patients in their practice decreases the doctors' incomes.

Do we really want to go down that road? How judgmental do we want to be? Given the difficulty of behavioral change in human beings, I think most people would find such policies harsh.

A recent study looked at the degree of adherence to a healthy lifestyle in US adults. People were surveyed about whether they complied with these five recommendations for a healthy lifestyle: eating more than five fruits or vegetables per day, maintaining healthy body weight, regularly exercising more than twelve times per month, moderate or no alcohol consumption, and not smoking. Only eight percent of US adults adhere to these widely known health recommendations. People with diabetes, heart disease, and high blood pressure were no more likely to adhere to recommendations than those without these diseases. (11)

Many addiction professionals, including myself, have compared drug addiction to a chronic disease, like diabetes. *Perhaps the more appropriate thing would be to compare diabetes to addiction.* We are very harsh when we fault people for failing to make a behavioral change quickly when it's in both the patient's and society's best interests to do so. But behavior change is hard for most humans. We like doing fun things, like eating and relaxing and taking drugs that numb emotional pain and produce a pleasurable feeling. Whether we call these behaviors "addictions" or "bad habits" sometimes depends on what socioeconomic class the person belongs to, whether we approve or disapprove of the behavior they're doing, or whether we struggle with the same behaviors.

Improving opioid treatment centers

Poorly run methadone clinics have caused part of the stigma against opioid treatment centers. It's easy to understand a community's opposition to a clinic, if it's poorly run. If all clinics re-evaluated their practices, perhaps changes could be made that would help both their patients, and their reputation in communities.

Clinic management should not turn a blind eye to what happens both inside and just outside their doors. Methadone clinics need to be safe places for addicts to get help. Many people argue we can never get rid of all drug dealing that occurs at a methadone clinic, but basic precautions will certainly reduce this, and other illicit activities.

Methadone clinics should be willing to pay for security guards, to patrol clinic parking lots at all hours the clinic is open. Patients caught selling drugs need to be directed to another form of treatment, for the safety of other clinic patients *and* the reputation of the clinic. Criminal activity should not be tolerated on clinic property, for the sake of patients, staff, and community relations.

Opioid treatment centers need to be more than "juice bars." That means the clinic must offer real counseling, not just methadone mixed in a fruit punch. Past studies show better patient outcomes with more counseling services, so clinics need to make counseling an integral part of treatment. Preferably, individual, group, and even family counseling sessions should be provided.

Federal regulations ask for a minimum standard of two counseling sessions per month, but to help patients change, more frequent counseling is usually needed. Patients at opioid treatment clinics tend to think their daily dosing fee pays for methadone, but that's not true. As mentioned above, methadone costs pennies for the clinics. The patients are really paying for the staffs' salaries. I tell patients that if they don't meet regularly with their counselor, they're not getting their money's worth

Federal regulations also ask for no more than fifty patients per counselor. Caseloads of less than fifty patients would make it easier for patients to see their counselor, because even fifty is a heavy load. The patients in an opioid treatment program can often be needy and mentally ill, and it can take time to help them. At least one group meeting should be held in the evening, so methadone patients who work during the day can attend. Group counseling is important, because there are some things addicts can learn in a group setting that they can't learn any other way. There is a particular sort of insight that occurs when we see ourselves in other people.

Large clinics containing more than two hundred and fifty patients should be broken into smaller clinics. Size makes a difference. The more patients attending a clinic, the more likely it is that chaos will ensue. Wise clinic directors limit their size, to give better care. Less chaos at opioid treatment centers would give these programs better reputations and better community support. Smaller and more numerous opioid treatment centers would give patients more choice, and possibly less distance to travel each day, because patients could pick the clinic closest to them.

Opioid treatment centers need to be good neighbors in their community. Some treatment centers work hard to initiate and sustain relationships with their community. At present, I work for a center that has had active community outreach, including an open house where community members were invited to take a tour of our facility, and get information about how our clinic operates.

Opioid treatment centers provide legitimate, evidence-based treatment. We shouldn't shrink from giving information to other treatment providers. Treatment professionals also need to take advantage of any opportunity to speak to community leaders, law enforcement, and social services providers, to educate them about methadone therapy. However, often this must be done with a great deal of tact. Clinic representatives need to be sensitive and collaborative in their approach to people in their community.

Medicaid rules regarding documentation requirements for methadone patients should be examined. These rules shouldn't create obstacles to patients' care. If the counselor must spend excessive time completing paperwork, he'll have less time to help his patients. Since Medicaid patients tend to have more illnesses, both physical and mental, they can benefit the most from treatment.

Successful methadone treatment programs have some characteristics in common, as we learned in previous chapters. They use adequate methadone doses, employ well-trained staff with low turnover, and make available a wide array of psychosocial services for their patients. They have good communication between counseling and medical staff. All methadone clinics should keep these factors in mind, and strive to keep improving the care they provide. Some of these things are expensive, like offering more services under one roof, and paying more to retain good counselors. But some improvements can be accomplished with little extra expenditures, like better communication and adequate dosing.

Clinics need to prescribe adequate doses of methadone. Multiple studies have shown that doses from eighty to one-hundred and twenty milligrams per day work better at retaining patients in treatment and reducing illicit opioid use. Many clinics are still rather stingy with their dosing, leading to poorer patient outcomes. Some patients prefer to keep their dose low, so they can still get high from continued illicit opioids.

Clinics need to hire qualified counselors and pay them enough so there won't be frequent turnover of counselors, which is a problem in many methadone clinics. The therapeutic relationship between patient and counselor has been found to be one of the most important factors for a successful patient outcome. If patients get new counselors repeatedly, they make less of an effort at counseling. The patients start to feel like they shouldn't bother repeating their life story, because they'll get a new counselor soon, anyway.

In the past, opioid treatment clinics were guilty of hiring poorly qualified counselors. In some states, a high school graduate can be a counselor in an opioid treatment center, with no other credentials required. Fortunately, many states are changing training requirements. Many treatment centers have hired people in recovery, but being in recovery isn't enough to assure competence in counseling. Recovering people can be excellent counselors, but they can be even better with training and experience. It's probably best to have a clinic with a mix of recovering counselors and counselors who don't have any past addiction issues, for more balance and objectivity. Counselors with no personal experience with addiction can still be extremely good at their jobs.

Working with addicts can be exhausting. Clinics should provide sufficient vacation time and other benefits, to help keep their counselors satisfied. This will pay off in the long run. Counselors who are contented with their work are more likely to counsel their patients effectively.

Opioid treatment clinics need to make sure their counselors know about all the studies relating to methadone treatment, both for overall education, and to assure them they're giving evidence-based treatment. If an opioid treatment center hires a counselor who is unsure or incompletely educated about methadone, that message will be transmitted to the patients, potentially causing harm.

Treatment centers of all types should refer patients to twelve step recovery fellowships. Not many patients will want to go, but the ones who do can find a rich and fertile environment for recovery. However, patients on methadone or buprenorphine need to be cautioned not to mention their medications, so they won't be ostracized by the group.

Clinics can encourage their patients to consider setting up their own Methadone Anonymous meetings, where recovering people on methadone can meet, with no clinic staff present, and run their own 12-step meetings. Sometimes people on prescribed medications feel more comfortable in Alcoholics Anonymous, since drugs are not usually discussed.

Mental health and physical health issues of opioid addicts should be addressed, starting on the first day of treatment. Untreated mental health issues often thwart efforts at addiction treatment. Pain patients who are maintained on either buprenorphine of methadone should have access to pain management programs that are opioid-free, to teach them how to manage their pain and concentrate on their function in daily life. Other medical issues should be assessed and treated. Studies show when more of these treatments can occur under one roof, the outcomes are better.

More opioid treatment centers are needed in some areas of the country. Government funded treatment centers would be ideal. Not only would this eliminate financial barriers to treatment, but it would be cost effective. As described in previous chapters, taxpayers save four dollars for each one dollar spent on addiction treatment. However, it seems unlikely this will happen anytime soon. Maybe our efforts would be better spent focusing on improving access to buprenorphine.

If government or non-profit clinics won't or can't fill the treatment void, we may need to encourage more for-profit clinics to pick up the slack. Hopefully, with new legislation aimed at removing barriers that have prevented opioid treatment centers from using buprenor-phine in addition to methadone, more patients will be started on the milder and safer buprenorphine, and those that fail this treatment can go to methadone, the stronger opioid.

Some patients are too sick for methadone maintenance. Some patients can't or won't quit drugs that can kill them if used while taking methadone, like benzodiazepines, alcohol, and other sedatives. In the past, information published by the Substance Abuse and Mental Health Services Administration indicated that ongoing drug use should rarely be used as a reason to dismiss a patient from methadone treatment, given the increased risk of death for dismissed patients. (12) Past stud-ies, done with heroin addicts, support that recommendation.

But rural addicts addicted to opioid pain pills may be different. It's possible they're more likely to misuse or be co-addicted to benzodi-azepines. After seeing a spate of overdose deaths at the methadone clinic where I worked, nearly always in patients also using benzodi-azepines, I've concluded the risk of methadone maintenance in patients with co-existing sedative addiction is too high. Because of this, the admitting physician at a methadone clinic needs to make a case-by-case determination of the risks versus benefits for these patients.

Physicians need to be able to make individual decisions about the appropriateness of methadone treatment. The clinic owners or admin-istrators shouldn't make that decision. The physician is ultimately responsible for the patients' wellbeing, and should not be pressured by the financial interests of the owners or managers. Physicians who work in opioid treatment centers must be able to do what they believe is in the best interests of the patient, without fear of being reprimanded or fired.

It's hard to say how much influence methadone clinic owners and administrators have over medical aspects of methadone maintenance treatment. Many clinics hire part-time or retired doctors to work for them, and many of these doctors are not addiction treatment specialists. If one of these doctors pushes administrators for a certain safety change which will cost the clinic money (for example, staying open seven days per week, instead of six days per week, or requiring EKGs on high risk patients), he or she runs the risk of being considered difficult to work with. That doctor may be released from employment, as soon as a replacement can be found.

If a doctor finds himself working at a clinic that needs changes for the safety of patients, what should he do? Should he continue to work inside a broken system and advocate for change? Or should he quit and let someone else deal with stubborn clinic owners or administrators?

At one methadone clinic where I worked, dysfunctional managers prevented some of the simplest of changes. For example, I noticed some of the treatment staff used the words "clean" and "dirty," when referring to urine drug screen results. I sent an email to all of the counselors, asking them to please use the phrases "positive" and "negative," when speaking of urine drug test results, because the language is more professional, and not pejorative.

Within the hour I got a haughty email from an administrator, saying that though he agreed with me in principle, all such policy changes needed to go through administrative channels, up the chain of command. I was dumbfounded at his hubris.

Doctors weren't links in their chain of command. Other doctors working there, certified in addiction medicine, also felt the administrators of this clinic saw doctors as "necessary evils." We were essential to the running of the clinic, but administrators preferred that we keep quiet about any problems we saw, and admit any addict who wanted treatment, regardless of their appropriateness. To refuse admission of an addict was called "denying treatment," even if the admitting physician felt the addict was not appropriate for treatment with methadone.

I've faulted the abstinence-based treatment centers and their personnel for not being open-minded, but at times, opioid treatment centers and their personnel can be equally close-minded. *Methadone and buprenorphine are not the best treatment choices for all opioid-addicted patients. One cure does not fit all. No treatment works for all addicts, but all legitimate and evidence-based treatments help some addicts. There are many paths to recovery.*

As we learn more about the brain in addiction, we may develop more medications that can help people recover from addiction. Since this disease is psychological, as well as physical, counseling must be the cornerstone of successful recovery. Good treatment centers will inform patients about all treatment options, both abstinence-based and medication-assisted, and help patients access the best treatment for them. An attitude of tolerance and open-mindedness can get addicts into a form of treatment that is acceptable to them. It can also help retain them in treatment, whether that treatment is inpatient, medication-assisted, or a creative combination of both.

While we do need to be open-minded, we don't want to be so open-minded that we ignore the need for evidence-based clinical trials to prove the efficacy of new treatments. In the past, patients were preyed upon by unscrupulous purveyors of "cures," which later turned out to have no benefit at all. We need to demand evidence-based research to support any new treatment for addiction. Science has evolved. Studies can be performed to tell us which methods work and which don't. Unproven methods have no place in addiction treatment. Historically, there have been many new "cures" for addiction, promising much and delivering little.

The marketing of a new treatment for addiction should not outstrip the science supporting it.

Maintenance to Abstinence?

Let's turn again to an extremely controversial topic, even among addiction medicine specialists. Should patients, doing well on medication-assisted treatment with either methadone or buprenorphine, ever attempt to taper off of them?

In 2009, I attended an ASAM conference where this was discussed. Addiction medicine specialists argued passionately and eloquently on both sides of this issue.

The studies of IV heroin addicts clearly show people who taper off of methadone have high relapse rates. Doctors who support indefinite methadone maintenance say that since opioid addiction is potentially fatal, and we know death and complication rates go down for patients who stay on methadone, it's careless and irresponsible to suggest these patients come off their medications. They argue it's the same as taking blood pressure medication, and the patient should continue medication for a lifetime.

Pro-maintenance clinicians point to the prolonged abstinence withdrawal syndrome that occurs in many patients, even after the acute withdrawal subsides. They postulate that some opioid addicts never start making their own endorphins again, and feel chronically bad, perhaps for a lifetime.

Yet, we know addicts who get lengthy inpatient treatment, like physicians and other professionals, are able to get past that post acute withdrawal period. These addicts don't feel chronically ill and most are able to return to work. In fact, they have one of the highest success rates, because of their monitoring programs. Similarly, thousands of opioid addicts recover in 12-step groups, without maintenance medications. These addicts found a way to get through post acute withdrawal and function normally.

Perhaps this post acute withdrawal doesn't last a lifetime in all addicts. We know that under the right circumstances, at least some opioid addicts are capable of complete abstinence from all drugs *and* replacement medications.

Also, at present, we can't be sure pain pill addicts will have the same outcomes as heroin addicts. Addicts who became addicted to prescription drugs often don't have the same degree of criminality, association and identification with the drug using culture as do the heroin users, who were the subjects of a great many of the early methadone studies. It's possible these patients have more resources, both emotionally and socially, to be able to withstand the post acute opioid withdrawal, after a slow taper from methadone or buprenorphine.

We need more information on the long-term outcomes of prescription pain pill addicts. To help answer our questions, the Prescription Opioid Addiction Treatment Study (POATS) was started in 2006. This study will examine outcomes for pain pill addicts, using different schedules of buprenorphine tapers. It will look at outcomes using a four week treatment with taper, and a twelve week treatment with stabilization for patients who don't do well with the four week taper. A long-term follow up is planned for one and a half years later, two and a half years later, and three and a half years after treatment. This study will look at the primary outcome of abstinence, but also look at withdrawal symptoms, cravings, and reduction of drug use. The study aims to see if co-existing chronic pain affects the outcomes. The study also plans to examine adverse events in the lives of the enrolled addicts.

The biggest uncertainty I face, in my work with medication-assisted treatment of opioid addiction, is whether, and when, to recommend tapering from buprenorphine or methadone. Hopefully, the results from the POATS study will help us decide if the risk of tapering a patient is worth the potential benefits. For now, if I have a patient who is strongly motivated to taper off either buprenorphine or methadone, I'll work with them, to help achieve that goal. I talk extensively about the importance of getting counseling, to help make the major life changes that need to be done prior to taper, to give the best chance of success, like cutting ties with the addicted community. I encourage the patient to taper slowly, so that withdrawal symptoms won't be as strong.

A few patients, after very bad relapse experiences, are willing to stay on medication and say, "This medication has helped me so much, I'm not going to risk my life by stopping it," as the successful buprenorphine patient interviewed in Chapter 11 said.

But most patients don't want to stay on replacement medications. Methadone and buprenorphine prescribers don't always realize how vulnerable their patients feel. Many patients feel they're at the whim of their treatment program, regarding the amount of medication they're given, and how many take home doses they're allowed. There is much stigma from family, friends, and even primary care and emergency room doctors, to get off the methadone or buprenorphine, even if that patient is doing well and his life is improving. It takes strong character to resist constant bombardment of negative opinions about your chosen treatment option and many patients prematurely terminate treatment in methadone clinics and relapse under the pressure.

In my experience, few patients on methadone or buprenorphine want to stay on this medication for life, even as they admit how much the medication has helped them.

This book has included a brief history of opioid addiction and past attempts at control of opioid addiction by the U.S. Some attempts have had successes, some have had failures, but most have had a mixture of both.

We didn't learn from the past, and repeated the iatrogenic (doctor created) wave of prescription opioid addiction in the late 1990's and early 21st century. This wave of addiction mirrored – though on a larger scale – the wave of prescription opioid addiction seen in the late 1800's and early 1900's. With the worthy goals of adequate treatment of pain, doctors and patients forgot that when humans are exposed to drugs that can trigger the pleasure center of the brain, addiction will happen.

People like to feel pleasure. Doctors, trying to alleviate suffering, had good intentions during both time periods, but vastly underestimated the addictive potential of opioids. In the late 1990's, the statistics that experts quoted were faulty, based on bad science. Primary care doctors still have little training in either pain management or addictive disorders and are poorly equipped to properly treat pain patients who become addicted, or any other addicts who cross their paths.

Methadone and buprenorphine reduce mortality rates of opioid addicts, as we saw from the information in these chapters. Even if society frowns on medication-assisted treatments, it clearly helps keep addicts alive. We now have forty years of history that prove the benefits of medications like methadone and buprenorphine. And if the addict is alive, then change and recovery are still possible, whether it occurs on or off medications.

Let's not forget the lesson we've had to learn and re-learn. The ultimate prevention would be if future generations are able to learn from the past, both from the late 1800's and from the late 1900's. Maybe doctors of the future will learn better ways to treat pain, without creating addicts. Maybe they'll do a better job of monitoring patients who do need strong opioids. Perhaps the U.S. society will never again have another plague of pain pill addiction.

Endnotes:

1. Martell, BA, O'Conner, PG, Kerns, KD, et. al., "Systematic review: Opioid treatment for chronic back pain: prevalence, efficacy, and association with addiction," *Annals of Internal Medicine*, 2007; 146: pp. 116-127.

2. Chou, R, Fanciullo, G, Fine, P, et. al., "Opioid Treatment Guidelines: Clinical guidelines for the use of Chronic Opioid Therapy in chronic, non-cancer pain." *The Journal of Pain*, 2009, Vol. 10, No. 2, pp. 113-130.

3. "Index to Drug Specific Information": accessed on 8/19/09.http://www.fda.gov/Drugs/DrugSafety/PostmarketD rugSafetyInformationforPatientsand-Providers/ucm111085.htm.

4. Substance Abuse and Mental Health Services Administration. (2009). *Results from the 2008 National Survey on Drug Use and Health: National Findings* (Office of Applied Studies, NSDUH Series H-36, HHS Publication No. SMA 09-4434). Rockville, MD http://oas.samhsa.gov/nsduh

5. National Prescription Drug Threat Assessment, 2009, Drug Enforcement Administration, http://www.usdoj.gov/ndic/pubs33/33775/index.htm

6. National Survey of Drug Use in Households, 2008, *Non-Medical Use of Pain Relievers in Sub-state Regions, 2004 – 2006*.

7. National Drug Control Strategy, 2009 Annual Report, available as a pdf file: http://www.whitehousedrugpolicy. gov/publications/ policy/ndcs09/2009ndcs.pdf .

8. Ganely, Oswald H, Pendergast, Warren J, Mattingly, Daniel E, Wilkerson, Michael W, "Outcome study of substance impaired physicians and physician assistants under contract with North Carolina Physicians Health Program for the period 1995-2000," *Journal of Addictive Diseases*, Vol 24(1) 2005.

9. McLellan, AT, Skipper, GS, Campbell, M, DuPont, RL, "Five Year outcomes in a cohort study of physicians treated for substance abuse disorders in the United States," *British Medical Journal*,2008;337: a 2038.

10. Treatment Episode Data Set, 1997-2007, National Admissions to Substance Abuse Treatment Services, Department of Health and Human Services, SAMHSA, Office of Applied Studies, Rockville, MD, August, 2009, p 117. www.oas. samhsa.gov/copies.com

11. King, Dana E., Mainous, Arch G. III, Carnemolla, Mark, Evererr, Charles J, "Adherence to Healthy Lifestyle Habits in US Adults, 1988-2006" *The American Journal of Medicine*, (2009) 122, pp. 528-534.

12. U.S. Department of Health and Human Services, Substance Abuse and Mental Health Services Administration, *Medication-Assisted Treatment for Opioid Addiction in Opioid Treatment Programs: TIP 43* (Rockville, MD, 2005) p 186.

APPENDIX A

Summary of the Data
Supporting Methadone Treatment

This appendix lists some of the major studies that first suggested the benefits of methadone in the treatment of opioid addiction. It's not meant to be a complete listing, as that would require a book itself, but a summary of the most prominent studies.

Amato L, Davoli, et. al., An overview of systematic reviews of the effectiveness of opiate maintenance therapies: available evidence to inform clinical practice and research. *Journal of Substance Abuse Treatment* 2005; 28 (4):321-329. In this overview of meta-analyses and other reviews, they conclude that methadone maintenance is more effective in the treatment of opioid addiction than methadone detoxification, buprenorphine, or no treatment. Higher doses of methadone are more effective than low or medium doses.

Baewert A, Gombas W, Schindler S, et.al., Influence of peak and trough levels of opioid maintenance therapy on driving aptitude, *European Addiction Research* 2007, 13(3),127-135. This study shows that methadone patients aren't impaired at either peak or trough levels of methadone.

Bale et. al., 1980; 37(2):179-193. "Therapeutic Communities vs Methadone Maintenance" *Archives of General Psychiatry* Opioid-addicted veterans who presented to the hospital for treatment were assigned to either inpatient detoxification alone, admission to a therapeutic community, or to methadone maintenance. One year later, patients assigned to therapeutic communities or methadone maintenance did significantly better than patients whose only treatment was detoxification. Patients in these two groups were significantly more likely to be employed, less likely to be in jail, and less likely to be using heroin, than the patients who got only detox admission. Patients in the therapeutic communities needed to stay at least seven weeks to obtain benefit equal to patients assigned to methadone maintenance.

Ball JC, Ross A., *The Effectiveness of Methadone Maintenance Treatment.* New York, NY: Springer-Verlag Inc., 1991. This landmark study observed six hundred and thirty-three male patients enrolled in six methadone maintenance programs. Patients reduced their use of illicit opioids 71% from pre-admission levels, with the best results (no heroin use) seen in patients on doses higher than 70 milligrams. Longer duration of treatment with methadone showed the greatest reductions in heroin use. Of patients who left methadone maintenance treatment, 82% relapsed back to intravenous heroin use within one year. This study also found a dramatic drop in criminal activity for addicts in methadone treatment. Within one year, the number of days involved in criminal activity dropped an average of 91% for addicts maintained on methadone. This study showed that methadone clinics vary a great deal in their effectiveness. The most effective clinics had adequate dosing, well-trained and experienced staff with little turnover, combined medical, counseling and administrative services, and a close and consistent relationship between patients and staff.

Bernard JP, Morland J et. al. Methadone and impairment in apprehended drivers. *Addiction* 2009; 104(3) 457-464. This is a study of 635 people who were apprehended for impaired driving who were found to have methadone in their system. Of the 635, only 10 had *only* methadone in their system. The degree of impairment didn't correlate with methadone blood levels. Most people on methadone who had impaired driving were using more than just methadone.

Caplehorn JR, Deaths in the first two weeks of maintenance treatment in New South Wales in 1994: Identifying cases of iatrogenic methadone toxicity. *Drug and Alcohol Review*, 1998, 17(1) p. 9-17. This study found that most deaths in opioid treatment centers occurred in the first two weeks of treatment. The rate of fatal toxicity was 2.2 per 1000 admissions.

Caplehorn JRM, Bell J. Methadone dosage and retention of patients in maintenance treatment. *The Medical Journal of Australia 1991; 154: pp. 195-199.* Authors of this study concluded that higher doses of methadone (80 milligrams per day and above) were significantly more likely to retain patients in treatment.

Caplehorn JR, Dalton MS, et. al., Methadone maintenance and

addicts' risk of fatal heroin overdose. *Substance Use and Misuse*, 1996 Jan, 31(2):177-196. In this study of heroin addicts, the addicts in methadone treatment were one-quarter as likely to die by heroin overdose or suicide. This study followed two hundred and ninety-six methadone heroin addicts for more than fifteen years.

Cheser G, Lemon J, Gomel M, Murphy G; Are the driving-related skills of clients in a methadone program affected by methadone? *National Drug and Alcohol Research Centre*, University of New South Wales, 30 Goodhope St., Paddington NSW 2010, Australia. This study compared results of skill performance tests and concluded that methadone clients aren't impaired in their ability to perform complex tasks.

Clausen T, Waal H, Thoresen M, Gossop M; Mortality among opiate users: opioid maintenance therapy, age and causes of death. *Addiction* 2009; 104(8) 1356-62. This study looked at the causes of death for opioid addicts admitted to opioid maintenance therapy in Norway from 1997-2003. The authors found high rates of overdose deaths both prior to admission and after leaving treatment. Older patients retained in treatment died from medical reasons, other than overdose.

Condelli, Dunteman, 1993: examined data from TOPS, the Treatment Outcome Prospective Study, assessed patients entering treatment programs from 1979 – 1981 and found data on improvement similar to DARP; longer duration of treatment in methadone maintenance shows lower use of illicit opioids.

Dittert S, Naber D, Soyka M., Methadone substitution and ability to drive. Results of an experimental study. *Nervenartz* 1999; 70: pp. 457-462. Patients on methadone substitution therapy did not show impaired driving ability.

Dole VP, Nyswander ME, Kreek, MJ, Narcotic Blockade. *Archives of Internal* Medicine, 1966; 118:304-309. Consisted of thirty-two patients, with half randomized to methadone and the other half to a no-treatment waiting list. The methadone group had much higher rates of abstention from heroin, much lower rates of incarceration, and higher rates of employment.

Faggiano F, Vigna-Taglianti F, Versino E, Lemma P, Cochrane Database Review, 2003 (3) Art. No. 002208. This review article was based on a literature review of randomized controlled trials and controlled prospective studies that evaluated the efficacy of methadone at different doses. The authors concluded that methadone doses of 60 – 100mg per day were more effective than lower doses at prevention of illicit heroin and cocaine use during treatment.

Goldstein A, Herrera J, Heroin addicts and methadone treatment in Albuquerque: a year follow-up. *Drug and Alcohol Dependence* 1995 Dec; 40 (2): p. 139-150. A group of heroin addicts were followed over twenty years. One-third died within that time, and of the survivors, 48% were on a methadone maintenance program. The author concluded that heroin addiction is a chronic disease with a high fatality rate, and methadone maintenance offered a significant benefit.

Gordon NB, Appel PW., Functional potential of the methadone-maintained person. *Alcohol, Drugs and Driving* 1995; 11:1: p. 31-37. This is a literature review of studies examining performance and reaction time of patients maintained on methadone, and confirms that these patients don't differ from age-matched controls in driving ability and functional capacity.

Gowing L, Farrell M, Bornemann R, Sullivan LE, Ali R., Substitution treatment of injecting opioid users for prevention of HIV infection. *The Cochrane Database of Systematic Reviews*, 2008, Issue 2, Ar. No. CD004145. Authors reviewed twenty eight studies, concluded that they show patients on methadone maintenance have significant reductions in behaviors that place them at risk for HIV infection.

Gronbladh L, Ohlund LS, Gunne LM, Mortality in heroin addiction: Impact of methadone treatment, *Acta Psychiatrica Scandinavica* Volume 82 (3) p. 223-227. Treatment of heroin addicts with methadone maintenance resulted in a significant drop in mortality, compared to untreated heroin addicts. Untreated addicts had a death rate 63 times expected for their age and gender; heroin addicts maintained on methadone had a death rate of 8 times expected, and most of that mortality was from diseases acquired prior to treatment with methadone.

Gruber VA, Delucchi KL, Kielstein A, Batki SL; A randomized trial of six month methadone maintenance with standard or minimal counseling versus twenty-one day methadone detoxification. *Drug and Alcohol Dependence*, 2008 94(1-3) p. 199-206. The authors found that six months of treatment with methadone treatment reduced heroin use more than twenty-one day methadone detoxification. The addition of increased counseling in one of the six-month groups didn't seem to improve outcomes any more than minimal counseling.

Gunne and Gronbladh, 1981: The Swedish Methadone Maintenance Program: A Controlled Study, *Drug and Alcohol Dependence*, 1981; 7: pp. 249 – 256. This study conducted a randomized controlled trial on inpatient opioid addicts to methadone maintenance with intensive vocational rehabilitation counseling, or a control group that were referred to drug-free treatment. Over 20 years, this study consistently showed significantly higher rates of subjects free from illicit opioids, higher rates of employment, and lower mortality in the group maintained on methadone than the control group.

Hartel D, Selwyn PA, Schoenbaum EE, Methadone maintenance treatment and reduced risk of AIDS and AIDS-specific mortality in intravenous drug users. Abstract number 8546, Fourth Annual Conference on AIDS, Stockholm, Sweden, June 1988. This was a study of 2400 opioid addicts followed over fifteen years. Opioid addicts maintained on methadone at a dose of greater than 60mg showed longer retention in treatment, less use of heroin and other drugs, and lower rates of HIV infection.

Hubbard RL, Marsden ME, et.al. *Drug Abuse Treatment: A National Study of Effectiveness*. Chapel Hill: University of North Carolina Press, 1989. Shows decreased use of illicit drugs (other than opioids) while in methadone treatment, and increased again after discharge.

Kosten TR, Rounsaville BJ, and Kleber HD. Multidimensionality and prediction of treatment outcome in opioid addicts: a 2.5-year follow-up. *Comprehensive Psychiatry* 1987; 28: pp. 3-13. Addicts followed over two and a half years showed that methadone maintenance resulted in significant improvements in medical, legal, social, and employment problems.

Lenne MG, Dietze P, Rumbold GR, et.al. The effects of the opioid pharmacotherapies methadone, LAAM and buprenorphine, alone and in combination with alcohol on simulated driving. *Drug Alcohol Dependence* 2003; 72(3):271-278. This study found driving reaction times of patients on methadone and buprenorphine don't differ significantly from non-medicated drivers; however, adding even a small amount of alcohol (.05%) did cause impairment.

Marsch LA. The efficacy of methadone maintenance in reducing illicit opiate use, HIV risk behavior and criminality: a meta-analysis *Addiction* 1998; 93: pp. 515-532. This meta-analysis of studies of methadone concludes that methadone treatment reduces crime, reduces heroin use, and improves treatment retention.

Mattick RP, Breen C, Kimber J, et. al., Methadone maintenance therapy versus no opioid replacement therapy for opioid dependence. *The Cochrane Database of Systematic Reviews, 2003*; (2): CD002209. This is a meta-analysis of studies of methadone treatment. The authors concluded that treatment of opioid dependence with methadone maintenance is significantly more effective than non-pharmacologic therapies. Patients on methadone maintenance are more likely to be retained in treatment and less likely to be using heroin. This study did not find a reduction in crime between the two groups.

McGlothlin WH, Anglin MD. Shutting off methadone: costs and benefits. *Archives of General Psychiatry* 1981; 38: pp. 885-892. Authors conclude that methadone maintenance treatment is effective at reducing crime, reducing narcotic use, increasing employment, reducing incarceration and drug dealing.

Metzger DS, Woody GE, McLellan AT, et. al. Human immunodeficiency virus seroconversion among intravenous drug users in- and out- of- treatment: an 18-month prospective follow up. *Journal of Acquired Immune Deficiency Syndrome* 1993; 6: pp. 1049-1056. Patients not enrolled in methadone maintenance treatment converted to HIV positivity at a rate of 22%, versus a rate of 3.5% of patients in methadone maintenance treatment.

Powers KI, Anglin MD. Cumulative versus stabilizing effects of methadone maintenance. *Evaluation Review* 1993: Heroin addicts admitted to methadone maintenance programs showed a reduction in illicit drug use, arrests, and criminal behavior, including drug dealing. They showed increases in employment. Addicts who relapsed showed fewer improvements in these areas.

Scherbaum N, Specka M, et. al, Does maintenance treatment reduce the mortality rate of opioid addicts? *Fortschr Neurol Psychiatr,* 2002, 70(9): pp. 455-461. Opioid addicts in continuous treatment with methadone had a much lower mortality rate (1.6% per year) than opioid addicts who left treatment (8.1% per year).

Sees KL, Delucchi KL, et.al. "Methadone maintenance vs 180-day psychosocially enriched detoxification for treatment of opioid dependence" *Journal of the American Medical Association,* 2000, 283:1303-1310. Compared the outcomes of opioid addicted patients randomized to methadone maintenance or to180-day detoxification using methadone, with extra psychosocial counseling. Results showed better outcomes in patients on maintenance. Patients on methadone maintenance showed greater retention in treatment and less heroin use than the patients on the 180 day taper. There were no differences between the groups in family functioning or employment, but maintenance patients had lower severity legal problems than the patients on taper.

Sells SB, Simpson DD (eds). *The Effectiveness of Drug Abuse Treatment.* Cambridge, MA: Ballinger, 1976: This was an analysis of information from DARP, the Drug Abuse Reporting Program, which followed patients entering three types of treatment from 1969 to 1972 and showed that methadone maintenance was effective at reducing illicit drug use and criminal activity. This study also demonstrated that addicts showed more improvement the longer they were in treatment.

Strain EC, Bigelow GE, Liesbon IA, et. al. Moderate- vs high –dose methadone in the treatment of opioid dependence. A randomized trial. *Journal of the American Medical Association* 1999; 281: pp. 1000-1005. This study showed that methadone maintenance reduced illicit opioid use, and more of a reduction was seen with the addition of psychosocial counseling. Methadone doses of 80mg to 100mg were more effective than doses of 50mg at reducing illicit opioid use and improving treatment retention.

Strain, Stitzer, Liebson and Bigelow, 1993: Authors conducted a trial of 247 opioid addicts randomized to either no methadone, low dose methadone at 20mg, or methadone dosed at 50mg (which we know today from later studies is also relatively low dose). The group on methadone 50mg was significantly more likely to stay in treatment, significantly less likely to screen positive for illicit opioids or cocaine, and had a dramatic drop in involvement in criminal activities.

Stine, Kosten; Medscape Psychiatric and Mental Health eJournal: article reminds us that though it's clear that better outcomes for methadone patients are seen with higher doses (more than 80mg), many opioid treatment programs still under dose their patients.

Vanichseni S, Wongsuwan B, Choopanya K, Wongpanich K. A controlled trial of methadone maintenance in a population of intravenous drug users in Bangkok: implications for prevention of HIV. *International Journal of the Addictions* 1991; 26 (12): pp. 1313-1320. This study compared drop out from treatment of addicts maintained on methadone for forty-five days versus addicts tapered from methadone over forty-five days. The maintained patients had a significantly higher retention in treatment and lower rates of positive urine drug screens for heroin. The study was limited by its short duration.

Zanis D, Woody G; One-year mortality rates following methadone treatment discharge. *Drug and Alcohol Dependence,* 1998: vol.52 (3) 257-260. Five hundred and seven patients in a methadone maintenance program were followed for one year. In that time, 110 patients were discharged and were not in treatment anywhere. Of these patients, 8.2% were dead, mostly from heroin overdose. Of the patients retained in treatment, only 1% died. The authors conclude that even if patients enrolled in methadone maintenance treatment have a less-than-desired response to treatment, given the high death rate for heroin addicts not in treatment, these addicts should not be kicked out of the methadone clinic.

APPENDIX B

Other medications to treat opioid addiction

This appendix describes medications other than methadone and buprenorphine that are used to treat opioid dependency. None of these medications are opioid stimulating drugs, and therefore have no potential for addiction.

Clonidine

Clonidine has been used for decades as a blood pressure medication. It's cheap and effective, but has some unpleasant side effects: sedation, dry mouth, and constipation. Because newer blood pressure medications have fewer side effects, clonidine is used less today than in the past to treat high blood pressure. However, it's at least moderately effective at treating many of the symptoms of opioid withdrawal.

Among many other places in the central nervous system, opioids act on a part of the brain called the locus ceruleus. The locus ceruleus, which in Latin means the "blue place," is part of the autonomic nervous system. When locus ceruleus neurons are stimulated, norepinephrine is released into the brain, and this causes overall stimulation of the brain. Opioids slow the firing of these neurons in the locus ceruleus, reducing the release of norepinephrine. When the body gets opioids regularly from an outside source, the locus ceruleus makes adjustments, to make up for extra opioids. Then, if the supply of opioids is suddenly stopped, the locus ceruleus becomes unbalanced, and releases an overabundance of norepinephrine. The heart rate and blood pressure increase, along with other symptoms: runny nose, yawning, tearing of the eyes, diarrhea, and nausea.

Since clonidine works by calming the locus ceruleus, clonidine reduces many of these unpleasant opioid withdrawal symptoms, though it rarely eliminates all withdrawal symptoms. In the past, when it was the only medication available for opioid withdrawal management, patients rarely stayed at a detox facility long enough to complete their withdrawal. It was difficult to retain the addict in treatment. Now,

most state-of-the-art detoxification units use Suboxone to ease withdrawal symptoms because it's more effective, and helps retain patients
in detoxification, a necessary step prior to the more intense inpatient
rehabilitation.

Opioid antagonists (blockers)

Opioid antagonists are drugs that firmly attach to the opioid
receptors, but don't activate these receptors. Antagonists prevent other
opioids from reaching and activating the receptors. Antagonists remove
opioids from the receptors, so if antagonists are given to an actively
using opioid addict, the addict will become sick with withdrawal. This
is called "precipitated withdrawal" because it was caused, or precipitated, by a medication.

Naltrexone is the most commonly used oral opioid blocker. It's
taken orally, in pill form. It's started after an opioid addict has completed opioid withdrawal. It can be a difficult medication to take,
because it may also block endorphins, our own naturally made opioids.
Some patients complain of headache, muscle aches, and fatigue while
taking naltrexone. Many times these unpleasant symptoms will subside,
with more time on the medication. The medication can be started at a
half dose for the first week or so, and then increased to the full dose.
Most patients tolerate this better.

Naltrexone has been used in this country mainly for relapse prevention, particularly for addicted professionals. Many professionals,
such as doctors and pharmacists, who have been treated for opioid
addiction, are started on naltrexone when they return to work. These
professionals may need to work around opioids, and if they relapse
while taking naltrexone, the opioids will have no effect. The antagonist
thus serves as extra insurance against a relapse. Many licensing boards
for impaired professionals insist they take naltrexone as a condition of
being allowed to return to work in their fields.

Naltrexone works well, but only if the patient takes it every day. If
the addict "forgets" to take her dose for one or two days, it's then possible for her to get high from ingested opioids. Because of this, the
medication is also available in an implantable form. Pellets containing
naltrexone are placed just under the skin and the medication is released
into the body over three months. With this method, compliance is

obviously higher, since the addict would have to dig the pellets out to be rid of the blocking drug.

Naloxone is the intravenous form of an opioid antagonist, better known by its brand name Narcan. It's injected to rapidly reverse the effects of opioids. Emergency workers often carry Narcan with them to use if they encounter a person who has overdosed with opioids. This medication can be life-saving, but it also puts the opioid addict into immediate withdrawal.

Detoxification under anesthesia

Because of the fear that many opioid addicts have of opioid withdrawal symptoms, some treatment programs have used a method of inducing physical withdrawal while the patient is under anesthesia.

With rapid or ultra-rapid detoxification, the patient is first given some type of general anesthesia, and then given doses of an intravenous opioid antagonist like naloxone. The naloxone puts the patient's body into withdrawal, but since he's unconscious, he won't be aware of it. Hours later, the patient is brought out of anesthesia. Proponents of this method of detoxification say that the patient has no further withdrawal once he is out of anesthesia. However, several studies show significant post-procedure symptoms, with nausea, vomiting, and insomnia. These symptoms can continue for days after the procedure. (1)

This method appeals to many addicts because it's advertised to be quick and painless. However, most evidence shows patient outcomes using rapid or ultra-rapid detoxification have the same results as techniques using buprenorphine to transition off of opioids and onto naltrexone. (2) Plus, ultrarapid detox costs *much* more. In many places, the procedure costs tens of thousands of dollars. This method also has the added risks of general anesthesia.

Treatment centers that perform rapid detox advertise claims of "100%" success, speaking of numbers of patients that complete treatment. But if the patient is under anesthesia, of course 100% will complete the treatment. They aren't going anywhere, since they are unconscious. Many proponents of rapid detox exaggerate and inflate success rates in this way. However, most studies show that at one year, success rates with rapid detox under anesthesia, compared to detox with a short course of buprenorphine are equal. They're equally dismal, with less than twenty percent of the addicts still abstinent from all opioids.

Most reputable treatment centers no longer use this expensive, and relatively riskier, method of detoxification under general anesthesia. Since the studies don't show greater abstinence rates with this method, it's difficult to justify its expense and risk. (2)

However, there may be some patients for whom this is an acceptable treatment. Perhaps if ultra-rapid detox is the *only* treatment option that an addict is willing to try, the potential benefits may outweigh risks, since we know continued active addiction is very risky. This method of detox may be most successful with a very motivated addict who, for whatever reason, has a deadline they want to meet for detoxification. Even though there's less than a twenty percent chance that he will be off opioids at one year after the procedure, that addict will still be introduced to the idea of addiction treatment

End notes:

1. Singh j, Ultra-rapid opioid detoxification: Current status and controversies, *Journal of Postgraduate Medicine* 2004; 50:227-232.
2. Collins ED, Kleber HD, Whittington RA, Heitler NE, Anesthesia-assisted vs buprenorphine- or clonidine-assisted heroin detoxification and naltrexone induction: A randomized trial, *Journal of the American Medical Association*, 2005; 294 (8) 903-913.
3. Cucchia AT, Monnat M, et.al; Ultra-rapid opiate detoxification using deep sedation with oral midazolam: short and long-term results. The authors conclude that patients still had withdrawal symptoms after the detoxification procedure, and eighty percent had relapsed back to opioid use at the six month follow up. *Drug and Alcohol Dependence*, 1998; 52(3) 243-250.

About the Author

Dr. Jana Burson is a medical doctor, certified by the American Board of Addiction Medicine, and by the American Board of Internal Medicine. Besides the practical knowledge she acquired working in primary care for many years, she has extensive experience treating prescription pain pill addiction. For the past six years, she's treated thousands of opioid addicts using all available forms of treatment. She has a special interest in medication-assisted treatments with methadone and buprenorphine.

Because so many opioid-addicted patients are eager to learn more about buprenorphine and methadone, she wrote this book, to give both patients and their families reliable information.

Dr. Burson graduated from Ohio University with a B.S. in Zoology and Microbiology in 1983, and then got her Medical Doctor degree from Ohio State University College of Medicine in 1987. She completed her Internal Medicine internship and residency at Carolinas Medical Center, Charlotte, NC, and has been board certified in Internal Medicine since 1990. She worked in primary care for many years before changing her focus to the treatment of addiction.

Since 2004, when she achieved certification by the American Society of Addiction Medicine, she has worked exclusively in Addiction Medicine. She is now the medical director of Stepping Stones Wellness Center, an opioid treatment program in Boone, NC which uses both methadone and buprenorphine to treat opioid addiction. She also works at Half Moon Medical Associates in Cornelius, NC, treating all types of addiction.

She lives in North Carolina, and trudges the road of happy destiny with the love of her life, Greg Moon, and her family and friends.

Index

A

abstinence-based treatment 17, 97, 119, 224–225. *see also* twelve-step groups

academic success and addiction 48

addiction (dependence), 11–15, 30, 39, 42–48, 52, 77–78, 218
    behaviors 12–15, 30
    caused by doctor. see iatrogenic addiction
    compared to abuse 14–16
    definition 42
    population changes 39, 52
    risk factors for 42–48, 77–78, 218
    signs and symptoms 11–13

Alcoholics Anonymous 66, 174. *see also* twelve-step programs

American Society of Addiction Medicine (ASAM) 42, 78, 82

Anslinger, Harry J 59–60

Anti-Drug Abuse Act (1988) 69

B

behaviors of addiction 12–15, 30

bipolar disorder. see psychiatric illness

Boggs Act (1951) 60

brain, changes during drug use and addiction 9–10

Buprenex 152. *see also* buprenorphine

buprenorphine 17, 19, 97, 99, 149–162, 163–173, 206, 227–229
    acute pain treatment 152
    compared to methadone 159–160, 206, 227–228
    deaths 156
    drug interactions 154, 172
    opioid addiction treatment 17, 19, 97, 99, 149–162, 163–173, 206, 227–229
    side effects 156

Butler, Willis 56

C

chronic pain and opioid use 11, 74, 77–78, 87, 136, 218–219, 234

Clonidine 97, 250–251

cocaine 68–70

common opioids 8

commonly abused opioids 18–19, 39

Controlled Substance Act (1970) 63–64

controlled substances, lack of physician training in prescribing 91–92, 94, 124–125, 219–221

counseling in opioid addiction treatment, 106, 118, 120, 130, 151–152, 170–172, 231
    need for 106, 171, 231
    with buprenorphine treatment 151–152, 170–172

continued use 22, 52
first use 19–21, 49
heroin 62
pain pills 19–20
recognizing addiction, lack of
physician training in 91–94,
219
recovery meetings
secular groups 185–186
twelve-step groups 174–190
relapse 20, 28, 36, 42, 97, 105, 119,
145, 171, 190, 195, 226, 229
incidence of 20, 42, 105, 145,
171, 190, 195, 226, 229
triggers 97, 119
replacement therapies 57, 61,
97–99, 129, 159–161, 170–172,
206, 227–229
residential treatment. see inpatient treatment
risk factors for addiction 42–48,
77–78, 218
chronic pain 77–78
environmental 47–48
academic success 48
affordability of drugs 47
availability of drugs 47
divorce 48
parenting 48
genetic 43–45, 218
personal 46–47, 218
domestic violence 46
serious illness 46
Rockefeller Laws 102, 182
Ryan Haight Act (2008) 86–87

S

schizophrenia. see psychiatric illness

social influences on addiction. see
risk factors, environmental
SOS (Secular Organizations for
Sobriety or Saving Ourselves)
185
sources of opioids 21–22, 73,
89–90, 221
stigmatization of maintenance
therapies 194–215, 228–229
addiction treatment community 208–215, 228–229
family 194–196
healthcare workers/medical
community 195–198, 229
law enforcement, legal community 199–203
local communities 203–205
patients 205–208, 229
pregnancy 195–196, 199–200
twelve-step programs
198–199, 229
Suboxone 152–153, 163–171. see
also buprenorphine
substance abuse, compared to
addiction (dependence) 14–16
Substance Abuse and Mental
Health Services Administration (SAMHSA) 69, 90, 103,
125
Subutex 152–153. see also
buprenorphine
Syanon 64–66

T

Talwin 80–81
therapeutic communities 64–68,
101, 226
treatment in doctors' offices 19,
56, 149–152, 156–162, 206

twelve-step groups 174–190
   effectiveness of 179–181
   patients on medication-assisted
   therapy in 175–177

U

United States Narcotic Farm. see
   Narcotic Farm
urine drug screening. 62, 88,
   117–118, 135

U.S. Public Health Service Narcotics Hospital. see Narcotic
   Farm

V

Vicodin. see hydrocodone

W

withdrawal 10, 16–17, 19, 97–98,
   229
   opioid 10, 16, 19
   post-acute 16–17, 97–98, 229
Women for Sobriety (WFS) 186

Z

Zuppardi, Melissa 141

CPSIA information can be obtained at www.ICGtesting.com
226113LV00003B/1/P